The Idea of International Society

This book offers the first comprehensive account and reappraisal of the formative phase of what is often termed the 'Grotian tradition' in international relations theory: the view that sovereign states are not free to act at will, but are akin to members of a society, bound by its norms. It examines the period from the later fifteenth to the mid-seventeenth centuries, focussing on four thinkers – Erasmus, Vitoria, Gentili and Grotius himself – and is structured by the author's concept of international society. Erasmus's views on international relations have been entirely neglected, but underlying his work is a consistent image of international society. The theologian Francisco de Vitoria concerns himself with its normative principles, the lawyer Alberico Gentili – unexpectedly, the central figure in the narrative – with its extensive practical applications. Grotius, however, does not reaffirm the concept, but wavers at crucial points. This book suggests that the Grotian tradition is a misnomer.

Ursula Vollerthun (1937–2011) came relatively late to international relations. With a background in political science and the history and philosophy of science, she pursued the present topic for her thesis in the Department of International Relations in the then Research School of Pacific Studies at the Australian National University.

James L. Richardson was Professor of Political Science (1975–85) and later of International Relations (1986–98) at the Australian National University. He is the author of *Germany and the Atlantic Alliance* (1966), *Crisis Diplomacy* (1994) and *Contending Liberalisms in World Politics* (2001). After Ursula Vollerthun's death, he devoted himself to this work.

The Idea of International Society

Erasmus, Vitoria, Gentili and Grotius

Ursula Vollerthun

Edited by James L. Richardson

CAMBRIDGE
UNIVERSITY PRESS

CAMBRIDGE
UNIVERSITY PRESS

University Printing House, Cambridge CB2 8BS, United Kingdom

One Liberty Plaza, 20th Floor, New York, NY 10006, USA

477 Williamstown Road, Port Melbourne, VIC 3207, Australia

314-321, 3rd Floor, Plot 3, Splendor Forum, Jasola District Centre, New Delhi - 110025, India

79 Anson Road, #06-04/06, Singapore 079906

Cambridge University Press is part of the University of Cambridge.

It furthers the University's mission by disseminating knowledge in the pursuit of education, learning and research at the highest international levels of excellence.

www.cambridge.org
Information on this title: www.cambridge.org/9781108417143
DOI: 10.1017/9781108264945

First published 2017

A catalogue record for this publication is available from the British Library

ISBN 978-1-108-41714-3 Hardback
ISBN 978-1-108-40463-1 Paperback

Contents

Preface

This work is based on the author's doctoral thesis, written in the Department of International Relations at the Australian National University, and completed in 1992. At that time it did not find a publisher: there was only limited interest in the history of international thought, and it seemed unlikely to attract a sufficient readership. Since then the interest in the history of ideas in international relations has increased immeasurably, but the present topic remains unexplored. The thesis was highly regarded in the Department for its originality and scholarship – the latter enhanced by the author's command of the relevant languages, Latin and Spanish as well as French and German – and after her death in 2011, a number of colleagues and friends encouraged me to edit it for publication.

The original intention was to remain as close as possible to the author's text, subject to reducing its length and other changes of presentation necessary for publication, limiting editorial intervention to notes drawing attention to more recent literature and an Introduction locating the work in this context. However, the publisher's readers persuaded me that this was not sufficient; the subject had moved on and there were new perspectives that a work published today would be expected to take into account, and thus a much more thoroughgoing revision was necessary.

This makes for a more complex relationship between the contributions of the author and the editor. The overall argument and the interpretation of the four thinkers remain entirely those of the author, as do the formulation and style of the interpretations, and thus the main body of the text of these four chapters, as well as Chapter 1, are essentially in the author's words. The editor has provided a more elaborate frame. The Introduction and Conclusion, while incorporating certain passages from the author, are essentially oriented to the present state of the literature. And each of the chapters on the four thinkers is placed in a new context, prompting some further comments in the course of the chapters.

I remain persuaded by the author's interpretations, but I have very infrequently qualified a specific point which seemed to me to go beyond what the text in question could support: rather more often I have reinforced the argument by including a further comment or reference.

James L. Richardson
Hamburg, June 2017

Acknowledgements

My thanks go first and foremost to my two supervisors, Professors H. N. Collins at Murdoch University, WA, and J. D. B. Miller at the Australian National University, for their advice and assistance. The former's support and encouragement in difficult circumstances have been especially appreciated. I also wish to thank Dr C. Holbraad and Professor K. Holsti for finding the time, when visiting the Department of International Relations, to read parts of the manuscript and offer their comments. Across the campus, at the Faculties, Mr W. C. Craven, History, and Dr T. R. Mautner, Philosophy, were helpful in canvassing some aspects of the topic. Professor H. Bull, who read the first chapter, I can no longer thank; but I did so at the time.

Of the libraries that I have used while undertaking this study I wish to thank the National Library of Australia, the Bayerische Staatsbibliothek Munich and the Universitaetsbibliothek Hamburg for assisting my research and responding to my inquiries.

Ursula Vollerthun
Canberra, July 1992

I am grateful to colleagues and friends who encouraged me at the outset to embark on this project, and to Hugh Collins, Jim George, John Groom, Andrew Hurrell and Andrew Linklater for their helpful comments on an initial outline. I am greatly indebted to the Department of International Relations, Coral Bell School of Asia Pacific Affairs, the Australian National University, for its generous support, and wish to thank Professor William Tow, Dr Mathew Davies and in particular Mary-Louise Hickey, the Department's Editor, for her invaluable work on the manuscript, assistance and advice, extending to proofreading when my eyes could no longer cope. And I owe special thanks to the publisher's readers for the exemplary care with which they assessed an earlier draft of the manuscript, combining cogent critique with constructive stimulus, all the more appreciated in view of the intense pressures on the time of senior scholars in the present era. Finally, I should like to thank John

Haslam, Executive Publisher, Political Science and Sociology, Cambridge University Press, for his attentive supervision of the publishing process, resolving problems that arose from time to time, and Trevor Matthews for compiling the index under time pressure at the end.

James L. Richardson
Hamburg, June 2017

Prologue: A Word about Words

Words are the means by which thinkers give expression to their ideas, and 'discontinuity' is perhaps the word which best describes the relationship that holds between the words chosen by Otto von Gierke, Martin Wight and Hedley Bull to present the idea of international society, using the English language, and those employed by Desiderius Erasmus, Francisco de Vitoria, Alberico Gentili and Hugo Grotius in their Latin writings, or, to put the same idea more descriptively, there are few direct lines connecting the vocabularies of the two groups of thinkers separated by centuries – and this despite the 'Latinate reaches'[1] of the English language. While there are words that have the same meaning for both groups, their derivations may differ; words used as a matter of course by one group are not available to the other; words that are at the disposal of both have different meanings; and words that survive the passage of time unchanged are given a different currency. The art of translation is often undervalued. Some less than satisfactory translations are noted in the course of the study.

Here I offer a comparison of words used by Gierke, Wight and Bull with those employed by one of the early thinkers – Vitoria has been chosen, as his writings are less extensive than those of the other three thinkers.[2] The emphasis is on those key words which denote important ideas within the idea of international society.

[1] A formulation found in R. Williams, *Politics and Letters: Interviews with New Left Review* (London: N.L.B., 1979), p. 178.

[2] The following four texts in Latin have been used: 'De Indis Recenter Inventis: Relectio Prior' [On the Indians Lately Discovered: First *Relectio*], hereafter 'De Indis' [On the Indians], and 'De Indis, Sive de Iure Belli Hispanorum in Barbaros: Relectio Posterior' [On the Indians, Or On the Law of War Made by the Spaniards on the Barbarians: Second *Relectio*], hereafter 'De Iure Belli' [On the Law of War], both in E. Nys (ed.), *Francisci de Victoria De Indis et De Iure Belli Relectiones* [Relectiones on the Indians and the Law of War by Franciscus de Victoria], The Classics of International Law (Washington, DC: Carnegie Institution, 1917, reprinted New York: Oceana Publications, 1964), pp. 217–68 and 269–97; 'De Potestate Civili' [Concerning Civil Power] and 'De Potestate Ecclesiae: Relectio Prior' [Concerning the Power of the Church: First *Relectio*], hereafter 'De Potestate Ecclesiae, I', both in T. Urdánoz, *Obras de Francisco de Vitoria*: *Relecciones Teológicas* [Works by Francisco de Vitoria: Theological Relectionnes] (Madrid: Autores Cristianos, 1960), pp. 150–95 and 290–316.

International, Society, Community

International

'International' is one of the constituents of the term 'international society'. Wight and Bull use the word, a creation of the late eighteenth century,[3] in the sense of that which appertains to relations among states. Both its formative elements, 'inter' and 'national', go back to the Latin language, the former directly, as it is the Latin for 'between', 'among', 'amidst', while the latter, along with the older word 'nation', is derived by adaptation from *natio*, 'nation', 'people', 'race'.

The Latin language does not have an adjective corresponding to 'international', but it has the word *inter*, and Vitoria uses it in conjunction with nouns which denote the specific entities with which he is concerned. Thus he speaks of the peace which is to be conserved 'among princes', *pax inter principes*, of the victor who sits as judge 'between the states' who went to war, *iudex inter respublicas*; and of the law that reason has established 'among all nations', *ius inter omnes gentes*. He also makes use of the genitive plural, for example, when he speaks of 'the mutual accord of nations', *consensus mutuus gentium*; of 'the intention of nations', *intention gentium*; and of 'the law of nations', *ius gentium* – a way of expressing himself which Gierke, writing nearly 400 years later, also chooses, for he speaks of the society 'of states' rather than 'international' society.

Society

'Society', the other constituent of the term 'international society' or 'society of states', is used by Gierke, Wight and Bull interchangeably with 'community' to describe the nature of the relationship held to exist among states – a usage which dictionaries have not yet added to the lists of meanings and changes of meanings attributed to the two words since they appeared in the fourteenth century. At their origin are the Latin words *societas* and *communitas* respectively.

The word *societas* is part of Vitoria's vocabulary, but when he uses it, he does not tie it to other nouns denoting political entities. *Societas gentium*, to mention just one possibility, is not among his expressions. When he uses the word *societas*, he gives it other companions. Thus it appears together with the adjective *naturalis*. *Societas naturalis*, 'natural society',

[3] Unless otherwise indicated, the information on the etymology of words is from C. T. Onions (ed.), *The Shorter Oxford English Dictionary on Historical Principles*, 3rd edn, 2 vols (Oxford: Clarendon Press, 1967).

is inclusive of all human beings. Or it is accompanied by the words *humanus* or *homines*. *Societas humana*, 'human society', or *societas hominum*, 'society of human beings', is exclusive of all who live 'in solitude', in 'the manner of wild beasts'. Or, thirdly, it is joined by the word *civilis*. *Societas civilis*, 'civil society', is 'of all societies that which best provides for the needs of men'.[4]

Community

Communitas occurs in Vitoria's vocabulary in mainly one sense: *communitas perfecta*, 'the perfect community', *communitas quae habet proprias leges, proprium consilium et proprios magistratus*, 'the community which has its own laws, its own council and its own magistrates'[5] – which is his definition of the state.

As used by Vitoria, *societas* and *communitas* may relate to the same entity, but if they do, they emphasize different aspects of it.

World, Christendom

Gierke, Wight and Bull make little use of two words which are prominent in the vocabulary of Vitoria: 'the world' and 'Christendom'.

World

Vitoria uses the word *orbis*, which he prefers to *mundus*, when he speaks of 'the beginning of the world', *principium orbis*, when he contrasts 'the New World', *Novus Orbis*, with 'our world', *noster orbis*, or when he refutes claims by emperor and pope to universal empire. *Imperator non est dominus totius orbis*, 'the Emperor is not lord of the whole world'.[6] *Papa non est dominus civilis aut ternporalis totius ortis*, 'the Pope is not civil or temporal lord of the whole world'.[7] He also uses the word *orbis* as a metonym for 'mankind'. *Una respublica (est) pars totius orbis*, 'a state is a part of the world as a whole'.[8] *Totus orbis ... aliquo modo est una respublica*, 'the world as a whole is in a way a state'.[9] He speaks of its 'authority', *auctoritas totius orbis*, and of its 'end and good', *finis et bonum totius orbis*.

[4] 'De Potestate Civili', p. 156.
[5] 'De Iure Belli', p. 277.
[6] 'De Indis', p. 235.
[7] Ibid., p. 240.
[8] 'De Potestate Civili', p. 168.
[9] Ibid., p. 191.

Christendom

Ecclesia, 'the Church', *respublica christiana*, 'the Christian state', *respublica spiritualis*, 'the spiritual state', *christianitas*, 'Christianity' – these are the words which Vitoria uses when he refers to Christians collectively or to the Christian domain. *Tota Ecclesia est quodammodo una respublica*, 'the Church as a whole is in a certain way a state'.[10] *Provincia christiana (est) pars reipublicae (christianae)*, 'a Christian province is a part of the Christian state'.[11] *Respublica spiritualis debet esse perfecta*, 'the spiritual state must be perfect'.[12] And the word *christianitas* appears in expressions such as *invadere christianitatem*, 'invading Christianity', or *cum damno christianitatis*, 'to the detriment of Christianity'.

State, Sovereignty

State

The word 'state', in the sense of 'body politic' used since the sixteenth century, is employed by Gierke, Wight and Bull to identify the members of international society. It is derived from the Latin word *status*.

Status is part of Vitoria's vocabulary, but for him it only means 'standing', 'position', 'condition'. Thus one meets with formulations such as *status reipublicae*, 'the position of the state', or *status felix*, 'a happy condition'.

When Vitoria refers to those public entities which he endows with rights and obligations in relation to one another, he uses a number of words other than *status*. Foremost amongst these is the word *respublica*. *Quid est respublica*? 'What is a state?' he asks.[13] *Respublica proprie vocatur perfecta communitas*, 'a state is properly called a perfect community'.[14] *Quaelibet respublica habet auctoritatem indicendi et inferendi bellum*, 'every state has the authority to declare and make war'.[15] Apart from using it in this general sense, he also applies it to particular states, for example, when he identifies 'the French' and 'the English' as 'two distinct and separate states', *duae respublicae disparatae et differentes, ut gallorum et anglorum*.[16]

Nearly as prevalent as *respublica* is the word *civitas*. It appears in general statements such as *nihil est illi principi Deo ... acceptius quam concilia*

[10] Ibid., p. 180.
[11] Ibid., p. 168.
[12] 'De Potestate Ecclesiae, I', p. 308.
[13] 'De Iure Belli', p. 277.
[14] Ibid.
[15] Ibid., p. 276.
[16] 'De Potestate Ecclesiae, I', p. 302.

coetusque … quae civitates appellantur, 'nothing is more acceptable in the sight of God our King than are those associations called states',[17] or *civis (est) qui natus est in civitate*, 'a citizen is he who is born in a state'.[18] And it occurs in reference to specific states, for example, when he speaks of 'free states such as Venice and Florence', *liberae civitates ut sunt Venetiae et Florentiae.*

Sovereignty

The states which Gierke, Wight and Bull identify as members of international society are 'sovereign'. This word, which goes back to Middle English,[19] has at its origin the popular Latin *superanus*, from *super* 'above'.

Vitoria does not have the word *superanus*, nor does he have another specific word to take its place. His way of giving expression to this Janus-faced idea comprises a number of words and expressions. When he speaks of the state, people or nation, which does not have another 'above' itself, he describes it as *liber*, 'free', *sui iuris*, 'independent', *per se totum*, 'complete in itself', *perfectus*, 'perfect', *sibi sufficiens*, 'self-sufficient'; *non esse pars alterius reipublicae*, 'not being a part of another state', *non esse subiectus alicui extra se*, 'not being subject to any one outside itself'; *habere potestatem gubernandi se*, 'having the power to govern itself', and by power he means *facultas, auctoritas, sive ius*, 'ability, authority, or right'.

When he refers to the prince or ruler who does not have another 'above' himself and who is 'above' everyone else in the community, he mainly makes use of the word *princeps*. *Princeps … non habent superiors*, 'princes do not have superiors';[20] *praesunt reipublicae*, 'they are at the head of the state'. King, emperor and pope are *principes*.

Interchangeably with, but less frequently than *princeps*, occurs the word *dominus*. King, emperor and pope are *domini*.

His main words for 'supreme rule', the rule of *princeps* or *dominus*, are *principatus*, *dominium*, *regnum* and *imperium*, and of these *dominium* and *principatus* occur far more often than *regnum* and *imperium*.

And when Vitoria treats of the state, people or nation which is deprived by another of its *status* of being 'sovereign', he uses expressions such as *venire in potestatem aliorum*, 'to come under the power of others', *venire in dicionem aliorum*, 'to come under the sway of others';[21] and he uses

[17] 'De Potestate Civili', p. 158.
[18] 'De Indis', p. 260.
[19] The Middle English period extends from ca. 1150 to ca.1450.
[20] 'De Iure Belli', p. 284.
[21] 'De Indis', p. 218.

further expressions such as *occupare principatum*, 'seizing supreme rule',[22] *dominos priores deponere et novos constituere*, 'deposing former lords and setting up new ones'[23] – combinations which intimate that he sees sovereignty as having two faces: an external and an internal.[24]

International Law, Commerce, Diplomacy, Balance of Power, Great Powers and War

The terms included under this heading are used by Gierke, Wight and Bull to denote the common rules and institutions ascribed to international society. A comparative glance across the centuries identifies only one of these readily – *commercium* – while the others are found to have either quite different corresponding words or none at all.

International Law

'International', as mentioned above, is a creation of the eighteenth century. 'Law', on the other hand, goes back to a distant past, at its origin being the Old English[25] word *lagu*, plural *laga*. 'International law', like its component 'international', is an eighteenth-century invention. Older than it are the expressions 'the public law of Europe' and 'the law of nations'.

Ius gentium is the corresponding term in Vitoria's vocabulary. *Quod naturalis ratio inter omnes gentes constituit, vocatur ius gentium*, 'what natural reason has established among all nations is called the law of nations'.[26] He uses the word *ius* in other expressions such as *ius divinum*, 'divine law', *ius humanum*, 'human law', *ius canonicum*, 'canon law', *ius civile*, 'civil law', and *ius belli*, 'the law of war'. But he employs the word *lex* when he refers to that body of law that constitutes the Christian religion. This is *lex christiana*, 'the Christian law', or *lex Evangelica*, 'the Evangelical law'. In the case of 'the law of nature', or 'natural law' one meets with both *ius naturae* or *ius naturale* and *lex naturae* or *lex naturale*. *Ius gentium*, however, never becomes *lex gentium*, but *ius gentium*, as Vitoria puts it, *habet vim legis*, that is, it 'has the force of law'.[27]

22 Ibid., p. 262.
23 Ibid., p. 261.
24 The term 'sovereignty' came to be widely used only after the publication of Jean Bodin's theory in 1576, i.e., after Vitoria but before Gentili and Grotius, who are both familiar with it.
25 The Old English period: before the middle of the twelfth century.
26 'De Indis', p. 257.
27 'De Potestate Civili', p. 191.

Commerce

The word 'commerce', in the sense of exchange of merchandise, especially on a large scale between countries, has been in use since the sixteenth century. It is derived from the Latin *commercium*.

Vitoria's vocabulary includes the word *commercium*, and he gives it the same meaning as his twentieth-century counterparts to its derivative. *Et Lusitani magnum commercium habent cum similibus gentibus, quas non subiecerunt*, 'and the Portuguese maintain a huge commerce with similar nations (as the Spaniards), without reducing them to subjection'.[28]

Diplomacy

The English language acquired the word 'diplomacy', from French *diplomatie*, in the late eighteenth century. Older than it and its cognates 'diplomatic' and 'diplomat' are 'embassy', 'ambassade', 'ambassador' and 'legation', 'legate'. Both of these groups of words are of Latin origin, the respective etymons being *ambactus* and *legatus*.

Vitoria uses the word *legatus*, and the point that matters to him is that *legati iure gentium sunt inviolabiles*, that is, 'ambassadors are by the law of nations inviolable'.[29]

Balance of Power

The first usage of the term 'balance of power' has not yet been ascertained by scholarship. David Hume, writing in the 1740s, credits 'these later ages' with the invention of the 'phrase', which he distinguishes from the idea to which he assigns a long history;[30] Frank Parkinson identifies it in the Treaty of Utrecht which was concluded in 1713 to end the War of the Spanish Succession[31] – hints that the term 'balance of power' may not have originated before the eighteenth century.

Vitoria does not give expression to the idea of the balance of power.

Great Powers

Not much is known about the beginnings of the term 'great powers'. *The Shorter Oxford English Dictionary* mentions that the word 'power', in

[28] 'De Indis', p. 268.
[29] Ibid., p. 262.
[30] D. Hume, 'Of the Balance of Power', in P. Seabury (ed.), *Balance of Power* (San Francisco, CA: Chandler, 1965), p. 32.
[31] F. Parkinson, *The Philosophy of International Relations: A Study in the History of Thought* (London: Sage, 1977), p. 45.

the sense of a state or nation having international authority or influence, was not used before the early eighteenth century.[32] It offers no information on the term 'great powers'. In his essay of 1833, entitled 'The Great Powers', Leopold von Ranke expresses the view that it is 'our century' that 'called the great powers into being',[33] but he says nothing about the term which he uses to give expression to that phenomenon. The essay seems to have been first translated into English in 1950.

Vitoria's vocabulary does not include a word or combination of words corresponding to 'great powers'.

War

'War', like 'law', does not have a Latin origin. It is a native word going back to the late Old English *werre*.

Vitoria's word for 'war' is *bellum*. He speaks of 'defensive war', *bellum defensivum*, and of 'offensive war', *bellum offensivum*; of 'the law of war', *ius belli*, and of 'the rules of war', *regulae belli*; of 'the just war', *bellum iustum*, and of 'the justice of war', *iustitia belli*. He does not use the words *privatus*, 'private', and *publicus*, 'public', in conjunction with *bellum*, but his concern is with the latter, public war.

[32] 'Power', in Onions (ed.), *Shorter Oxford English Dictionary*, vol. 2, p. 1559.

[33] L. von Ranke, 'The Great Powers', in G. G. Iggers and K. von Moltke (eds), *The Theory and Practice of History by Leopold von Ranke* (Indianapolis and New York: Bobbs-Merrill, 1973), p. 99.

Introduction

The English School's concept of international society, little known in the discipline of international relations a generation ago, has become familiar to today's students of the subject, as has Martin Wight's idea of three traditions of international thought. Since the emergence of the modern states system, as Wight sees it, there have been three contending schools of thought: realism, revolutionism and rationalism; he sometimes refers to these by the names of emblematic thinkers: the Machiavellian, Kantian and Grotian traditions. The post-1945 'great debate' between exponents of realism and idealism exemplifies the opposition between the first two traditions; Wight's claim that there was a third outlook, equally long-standing, in some sense a *via media* between the two, was then novel and had little immediate resonance. More recently, the thesis of the three traditions has become a topic of lively controversy.

Hedley Bull, while taking Wight's position as the framework for his own theorizing, on occasion raised the question: 'Is it true? Can one really categorize the history of thought about international politics in this way?' Is this really an exercise in the history of ideas or just 'an imaginary philosophical conversation, in the manner of Plato's dialogues'?[1] English School theorists have not squarely addressed this question. They tend to see the three traditions as an ideal type highlighting certain fundamental differences among theories without troubling themselves about its historical validity. They have not sought to substantiate Wight's thesis through studies in the history of international thought.

This is not the aim of the present work; its aim, rather, is to take up Bull's challenge, but with no preconceived answer – in other words, to treat Wight's thesis of the three traditions as a hypothesis to be examined. It investigates several thinkers identified with the tradition most characteristic of the English School, the *via media*, whose central concept

[1] H. Bull, 'Martin Wight and the Theory of International Relations', in M. Wight, *International Theory: The Three Traditions*, ed. G. Wight and B. Porter (Leicester: Leicester University Press for the Royal Institute of International Affairs, London, 1991), p. xviii.

is international society, inquiring whether indeed their writings give expression to a concept of international society as understood by Wight and Bull – an overarching concept which guides their thinking on international relations. Or are the metaphors and colourful expressions which suggest this merely rhetorical flourishes, rather as contemporary politicians like to invoke the international community?

One of the attractions of Wight's thesis of the three traditions is that it refers to the whole history of the modern states system since its emergence in Europe, a gradual process usually taken to span the period from the later fifteenth to the mid-seventeenth centuries. Wight and Bull name only four thinkers in the Grotian tradition in this period: Francisco de Vitoria, Francisco Suárez, Alberico Gentili and Hugo Grotius himself. This period has been chosen for the present study for several reasons. First, it makes for an important test of Wight's thesis: can the traditions really be traced back as far as he maintains? Second, it is of particular interest to see how the earliest thinkers ascribed to this particular tradition envisaged its central idea – international society. Third, while the period is of special interest to historians of political thought, they have paid relatively little attention to the thinking about international relations at that time: it may be hoped that the study can go some way towards correcting this imbalance.

The four authors chosen for this study include three named by Wight and Bull, all of them writing on what came to be termed international law – then *ius gentium*, the law of nations. In later periods, Wight and Bull include a wide variety of thinkers in this tradition, as in the other two: for example, statesmen and diplomats, historians and publicists, as well as political theorists and international lawyers. The question naturally arises whether there may have been other kinds of authors in this period. The name of Desiderius Erasmus, the renowned humanist scholar and most prominent writer of the time, naturally suggests itself, and an initial impression of his writings suggested that he might well be an exponent of the *via media* outlook. The authors chosen satisfy two criteria: a balance between the two main intellectual schools of the time, the scholastics and the humanists; and a balance between the earlier and the later years of the period. Vitoria, Professor of Theology at Salamanca and the foremost scholastic theorist of the time, offers a counterweight to the humanist, Erasmus. Gentili and Grotius were more eclectic, taking much from the humanists but not free from scholastic influences. The former two, born in the later fifteenth century, wrote mainly in the earlier sixteenth century – that is to say, in the earlier half of the period; Gentili wrote in the later sixteenth century, and Grotius in the early years of the seventeenth – both thus in the later half of the period. The inclusion of

Suárez, the second outstanding member of the Salamanca School, at the expense of his contemporary, Gentili, would have placed excessive emphasis on the scholastics and reduced the intellectual diversity of the sample.

Four was the maximum number of thinkers it was practicable to include. The idea of international society is not present on the surface of their writings; whether it is indeed present, and how they envisage it, has to be teased out by a painstaking interpretation of the texts. The conceptual vocabulary of the period has to be mastered, followed by the particular problems posed by each author's unfamiliar mode of reasoning.

Before embarking on the inquiry, it is necessary to take note of the recent critical discussion of the concept of tradition and of the criticisms that have been advanced against Wight's three traditions in particular. For example, John Gunnell maintains that supposed scholarly traditions are a 'retrospective analytical construction ... a rationalized version of the past ... calculated to evoke a particular image of ... the political condition of our age'.[2] These have been termed 'analytical traditions', patterns discovered or imposed by today's theorist, in contrast to 'historical' or 'self-constituted' traditions, where the participants formulate the ideas and are conscious of belonging to a particular school of thought.[3] Bull's question, it should be noted, is not whether the three traditions are historical or analytical, as thus defined. It is not whether or not the thinkers were conscious of sharing a common outlook, or pattern of ideas; it is whether their writings actually exemplify the pattern of ideas in question. These issues will be taken up in the Conclusion. The final assessment should not turn on a matter of verbal definition, but on as clear as possible an account of the substantive findings.

Some, but not all, of the specific criticisms of the three traditions raise questions that need to be taken into account at the outset. Provocative but in the end tangential is David Boucher's critique of Wight's 'intellectual egalitarianism': precisely that diversity of those Wight includes in the tradition that has just been noted. He fails to distinguish the genuinely philosophical from the merely polemical.[4] Wight's fault is to focus on the end product, the theories' conclusions – anarchy, international society or universalist values – not on their philosophical foundations.[5] Boucher proceeds to write the history that Wight should have written; he also posits three traditions, defined by their philosophical fundamentals: empirical

[2] J. G. Gunnell, quoted in R. Jeffery, *Hugo Grotius in International Thought* (New York: Palgrave Macmillan, 2006), p. 22.

[3] Ibid., pp. 24, 141, discussing the distinction drawn by Brian Schmidt.

[4] D. Boucher, *Political Theories of International Relations: From Thucydides to the Present* (Oxford: Oxford University Press, 1998), p. 8.

[5] Ibid., pp. 16, 19.

realism, universal moral order and historical reason. This is an important undertaking, but his critique is beside the point. This was never intended by Wight and Bull: their interest was in different conceptions of international relations, in the everyday political discourse as much as in political philosophy. Moreover, it is evident that each of their three traditions draws on a variety of philosophical schools over the centuries.[6]

Michael Doyle also proposes three traditions – realism, liberalism and socialism – seemingly the kind of twentieth-century perspective on the subject which Wight sought to avoid. But one of Doyle's criticisms of Wight points to a problem, namely that some of the major thinkers placed in the realist or revolutionist traditions are simply misplaced because in some respects they take up the rationalist viewpoint.[7] He offers Immanuel Kant, Karl Marx and Thomas Hobbes as examples, and others have made the same point regarding these authors. In other words, the three traditions do not offer a genuine typology. Wight, however, is well aware of this, and goes so far as to say that most of the great political theorists transcended their own systems, bringing in themes from a second tradition.[8] In another context he proposes to subdivide revolutionism into hard and soft variants (e.g., Vladimir Lenin against Kant, the latter being closer to rationalism) and to subdivide realism into moderate and extreme variants.[9] He does not subdivide rationalism, but Bull's distinction between pluralism and solidarism suggests itself, the former tending towards realism, the latter towards revolutionism.[10]

This modification of the three traditions raises the question whether the range of viewpoints is now envisaged as a continuum, the boundary between them becoming imperceptible, or whether the three basic outlooks remain quite distinct, despite internal variations. There is the further question, whether the elements from the second tradition are integrated into a coherent viewpoint or remain undigested, such that no coherent account can be discerned.

In the light of these complications, the statement of this study's central question needs to be extended. It is not just a question of whether

[6] This is evident, for example, from a perusal of Meinecke's classic history of realism. F. Meinecke, *Machiavellism: The Doctrine of Raison d'État and Its Place in Modern History*, transl. from German D. Scott, intro. W. Stark (New York and Washington, DC: Praeger, 1965), or from noting the variety of philosophical schools in the history of liberal thought.

[7] M. W. Doyle, *Ways of War and Peace: Realism, Liberalism, Socialism* (New York: Norton, 1997), pp. 11–12.

[8] Wight, *International Theory*, p. 259.

[9] Ibid., p. 47.

[10] H. Bull, 'The Grotian Conception of International Society', in H. Butterfield and M. Wight (eds), *Diplomatic Investigations: Essays in the Theory of International Politics* (London: George Allen & Unwin, 1969).

an author's thinking is shaped by a genuine conception of international society, or whether language suggesting this is misleading. There are further possibilities: there may be an admixture of two traditions, and this may either be coherent or shot through with inconsistencies.

A further line of criticism, frequently recurring in comments by English School authors as well as critics from outside, takes up the danger of 'pigeonholing', allocating thinkers to one or other tradition with little reflection or close reading, with adverse effects both for teaching and scholarly inquiry.[11] Instead of arousing students' curiosity and sense of the magnitude of the issues, too ready an assigning of thinkers to traditions may present a rather lifeless image of the subject, as if the main outlines are already known. And it may channel research in familiar directions, discouraging potentially more significant lines of inquiry. It might be thought that there is a simple response to this latter concern: that it is surely up to the critic to propose such lines of inquiry. But this may underestimate the effects of established frameworks of thought. The danger that the three traditions, like other frameworks, may be misused is a real one. What was inspiring to one generation may be oppressive to the next. Many of those who heard Wight's lectures have testified to their inspiring effect, and something of this comes through in the published version. By treating the three traditions as hypothesis, not established historical fact, the present study circumvents these potential drawbacks of classification: the hypothesis requires a searching reading of the texts with other possibilities in mind – thus recovering something of the sense of discovery communicated by Wight's lectures.

The organization of the study requires little explanation. Chapter 1 outlines the idea of the three traditions presented by Wight and Bull and also their nineteenth-century predecessor, Otto von Gierke and, in greater detail, their account of the rationalist tradition. It seeks to identify the key elements of their concept of international society and, in the light of this breakdown, formulates the questions to be raised in relation to each of the four authors.

Chapters 2 to 5 explore the writings of Erasmus, Vitoria, Gentili and Grotius in turn, inquiring whether each presents a coherent account of international society and presenting the findings under a varying number of headings to give expression to differences in their thought and mode of expression. Although the concept of international society is not part of their political vocabulary, they comment on its various elements. These comments need to be identified and brought together, taking account of whether they are supported by the author's thought as a whole.

[11] Jeffery, *Hugo Grotius in International Thought*, pp. 19–20, refers to several examples.

Quotations are used quite extensively in these chapters to illustrate the authors' mode of reasoning and to acquaint readers with the problems of translating the language of the time into today's concepts. Quotations also convey impressions of the personalities and thus help bring them to life.

The Conclusion draws together the findings on the extent to which the pattern of ideas comprising international society has been discovered in the texts, and suggests an additional element that might be included in the pattern. The principal finding is highly positive: three of the four authors do indeed present a quite coherent image of international society. Although this cannot be extrapolated to later periods, it is surely significant in relation to this initial phase of the modern states system. The Conclusion also considers wider implications of the findings – for the history of international thought and for English School theory – and questions which the study may suggest concerning the contemporary discipline.

The study is based mainly on primary sources, in particular the writings of the four thinkers, not only their main works but also lesser writings and correspondence, taking account of the political and intellectual context as well as existing interpretations. Wherever possible, references are to English translations, and in their absence to French, Spanish and German translations. The original languages are referred to only where there are no translations or where these need to be clarified. All quotations are in English – the author's translation where non-English texts have been used.

1 Three Ways of Thinking about International Relations

The origins of the idea of three traditions of thought on international relations are not clear. Martin Wight describes it as a 'familiar aspect' of the intellectual history of modern Europe and even as 'strikingly plain',[1] but his only reference is to the German jurist and historian Otto von Gierke.[2] Gierke himself, the first author known to have expounded the thesis, gives no indication, and Hedley Bull refers only to these two.[3] Despite his questioning of the historical validity of the three traditions noted above, Bull later treats them as a matter of fact: 'Throughout the history of the modern states system there have been three competing traditions of thought.'[4]

This chapter first presents the accounts of the three ways of thinking by Gierke, Wight, and Bull; after comparing the three accounts, it identifies the essential elements of the concept of international society as they present it; and in the light of this it formulates the questions that guide the analysis of the writings of the four thinkers.

[1] M. Wight, *International Theory: The Three Traditions*, ed. G. Wight and B. Porter (Leicester: Leicester University Press for the Royal Institute of International Affairs, London, 1991), p. 7. See also M. Wight, *Systems of States*, ed. and intro. H. Bull (Leicester: Leicester University Press for the London School of Economics and Political Science, 1977), p. 38.

[2] M. Wight, 'An Anatomy of International Thought', *Review of International Studies*, vol. 13, no. 3, 1987, p. 227. For other references to Gierke, see, for example, Wight, *Systems of States*, pp. 21, 204, 214 and 215. No other scholar, either before or contemporary with Gierke, or between Gierke and Wight, is known to have presented the idea of the three ways of thinking about international relations. A variation of this idea is formulated by J. H. Herz, *Political Realism and Political Idealism: A Study in Theories and Realities* (Chicago: University of Chicago Press, 1951), pp. 17–42 and 129–53. See also the latter's autobiography, J. H. Herz, *Vom Ueberleben: Wie ein Weltbild entstand* [On Survival: How a View of the World Came into Existence] (Duesseldorf: Droste, 1984), pp. 160–68.

[3] H. Bull, *The Anarchical Society: A Study of Order in World Politics* (London: Macmillan, 1977), pp. ix, 28.

[4] Ibid., p. 24.

Gierke's Account

Gierke offers a concise account of three contending interpretations of the history of international law, initially in his monograph on Johannes Althusius, published in 1880,[5] and in greater details in his monumental work, *Das Deutsche Genossenschaftsrecht*, vol. 4, published in 1912.[6] In the first chapter of this volume, covering the period to the middle of the seventeenth century, Gierke writes:

> The medieval idea of a world monarchy was foreign to the natural-law theorists. They left it to the Imperial publicists to conjure up, on reams of paper, the lifeless shadow of the *imperium mundi*, while they themselves developed out of the indestructible core of that dying idea the new and fruitful idea of *voelkerrechtliche Gemeinschaft.*[7] Beginning with the sixteenth century, it became customary to base the binding force of the *jus gentium*[8] on a *societas gentium* in which the original and indestructible unity of mankind was held to continue to exist, while sovereignty had passed to the individual nations.[9]

Gierke mentions thinkers such as Omphalus, Connanus, Gregorius, Suárez, Winkler, Gryphiander and Grotius as representatives of this view.

After noting that the nature of this society of states remained unclear because no distinction was made between the concept of partnership and that of corporation,[10] Gierke continues: 'And it happened that, on the one hand, the inclination to compress this society into a world state with a world government organized along republican lines appeared again and again' – he thinks of theorists such as Vitoria, Gentili, Boxhornius and

[5] O. von Gierke, *Johannes Althusius und die Entwicklung der naturrechtlichen Staatstheorien* [Johannes Althusius and the Development of the Natural-Law Theories of the State], 5th edn (Aalen: Scientia, 1958), pp. 235–37.

[6] O. von Gierke, *Das Deutsche Genossenschaftsrecht* [The German Law of Cooperative Associations], vol. 4 (Graz: Akademische Druck und Verlagsanstalt, 1954), pp. 361–63, 535–41. In Gierke, *Natural Law and the Theory of Society 1500–1800*, transl. with intro. E. Barker, 2 vols (Cambridge: Cambridge University Press, 1934), the corresponding pages are vol. 1, pp. 85–86, 195–96; vol. 2 (notes), pp. 282–83, 394–95. For Gierke's word *Genossenschaft* a number of translations have been put forward, ranging from 'association' to 'fellowship'. Friedrich's 'co-operative association' may be the most satisfactory. See C. J. Friedrich, 'Gierke, Otto von', in E. R. A. Seligman (ed.-in-chief), *The Encyclopaedia of the Social Sciences*, vol. 6 (New York: Macmillan, 1931), p. 655. Gierke received the 'von' during his lifetime; hence one meets with both Otto Gierke and Otto von Gierke in the literature.

[7] There is no entirely satisfactory translation of *voelkerrechtlich*, but Gierke's meaning of *voelkerrechtliche Gemeinschaft* is perhaps best conveyed by translating it as the legal community of nations (or states).

[8] Translated: law of nations, society of nations.

[9] Gierke, *Das Deutsche Genossenschaftsrecht*, vol. 4, p. 361.

[10] For Gierke, a corporation is a juristic person, whereas a partnership is no more than the sum of its members. See O. von Gierke, *Das Deutsche Genossenschaftsrecht*, vol. 1 (Graz: Akademische Druck und Verlagsanstalt, 1954; first published 1868), p. 361.

Junius Brutus – 'while, on the other hand, the stricter adherents of the theory of sovereignty altogether rejected the idea of a natural community binding the states.'[11] The two examples which he gives are Bodin and Hobbes.

After this brief outline of the three ways of thinking about international relations, Gierke returns to 'the dominant theory, decisive for the future of the law of nations', to point out that its exponents maintained that

> there did exist an association based on natural law amongst nations, and that this association, while it did not produce any power of the whole over its parts, did generate mutual rights and obligations of a social kind. The law of nations was interpreted as natural law binding the states – which as a result of their sovereignty remained in the state of nature – just as the pre-state natural law had bound human beings in the state of nature.[12]

In the second chapter, which covers the period from the middle of the seventeenth century to the beginning of the nineteenth century, Gierke observes that the question relating to the existence and nature of *voelkerrechtliche Gemeinschaft* continued to be answered in different ways. On the one hand, there were those who altogether rejected the idea of a general society of states. Their reasoning was that 'if the state of nature was a state without a social life, and if the law of nations was nothing more than pure natural law which continued to be valid between states, who as *personae morales* lived in a state of liberty and equality, then there could be no general society of states'.[13] His research showed Gierke that, because of the esteem in which Samuel Pufendorf was held, it looked for a time as if such a view would carry the victory. Apart from Pufendorf, it was people such as Hornius, Spinoza, Hertius, Boehmer and Justi who expounded this view. However, in the long run, as he observed, the opposite view prevailed:

> It was argued that in as far as an original community amongst human beings was assumed, the state of nature which existed among states was also that of a natural society. Yet, even if one proceeded from the assumption of individualization, but saw in the creation of the social condition a development of natural law itself, one arrived at the idea of a society among nations established by natural law or at least postulated by natural law. The representatives of this view usually recognized a positive law of nations which was produced within this society by extending the natural law of nations through a process of express or tacit consent. In this way, the concept of a general society of states was successfully defended.[14]

[11] Gierke, *Das Deutsche Genossenschaftsrecht*, vol. 4, p. 362.

[12] Ibid.

[13] Ibid., p. 535. As E. Barker comments: 'The adjective "moral" is only used in a negative sense, as the antithesis of "natural" or "physical"'. See E. Barker, 'Introduction', in Gierke, *Natural Law and the Theory of Society*, vol. 1, p. lxv.

[14] Gierke, *Das Deutsche Genossenschaftsrecht*, vol. 4, pp. 535–36.

Gierke mentions Johann a Felde, Mevius, Praschius, Bossuet, Placcius, Leibniz and Thomasius as representatives of this view. 'Yet every so often', the account concludes, 'the idea of a *civitas maxima*,[15] whose citizens, the states, were subject to a true universal government, reappeared.'[16] Its advocates, Gierke notes, were thinkers such as Vico, Wolff, Achenwall, Kant and Fichte.

Wight's Account

The most concise formulation of Wight's view of the three traditions is in his chapter in *Diplomatic Investigations*, 'Western Values in International Relations', originally published in 1966.[17] His later posthumously published lectures offer variations on the theme and some useful clarifications, but no better outline. 'Ever since Machiavelli and Hobbes', the account begins,

> there have been those who take the view that there is no such thing as international society: that international relations constitute an anarchy whose social elements are negligible. The doctrine that the state is the ultimate unit of political society entails the doctrine that there is no wider society to embrace states.[18]

According to the exponents of this view, Wight goes on to say, the diplomatic system, the network of functional international organizations, the League of Nations and the United Nations furnish no evidence of an international society, and international law 'is only the sum of the principles and rules which states ... have agreed to regard as obligatory; and the basis of international obligation is purely contractual'.[19] Wight holds that, for example, Hegel, the Social Darwinists, the legal positivists and many a diplomat of the nineteenth and twentieth centuries represented this line of thinking.

'At the opposite extreme', Wight continues, there are those who believe that

> the society of states is the unreal thing – a complex of legal fictions and obsolescent diplomatic forms which conceals, obstructs and oppresses the real society of individual men and women, the *civitas maxima*.[20] On this view, international

[15] Translated: world state.

[16] Gierke, *Das Deutsche Genossenschaftsrecht*, vol. 4, p. 536.

[17] M. Wight, 'Western Values in International Relations', in H. Butterfield and M. Wight (eds), *Diplomatic Investigations: Essays in the Theory of International Politics* (London: George Allen & Unwin, 1969).

[18] Ibid., p. 92.

[19] Ibid., p. 93.

[20] Translated: community of mankind. Note the different meaning that Gierke ascribes to *civitas maxima* [world state].

society is none other than the community of mankind. If the community of mankind is not yet manifested, yet it is latent, half glimpsed and groping for its necessary fulfilment.[21]

According to Wight, the Huguenots, Kant and Turgot represent this view, and so do the Jacobins, Mazzini, President Wilson and the communists. The road to a world state may be peaceful or it may be marked by war, but whatever its nature, it is believed that, as Wight puts it, 'the community of mankind, like the kingdom of God, is the glory that shall be revealed'.[22]

More prosaically, in the published lectures Wight makes it clear that he envisages major variations in the political form this vision may assume and in the manner in which it is to be realized. It may harden into a world-state or consist in an association of like-minded political communities representing their individual citizens and living peacefully together (Kant's republics or Mazzini's nations) or, more radically, a cosmopolitan *civitas maxima* of individual citizens, yet not a state, the states as such, and along with them international relations, having been dissolved away. The vision may be realized peacefully or through violence, through doctrinal uniformity or through doctrinal imperialism.[23]

Having outlined the two extreme ways of thinking about international relations, Wight introduces the third tradition of thought which has the 'quality of a *via media*': 'Between the belief that the society of states is non-existent or at best a polite fiction, and the belief that it is the chrysalis for the community of mankind, lies a more complex conception of international society.'[24] It is a conception, Wight holds, which is expressed in a language which is imprecise and full of qualifications. It does not deny the sovereignty of states, but maintains that this sovereignty is relative and not absolute. It sees the states not as dissolving and merging into a world community, but rather as parts of a greater whole, and this greater whole, international society, exercises restraints upon its parts, the states.

Given 'such tension between opposites' an understanding of this conception of international society, Wight argues, can be arrived at only by extensive historical and sociological study. International society, on this view:

[I]s the habitual intercourse of independent communities, beginning in the Christendom of Western Europe and gradually extending throughout the world.

[21] Wight, 'Western Values', p. 93.
[22] Ibid., p. 94. The political organization advocated by universalists is discussed by Wight in his 1960 lecture, 'An Anatomy of International Thought', pp. 225–26.
[23] Wight, *International Theory*, pp. 40–48.
[24] Wight, 'Western Values', pp. 91, 95. See also his reference to it as 'the broad middle road of European thinking', in Wight, *International Theory*, pp. 14–15.

It is manifest in the diplomatic system; in the conscious maintenance of the balance of power to preserve the independence of the member-communities; in the regular operations of international law, whose binding force is accepted over a wide though politically unimportant range of subjects; in economic, social and technical interdependence and the functional international institutions established latterly to regulate it. All these presuppose an international social consciousness, a world-wide community-sentiment.[25]

As representatives of this way of thinking, Wight mentions Vitoria, Suárez, Gentili, Grotius, Locke, Callières, Halifax, Montesquieu, Burke, Gentz, Castlereagh, Coleridge, Tocqueville, Lincoln, Gladstone, Cecil of Chelwood, Ferrero, Churchill, Brierly, Harold Nicolson and Spaak.

Bull's Account

Bull's earliest discussion of the three traditions, his chapter in *Diplomatic Investigations*, 'Society and Anarchy in International Relations',[26] is notable for his sustained defence of the concept of international society, but his most succinct account of the traditions is that in *The Anarchical Society*:

Throughout the history of the modern states system there have been three competing traditions of thought: the Hobbesian or realist tradition … the Kantian or universalist tradition … and the Grotian or internationalist tradition.[27]

According to the Hobbesian tradition – Bull mentions Machiavelli, Bacon and Hegel and his successors in addition to Hobbes – international relations

represent pure conflict between states and resemble a game that is wholly distributive or zero-sum: the interests of each state exclude the interests of any other. The particular international activity that … is most typical of international activity as a whole, or best provides the clue to it, is war itself. Thus peace, on the Hobbesian view, is a period of recuperation from the last war and preparation for the next.[28]

To this Hobbesian description of the nature of international relations Bull adds the Hobbesian prescription for international conduct:

[T]he state is free to pursue its goals in relation to other states without moral or legal restrictions of any kind … If any moral or legal goals are to be pursued in international politics, these can only be the moral or legal goals of the state itself …

[25] Wight, 'Western Values', pp. 96–97.

[26] H. Bull, 'Society and Anarchy in International Relations', in Butterfield and Wight (eds), *Diplomatic Investigations*.

[27] Bull, *The Anarchical Society*, p. 24.

[28] Ibid., pp. 24–25.

The only rules or principles which ... may be said to limit or circumscribe the behaviour of states in their relations with one another are rules of prudence or expediency.[29]

At the other extreme, there is the Kantian or universalist way of thinking about international relations. As Bull presents it, the Kantian view is that

the dominant theme of international relations ... is only apparently the relationship among states, and is really the relationship among all men in the community of mankind – which exists potentially, even if it does not exist actually, and which when it comes into being will sweep the system of states into limbo.[30]

The Kantians hold that

within the community of all mankind ... the interests of all men are one and the same; international politics ... is ... a purely co-operative or non-zero-sum game. Conflicts of interest exist among the ruling cliques of states, but this is only at the superficial or transient level of the existing system of states ... The particular international activity which ... most typifies international activity as a whole is the horizontal conflict of ideology that cuts across the boundaries of states and divides human society into two camps – the trustees of the immanent community of mankind and those who stand in its way.[31]

For the Kantians, Bull claims, there do exist moral rules in international relations, but these rules do not enjoin the preservation of the system, but rather its overthrow and replacement by a universal society.[32]

Between the realist and the universalist traditions there is the Grotian or internationalist tradition. As Bull puts it,

The Grotian tradition describes international politics in terms of a society of states or international society. [This tradition contends] that states are not engaged in simple struggle ... but are limited in their conflicts with one another by common rules and institutions. [It accepts] the Hobbesian premise that sovereigns or states are the principal reality in international politics; the immediate members of international society are states rather than individual human beings.[33]

Neither complete conflict of interests between states nor complete identity of interests reflects international reality. Neither war between states nor horizontal conflict cutting across the boundaries of states is the most typical international activity, but rather 'trade – or, more generally, economic and social intercourse between one country and another'.

29 Ibid., p. 25.
30 Ibid.
31 Ibid., pp. 25–26.
32 Ibid., p. 26. Bull does not discuss the question of political organization in relation to universalism.
33 Ibid.

As far as their prescription for international conduct is concerned, the Grotians hold that

> all states, in their dealings with one another, are bound by the rules and institutions of the society they form ... States ... are bound not only by rules of prudence or expediency but also by imperatives of morality and law. But ... what these imperatives enjoin is not the overthrow of the system of states and its replacement by a universal community of mankind, but rather acceptance of the requirements of coexistence and co-operation in a society of states.[34]

Bull's list of representatives of this tradition of thought is long. It includes, for example, Vitoria, Suárez, Gentili, Grotius, Pufendorf, Callières, Bynkershoek, Wolff, J. M. Moser, Vattel, Burke, G. F. von Martens, Heeren, Gentz, Ancillon, Castlereagh, Ranke, Gladstone, Phillimore and Salisbury.

Comparing the Three Accounts

All three identify the same patterns of thought about international relations, or traditions, and agree in seeing international society as central to one of them, even though Gierke's terminology differs from the other two. He does not use the word 'tradition', which as we have seen raises questions that will require further discussion, nor does he use the word 'international', but rather *vöelkerrechtlich* (from *Völkerrecht*, the law of nations – *ius gentium*). Thus he uses the terminology of the period he was describing, to refer to what later came to be termed international law.

There is a second definitional question. It relates to the word 'society'. Gierke does not distinguish between *Gemeinschaft* (community) and *Gesellschaft* (society), nor does he use the word 'system'. Wight, like Gierke, uses 'society' and 'community' interchangeably: sociologists, in his view, had not agreed on a satisfactory distinction between the two.[35] And while he occasionally hints at a distinction between system and society/community, for the most part he treats them as synonymous. '[International society] has been variously called the family of nations, the states-system, the society of states, the international community.'[36]

Like Gierke and Wight, Bull does not distinguish between 'society' and 'community', but he does draw an important distinction between 'society' and 'system'. He defines the latter thus:

34 Ibid., p. 27.
35 Wight, 'Western Values', p. 92.
36 M. Wight, *Power Politics*, ed. and intro. H. Bull and C. Holbraad (Harmondsworth: Pelican, 1979), p. 105. See also Wight, *Systems of States*, pp. 21–22, 110–52; and Butterfield and Wight (eds), *Diplomatic Investigations*, p. 12.

[W]here states are in regular contact with one another, and where in addition there is interaction between them sufficient to make the behaviour of each a necessary element in the calculations of the other, then we may speak of their forming a system.[37]

'Society', in contrast, is defined in the following way:

A society of states (or international society) exists when a group of states, conscious of certain common interests and common values, form a society in the sense that they conceive themselves to be bound by a common set of rules in their relations with one another, and share in the working of common institutions.[38]

Since this is an important distinction and has been generally adopted by the English School, this study will follow this usage. Like all three authors, it will regard 'society' and 'community' as interchangeable.

The authors are in substantial agreement on the origins of the three ways of viewing international society. Gierke sees different views appearing in the sixteenth century, his representative thinkers being Bodin, Connanus and Vitoria. Wight does likewise, mentioning Machiavelli and Vitoria. Bull speaks of a first phase of the three traditions of thought, which he attaches to the fifteenth, sixteenth and seventeenth centuries. Machiavelli and Vitoria are his first spokesmen; like Wight, he does not name a universalist.

In Gierke's account, the three ways of viewing international relations remain anonymous. Wight initially called them the realist, rationalist and revolutionist traditions, later the Machiavellian, Grotian and Kantian traditions respectively.[39] In 'Western Values' he terms the Grotian tradition the 'constitutional tradition', adding that it has the quality of a *via media*.[40] Bull expressed a preference for Wight's second set of names but himself chose a slight variation: the Hobbesian or realist tradition, the Kantian or universalist tradition and the Grotian or internationalist tradition.[41] This study will retain the term 'realist', noting that it has been defined in a particular way. For the period chosen, the term 'universalist' seems more appropriate than revolutionist, but none of the three names for the third tradition is wholly satisfactory. Both rationalist and internationalist have too many other connotations, and the appropriateness of individual names has been questioned. In this study it will be termed, provisionally, the *via media* tradition, except where referring to comments by Wight and Bull.

[37] Bull, *The Anarchical Society*, p. 10.
[38] Ibid., p. 13.
[39] Wight, *International Theory*.
[40] Wight, 'Western Values', pp. 90–91.
[41] Bull, *The Anarchical Society*, p. 24.

The three accounts include the names of many thinkers. Yet neither Gierke nor Wight or Bull claims completeness for his lists. It is therefore not surprising to find that, while some names recur in each account in the same tradition (for example, Suárez, Hobbes, Grotius and Kant), other names recur in only two accounts in the same tradition (for example, Callières, Burke, Gentz and Hegel), and some other names again occur in only one account (for example, Leibniz, Halifax, Vattel and Fichte). However, there are some names which appear in different traditions in the three accounts. Vitoria and Gentili, for example, figure in Gierke's account amongst the universalists, whereas Wight and Bull mention them among the internationalists. Pufendorf is allocated to the realists by Gierke and to the internationalists by Bull. Do these differences reflect changing views on the part of those thinkers? Or do they result from different criteria of selection on the part of Gierke, Wight and Bull – criteria which they do not explain? These questions will be taken up in the relevant chapters.

The three accounts are in agreement that the traditions have not coexisted peacefully. The language that Gierke uses to describe the interaction of the three traditions – to be victorious and to die, to be dominant and to defend – reflects his general belief that, 'Just as all life, so all history is a struggle; and the struggle does not lead to harmony in the short run; more often it results in suppression of the vanquished and in tyranny of the victor ... Only in the long run, the growing intelligence, the growing consciousness of nations ... will achieve the longed-for harmony.'[42]

Wight shares Gierke's view that the three traditions have not lived quietly side by side. His language, however, is less dramatic. When thinking of the Grotian tradition, he says: 'This pattern of ideas is persistent and recurrent. Sometimes eclipsed and distorted, it has constantly reappeared and reasserted its authority,'[43] and later he adds: '[T]here are other patterns of ideas in international history for which persistence, recurrence and coherence can be claimed.'[44] But in contrast with Gierke, Wight sees no end to the struggle or debate, either in the short or the long run.

Bull prefers the term 'competition' when describing the relationship between the three traditions of thought: 'Throughout the history of the modern states system there have been three competing traditions of thought.'[45]

[42] Gierke, *Das Deutsche Genossenschaftsrecht*, vol. 1, p. 2.

[43] Wight, 'Western Values', p. 90.

[44] Ibid., p. 91. See also Wight's discussion, 'Varying relative strength of traditions', in Wight, *International Theory*, pp. 162–63, which includes words such as 'dominant', 'rival', 'recessive' and 'destroy'. See also the phrase 'the erosion of Rationalism', p. 260.

[45] Bull, *The Anarchical Society*, p. 24.

In the twentieth century as in the sixteenth and seventeenth centuries, the idea of international society has been on the defensive. On the one hand, the Hobbesian or realist interpretation of international politics has been fed by the two World Wars, and by the expansion of international society beyond its originally European confines. On the other hand, Kantian or universalist interpretations have been fed by a striving to transcend the states system so as to escape the conflict and disorder that have accompanied it in this century.[46]

Whether one sees the relationship between the three traditions as a struggle, a debate or a competition, there is a question which remains. The three accounts make it clear that the Hobbesian and Grotian traditions are incompatible with one another. They are less clear whether the universalist tradition is incompatible with the other two or rather is addressed to different concerns, that is to say, is less concerned with the character of the international system or society as it exists, and more concerned to transcend it. The reason for seeking to transcend it, however, is that the present condition, perceived in realist terms, is seen as intolerable, and from this perspective international society is a fiction or an illusion. Thus there is an extreme tension, if not outright incompatibility, between these two traditions, in contrast to the seeming compatibility between realism and universalism.

Differing Contexts

Gierke's account of the three traditions in international law is incidental to his main purpose: overall, a history of German cooperative associations, and in volume 4, the theory of state and corporations, where it forms part of a discussion of natural law theories. He makes it clear that he sees the natural law conception of the state and society in juristic terms, and does not enlarge on his brief account of the traditions in international law nor place it in a wider political context.

Wight, in contrast with Gierke, made the three traditions central to his thinking about international relations. In 'Western Values' it is the suggestion that the values of a society express themselves in its ideas rather than in the record of its practice which provides the context within which he presents his account of the three traditions, and he advances the proposition that, while the existence of these three traditions is a characteristic feature of the history of thought about international relations in modern Europe, the 'constitutional tradition' is 'specially representative of Western values'.[47] And he investigates this proposition by relating it to

[46] Ibid., p. 38.
[47] Wight, 'Western Values', p. 91.

questions such as order and how to maintain it, intervention and international morality.

In *Systems of States*, Wight places his account of the three traditions in the context of cultural questions, suggesting that '[w]e must assume that a states-system will not come into being without a degree of cultural unity among its members'.[48] We noted earlier that he treats the states-system as synonymous with international society.

In the published lectures, after a brief introduction on the relationship between international theory and political theory, and after commenting that 'one of the main purposes of university education is to escape from the *Zeitgeist*',[49] he structures his whole discussion of international theory in terms of the three traditions, comparing their characteristic views on a range of issues: human nature, international society, mankind, national power and national interest, diplomacy, war, international law and the balance of power.

Bull, in contrast with Gierke and Wight, was not so much concerned with showing the three traditions to be a historical experience of the Western mind as with exploring their role and significance in the context of present-day thinking and action in international relations. This is evident in his first discussion of the traditions, 'Society and Anarchy in International Relations', where he laments the prevalence of the view that the present system of sovereign states rules out the establishment of an acceptable international order. 'It exists ... where we might least expect to find it, in the pronouncements of the servants of sovereign states themselves, by whose daily acts the system is preserved.'[50] His account of the traditions seeks to counter this prevailing view, in some ways foreshadowing the argument in *The Anarchical Society*.

In this work, an 'inquiry into the nature of order in world politics', Bull's account of the traditions appears in chapter 2, 'Does Order Exist in World Politics?': he goes on to an extended discussion of the Grotian tradition, its history and its concept of international society as the framework for thinking about international order and the institutions which make it possible, the discussion of which occupies a large part of the book. The historical record provides the foundation, but in the end the focus is on the contemporary relevance of the ideas and the institutions.

From the foregoing comparison, it may be concluded that the differences among the three authors' accounts amount to differing emphases and styles, but there are no major differences of substance in the way

[48] Wight, *Systems of States*, p. 33.
[49] Wight, *International Theory*, pp. 1–6.
[50] Bull, 'Society and Anarchy in International Relations', p. 36.

they characterize the traditions. The common ground is far more significant. It remains to observe precisely how they characterize the traditions and how they spell out the essentials of the concept of international society central to the *via media* tradition.

The Concept of International Society

First, we may note how the authors characterize the rival traditions. Realism is presented as the doctrine that sovereignty entails the complete absence of restrictions on the sovereign state's freedom of action. International anarchy negates any wider community; there can be no binding moral or legal rules, since there is no society beyond the state. If states comply with international law, this is solely due to expediency. Further, the typical relationship among sovereigns is a state of war; peace is essentially a time of preparing for the next war. This depiction of realism will be contested by those who celebrate the richness and diversity of the realist tradition, but arguably its emphasis on conflict and the absence of moral and legal restraints brings out the central realist assumptions.

As regards universalism, Wight's distinctions make it clear that the *civitas maxima* or community of humanity can take a variety of forms: an association of like-minded states as well as a world government, the religious or political ideals of those for whom the overriding concern is to establish the true doctrine at home and abroad, confident that it embodies the true aspirations of humanity (here 'revolutionism' fits well). This still leaves the question whether all these variants really form one category, but it clarifies the otherwise rather disparate depictions of the tradition.

There is a remarkable congruence between the three accounts of the essentials of the third tradition. For Gierke, as we have seen, the binding force of the *ius gentium* rests on a *societas gentium* 'in which the original and indestructible unity of mankind' coexists with sovereignty's 'having passed to the individual nations'. He refers to an association based on natural law which does not entail any power of the whole over the parts but does generate mutual rights and obligations. For Wight, sovereignty remains with the states, but they form part of a greater whole that exercises restraints on the parts, the states. For Bull, sovereigns or states are the principal realities in international politics, but their actions are limited by common rules and institutions, not only rules of prudence or expediency but imperatives of morality and law. Both Wight and Bull refer to 'habitual intercourse among independent communities' or 'economic and social intercourse', not war or ideological conflict, as 'the most typical international activity'. Gierke, limiting himself to the legal dimension, does not mention this latter point.

This formulation of the essential elements of the concept of international society forms the basis for the following inquiry, whether the thesis of the three traditions, here treated as a hypothesis, is borne out by an examination of the thought of the four selected authors. A positive finding would not be conclusive but would strengthen the hypothesis; a negative finding would seriously weaken it.

Questions Suggested by the Hypothesis

The hypothesis derived from Gierke, Wight and Bull suggests a number of questions which relate partly to the pattern of ideas and partly to the thinkers.

1. Do the thinkers said to represent the *via media* have the idea of a plurality of political entities and, if so, what do they say about these entities?
   - Do they have the idea of that which links these entities and, if so, what content do they give to it?
   - Do they have the idea of rules and institutions shared by these entities and, if so, how do they present these?
   - How do they reconcile war with the idea of international society?
   - Are there other relevant ideas, not suggested by the hypothesis but present in the writings of these thinkers?
2. Do the thinkers said to represent the *via media* see themselves as taking up a position which differentiates them from both realism and universalism?
   - Are they familiar with one another's writings and, if so, what is their reaction to them? Do they regard themselves as forming a tradition of thought and, if so, when or with whom do they see it beginning?

These questions will guide the search for the idea of international society in this study, and the attempt to answer them will provide the structure of its chapters.

2 Desiderius Erasmus of Rotterdam

Erasmus stands out among the writers of the later Renaissance both for his renown at the time and for the unabated interest that he continues to attract. Numerous editions and translations of his work appeared at the time and continue to appear, accompanied by a stream of commentaries. Virtually all aspects of his thought have been examined in minute detail, but his ideas on international relations constitute a notable exception, notwithstanding the comment of a prominent Erasmus scholar, Margaret Mann Phillips, that

> he was the man of his century who could best survey the whole European scene. In the first flood of the spirit of nationalism, one person was watching the *entre-choc* of nations with a lucid and penetrating eye, and deriving from the prospect the first true idea of international relations on a general scale: and that man was Erasmus.[1]

Erasmus is usually seen as the central figure among the 'northern humanists' of the early sixteenth century, notably Thomas More and John Colet in England, Guillaume Budé in France and Johannes Reuchlin in Germany. Humanism – the promotion of classical literature and learning – originating in fourteenth-century Italy and coming to fruition in the Florentine Renaissance, had transformed the European intellectual world, challenging the dominance of the scholastic philosophy of the late middle ages. At the turn of the sixteenth century, scholasticism was still the orthodoxy in northern universities, but was on the defensive. Humanism was not a rival doctrine but an entirely different intellectual approach.[2]

Its foundation was the recovery and propagation of the classical Greek and Roman texts, taking full advantage of the new technology – printing.

[1] M. M. Phillips, *Erasmus and the Northern Renaissance* (New York: Collier Books, 1965), p. 129.

[2] On humanism, see, for example, Q. Skinner, *The Foundations of Modern Political Thought*, vol. 1, *The Renaissance* (Cambridge: Cambridge University Press, 1978), pp. 35–48, 69–112, 193–263. Humanism is discussed in all the works on Erasmus.

Humanist teaching emphasized classical philosophy and rhetoric: philosophy as a guide to the good life, rhetoric as persuasion through eloquence, or sometimes satire, not through the abstract logic of the scholastics. The Italian humanists, while not openly distancing themselves from Christianity, celebrated human achievement and proclaimed a view of the good life (*vir virtutis*) which was at odds with the Christian assumptions of human imperfection and original sin.

The northern humanists fully shared the commitment to classical learning, but for them Christianity was not just taken for granted but was the prior commitment, although there was no sense of a conflict between the two. The prince would acquire virtue through pondering Christ's teaching, and wisdom through studying the classics. For Erasmus, what was fundamental – the 'philosophy of Christ' – was the Christian ethic: the striving to live according to the spirit of Christ's words.[3] The close reading of the scriptures was basic; in his view the scholastics and the monks had lost sight of these simple truths, in the one case through abstruse argumentation, in the other through preoccupation with externals: rules and rituals. This normative stance lay behind Erasmus's thinking on politics.

Erasmus's reputation does not depend on any single work, but on the range and diversity of his writings exemplifying most of the humanist literary *genres*: treatises, essays, religious tracts, dialogues, satires, panegyrics, advice to the ruler, and book dedications. Their subject matter included education, religion, personal conduct, social life and themes from the ancient world. He wrote relatively little on politics directly – on monarchy and its problems, the education of the ruler, and his famous denunciations of war – but comments appear in many other contexts, especially in his voluminous correspondence.

In addition, he published new editions of many classical texts, for example, Aristotle, Euripides, Lucian, Cicero, Isocrates, Ovid, Plutarch and Suetonius, and writings of early Church Fathers such as Jerome, Arnobius, Irenaeus, Ambrose and Augustine. One of his major projects – a 'life work' – was his edition of the Greek New Testament, with his Latin translation, compiled by comparing the available imperfect manuscripts and constantly revised in the light of further manuscripts. Among his best-known works were the *Adages*, a collection of classical proverbs with his own comments, sometimes substantial essays, constantly revised and expanded, and the *Colloquies*, lively dialogues, likewise frequently

[3] See, for example, Phillips, *Erasmus and the Northern Renaissance*, pp. 57–93; A. G. Dickens and W. R. D. Jones, *Erasmus the Reformer* (London: Methuen, 1994), pp. 41–62; R. J. Schoeck, *Erasmus of Europe*, vol. II, *The Prince of Humanists, 1501–1536* (Edinburgh: Edinburgh University Press, 1993), pp. 28–40.

reissued. His most popular work, *The Praise of Folly*, was a satire whose targets included monastic, papal and political abuses.

His life may be seen as falling into three phases: his youth and intellectual formation, up to and including his first visit to England in 1499; his rapid rise to fame and authority a decade later; and a final period overshadowed by controversies over his attempt to find a middle way between Luther and orthodox Catholicism.[4]

Erasmus was born of an 'unlawful' and, as he called it, 'sacrilegious union'[5] – his year of birth is variously given as 1466, 1467 or 1469 – in Rotterdam, Holland, then part of the Burgundian Low Countries which came under Habsburg rule in 1477. His schooling took place mainly at Deventer, where he studied with the Brethren of the Common Life, a group of teachers regarded as the leading educators of the time. In 1487 he entered the Augustinian monastery at Steyn and stayed there for approximately six years. From this period date letters, and also *Antibarbarorum Liber* [The Book of the Antibarbarians], a treatise in which he sets out his position in support of the use of classical learning, a position which he never abandoned. In 1493 he was appointed secretary to Henry of Bergen, Bishop of Cambrai.

In 1495 Erasmus took leave of absence from the Bishop to study theology at the University of Paris for four years. Here he was required to study scholastic texts whose approach he rejected as arid, preoccupied with minor issues and remote from the central Christian message; but he was able to make contact with humanist scholars and develop his own approach. In 1499 he accepted an invitation to England and stayed for six months, studying Greek, the ancient Church Fathers and the Scriptures. His lifelong friendship with More and Colet dates from this visit. He returned to Paris in 1500 and published the first edition of the *Adagia* [*Adages*].

From 1501 to 1505 he was in the Low Countries, mainly in the university city of Louvain where, in 1503, he published his composition *Enchiridion Militis Christiani* [The Handbook of a Christian Soldier],

[4] For accounts of Erasmus's life and publications, see, for example, R. H. Bainton, *Erasmus of Christendom* (Glasgow: Fontana/Collins, 1977); R. J. Schoeck, *Erasmus of Europe*, vol. I, *The Making of a Humanist, 1467–1500* (Edinburgh: Edinburgh University Press, 1990); Schoeck, *Erasmus of Europe*, vol. II; C. Augustijn, *Erasmus: His Life, Works and Influence* (Toronto: University of Toronto Press, 1991); L. Halkin, *Erasmus: A Critical Biography* (Oxford: Oxford University Press, 1993); J. D. Tracy, *Erasmus of the Low Countries* (Berkeley, CA: University of California Press, 1996). For a comparison of interpretations of Erasmus in recent biographies, see B. Mansfield, *Erasmus in the Twentieth Century: Interpretations c1920–2000* (Toronto: University of Toronto Press, 2003), pp. 202–05, 218–24.

[5] Bainton, *Erasmus of Christendom*, p. 20.

a guide to Christian living. In 1504 he gave an oration, *Panegyricus* [The Panegyric], at Brussels, capital of Burgundy, on the safe return from Spain of Prince Philip, Duke of Burgundy and father of the future Emperor Charles V. In 1505 he visited England again.

The years 1506 to 1509 saw him in Italy, travelling and studying. From this period also dates his doctorate in theology from the University of Turin. In Bologna, he was deeply shocked to witness the triumphal entry, in full military splendor, of Pope Julius II, after his army had defeated the city's ruler. In 1509 he returned to England and spent the next five years there – a sojourn interspersed with journeys to the Continent. During this time he wrote *Moriae Encomium* [The Praise of Folly], published in Paris in 1511. Also credited to his account is the dialogue *Julius Exclusus e Coelis* [Julius Excluded from Heaven], a satire on the late Pope Julius II, which appeared anonymously in 1514 in Paris. In the same year the Augustinian canons made an unsuccessful attempt to regain Erasmus for the monastic life at Steyn, to which he was obliged, in principle, as a member of the Augustinian order, to return until granted a papal dispensation in 1517.

Between 1514 and 1521 he stayed at various places in the Low Countries, visited England three more times, and travelled in Germany and Switzerland. In 1516 he was appointed Councillor to Prince Charles. His response was the treatise *Institutio Principis Christiani* [The Education of a Christian Prince], which he dedicated to Charles. The same year also saw the publication of his editions of the Greek New Testament, with his translation into Latin, and of Jerome, an ancient Church Father. In 1517 he organized the *Collegium Trilingue* for the study of Hebrew, Greek and Latin at Louvain, and published his 'great denunciation of war', *Querela Pacis* [The Complaint of Peace].

It was also in 1517 that Martin Luther launched his challenge to papal authority, nailing his 95 Theses to the church door at Wittenberg. In 1519–20, Erasmus helped to formulate a policy of protection for Luther sought by the Duke of Saxony. His advice is contained in letters to various rulers and in what has come to be known as *Axiomata pro Causa Lutheri* [Propositions in Support of Luther].

In 1521 he left the Low Countries, as his reaction to Luther was viewed with suspicion at Louvain, and moved to Basel where he stayed until 1529. His support for Luther was in fact quite limited. He recognized the same clerical abuses but sought reform within the Church, privately deploring the immoderation of Luther and his followers. He was soon under fire from both sides, either for not condemning Luther or for not openly supporting his cause. In 1524 he published *De Libero Arbitrio* [On Free Will], criticizing a key Lutheran doctrine but refraining from any general condemnation. The response from the Lutherans, however, was vitriolic, and he found himself increasingly isolated between the two hostile camps. His publications, however, continued unabated. They included editions of further Church Fathers, some of his 'most piquant' *Colloquies*, which he had begun to publish in 1518, and his *Opus Epistolarum* – not the first but the largest edition of his letters during his lifetime.

Because of religious turbulence, Erasmus left Basel in 1529 and moved to Freiburg, which was then under the rule of the Austrian branch of the House of Habsburg. He stayed for six years, continuing to write and publish: for example, in 1530 the essay *Utilissima Consultatio de Bello Turcis Inferendo* [A Valued Discussion on War against the Turks]; in 1533 *De Sarcienda Ecclesiae Concordia* [On Mending the Peace of the Church]; and in 1535 *Ecclesiastes* [On Preaching].

In 1535 Erasmus returned to now reformed and tranquil Basel. He declined Pope Paul's III invitation to Rome, and died at Basel in 1536.

What Erasmus offers to those who pursue the idea of international society is not confined to his political writings, but is dispersed throughout his works. His ideas will be presented in the sections to follow. The first section is a response to the numerous references found in his writings to the events of his time rather than to a specific question suggested by the hypothesis. These references are instructive for the light which they throw on the historical context within which he lived and worked; they also suggest that thinkers other than 'realists' may be credited with the distinction of being realistic observers.

The second and third sections offer an answer to the question: do the thinkers who are said to represent the *via media* see themselves as taking up a position which differentiates them from both realism and universalism?

The next two sections formulate two ideas discovered in his writings in response to the question: Do the thinkers said to represent the *via media* have the idea of a plurality of political entities and, if so, what do they say about them?

The question of whether the thinkers said to represent the *via media* have the idea of that which links the entities constituting political plurality and, if so, what content do they give to it leads to findings presented in the final four sections.

Erasmus and the Events of His Time

Erasmus lived in a period which we now see as the formation of the modern states system, characterized by political plurality and intense conflict. The former expressed itself not only in the variety of forms of government which existed – according to the historian J. R. Hale there were monarchies, republics, confederations, cities, an emperor and a pope[6] – but was also reflected in the number of political units which constituted Europe. A list drawn up by Hale of Europe in about 1500 may be reproduced as follows:

Russia – Moldavia – Lithuania (ruled from and in conjunction with) Poland – Hungary – Bohemia – Germany (as chief component of the Holy Roman Empire theoretically under the authority of the emperor-elect, Maximilian of Habsburg, hereditary ruler of the duchies of Austria, Styria, Carinthia, Carniola and Tyrol; in practice a congeries of independent units comprising some thirty principates, fifty ecclesiastical territories, about one hundred counties and sixty self-governing cities) – The Netherlands (traditionally part of the Holy Roman Empire, now ruled jointly with Luxembourg and Franche-Comté by Prince Philip of Habsburg, son of Maximilian) – Switzerland – Denmark – Sweden – Norway – Italy shared by (to name the chief independent powers of the peninsula) Venice, Milan, Florence, the Papal States and Naples – Sicily – Spain comprising Aragon and Castile – Portugal – Navarre – France – England.[7]

And this was not all. As Hale points out, there were further political units functioning as 'independent states either by right … or because their nominal superiors were unable to control them'. His examples include Scotland and Savoy, Luebeck and the area controlled by the Teutonic Knights. And there was one state, he reminds his readers, 'which was not of, but was half in Europe, the empire of the Ottoman Turks'.[8]

The political plurality which Europe then knew was accompanied by conflict, and references to conflict run like a red thread through the writings of Erasmus. Studying these references means meeting a well-informed, discerning and sober observer, and not, as one commentator has suggested, a man who did not understand his time.[9] To convey this impression by means of a few examples is difficult, but this is all that can be offered in the context of this inquiry.

The Italian wars, which had begun in 1494 when Charles VIII, King of France, entered Italy with the intention of taking up a claim to Naples, were still continuing when Erasmus visited Italy from 1506 to 1509. In a letter of 1506 to Servatius Rogerus, Prior of Steyn, the Augustinian monastery where he had spent the years 1487 to 1493, Erasmus writes:

[6] J. R. Hale, *Renaissance Europe: 1480–1520* (London: Fontana/Collins, 1979), p. 55.
[7] Ibid., pp. 320–21.
[8] Ibid., pp. 321, 322.
[9] S. Dresden, 'Présence d'Érasme' [Presence of Erasmus], in Académie Royale Néerlandaise des Sciences et des Sciences Humaines, *Actes du Congrès Érasme, Rotterdam, 27–29 Octobre 1969* [Records of the Erasmus Conference, Rotterdam, 27–29 October 1969] (Amsterdam and London: North Holland Publishing Company, 1971), p. 11.

I came to Italy mainly in order to learn Greek; but studies are dormant here at present, whereas war is hotly pursued ... Bentivoglio has left Bologna; the French ... were driven back ... On St Martin's Day Julius, the supreme pontiff, entered Bologna ... The emperor's arrival is awaited. Preparations are afoot for a war against the Venetians.[10]

The League of Cambrai, concluded in 1508 by Louis XII, King of France, Ferdinand, King of Aragon and Regent of Castile, the Emperor Maximilian, Pope Julius II and the Duke of Mantua, with the purpose of partitioning Venice, was followed three years later by the Holy League which joined Julius II with Ferdinand, Maximilian, Venice and Henry VIII of England with the aim of expelling France from Italy. Erasmus, writing in 1511 from Cambridge to Andrea Ammonio, Latin secretary to Henry VIII, comments:

As to the war that has been set on foot, I am afraid that the Greek proverb about the moth in the candle-flame will soon be appropriate. For if anything happens to the Roman church, then who, I ask you, could more properly be blamed for it than the all-too-mighty Julius? But pray suppose the French are driven out of Italy, and then reflect, please, whether you prefer to have the Spaniards as your masters, or the Venetians, whose rule is intolerable even to their own countrymen ... I fear Italy is to have a change of masters and, because she cannot endure the French may have to endure French rule multiplied by two.[11]

The conflicts in Italy generated conflicts in other parts of Europe. In 1512 the Netherlands saw Henry VIII at war with the French, whom he defeated near Saint-Orner in 1513. In 1514 it seemed that the war would be resumed. Erasmus observes from London in a letter to Antoon van Bergen, Abbot of St Bertin, a man of influence with the Court at Brussels:

But the war that is being prepared for has brought about a sudden change in the character of this island. Here the price of everything is going up every day, while liberality declines ... Besides, while it is a kind of exile to live on any island, our confinement is closer still at present by reason of the wars, so that one cannot even get a letter out.[12]

In September 1517, nearly two months before Luther's theses became public knowledge, Erasmus writes from Antwerp, communicating his apprehensions to Thomas Wolsey, Cardinal of York: 'In this part of the

[10] Erasmus to Servatius Rogerus, 16 November 1506, in *Collected Works of Erasmus*, vol. 2, *The Correspondence of Erasmus: Letters 142 to 297, 1501 to 1514*, transl. R. A. B. Mynors and D. F. S. Thomson, annotated W. K. Ferguson (Toronto: University of Toronto Press, 1975), p. 125.

[11] Erasmus to Andrea Ammonio, 26 November 1511, in *Collected Works of Erasmus*, vol. 2, pp. 204–05.

[12] Erasmus to Antoon van Bergen, 14 March 1514, in ibid., pp. 279.

world I am afraid a great revolution is impending, unless the favour of Heaven and the piety and wisdom of our rulers provide for the interests of humanity.'[13] The Diet of Worms took place in 1521. Luther refused to retract his writings, was condemned and disappeared behind the walls of the Wartburg. The Emperor, now Charles V, and the French King, now Francis I, resumed the war in Italy, which came to a temporary end in 1525 when Francis was taken prisoner at Pavia. In the same year, 1521, the Turks moved to conquer Belgrade; in the following year, Rhodes; and, in 1525, they won a decisive victory at Mohacs against the Hungarians. Erasmus's *Colloquy* of 1526, 'The New Mother', contains advice on the care of babies, instructions on the nature of the soul and a brief survey of the political situation in Europe:

King Christian of Denmark, a devout partisan of the gospel, is in exile. Francis, King of France, is a 'guest' of the Spaniards ... Charles is preparing to extend the boundaries of his realm.[14] Ferdinand has his hands full in Germany. Bankruptcy threatens every court. The peasants raise dangerous riots ... The commons are bent on anarchy; the Church is shaken to its very foundations by menacing factions ... The Turks conquer and threaten all the while.[15]

Upon signing the peace treaty of Madrid in 1526, which brought his release from imprisonment, Francis I formed a league with Milan, Venice, Florence and the Pope, now Clement VII, against Charles V. The ensuing campaigns led in 1527 to the sacking of Rome by the imperial forces. Erasmus expresses the significance of this event in one sentence contained in a long letter which he addresses in 1528 to Jacobus Sadoletus, Bishop of Carpentras, Avignon, regarding 'this calamitous event': 'This surely was the destruction of a world rather than a city.'[16]

13 Erasmus to Thomas Wolsey, 9 September 1517, in F. M. Nichols, *The Epistles of Erasmus From His Earliest Letters to His Fifty-First Year Arranged in Order of Time: English Translations from the Early Correspondence with a Commentary Confirming the Chronological Arrangement and Supplying Further Biographical Matter*, vol. 3 (London: Longmans/Green & Co., 1918), p. 51.

14 The original version (1526) of this sentence was: 'Charles wants a new monarchy comprising the whole world' [*Carolus molitur nouam totius orbis monarchian*], but the word 'new', as Erasmus writes to Alfonso Valdes, the Imperial Chancellor's secretary, produced a 'chicanery' against him on the part of those who upheld the imperial cause. See Erasmus to Alphonse Valdes, 21 March 1529, in A. Gerlo (ed.), *La Correspondance d'Érasme* [The Correspondence of Erasmus], vol. 8 (Brussels: University Press, 1979), p. 121. For the original Latin text, see A. G. Weiler, 'Einleitung' [Introduction], to D. Erasmus, 'Vtilissima Consvltatio de Bello Tvrcis Inferendo, et Obiter Enarratvs Psalmvs XXVIII' [A Valued Discussion of War Against the Turks ...], in *Opera Omnia Desiderii Erasmi Roterodami* [The Complete Works of Desiderius Erasmus of Rottersam], V–III, vol. 15 (Amsterdam: North Holland Publishing Co., 1986), p. 9.

15 'The New Mother' (1526), in C. R. Thompson (transl.), *The Colloquies of Erasmus* (Chicago and London: University of Chicago Press, 1965), pp. 269–70.

16 Erasmus to Jacobus Sadoletus, 1 October 1528, in J. C. Margolin, *Guerre et Paix dans la Pensée d'Érasme* [War and Peace in the Thought of Erasmus] (Paris: Aubier Montaigne,

In 1530 the Diet of Augsburg met, leaving both the Lutherans and the Catholics even more intransigent than previously. And no change in their respective attitudes took place during the remaining years of Erasmus's life. In a letter from Basel in 1535 to Bartholomeus Latomus, the first professor of Latin in the College de France at Paris, Erasmus observes: 'It seems that the pope is seriously thinking of a council here. But I do not see how it is to meet in the midst of such dissension between princes and lands.'[17]

The red thread is nearing its end. As one leaves it behind, the impression stays that Erasmus was a realistic observer of events – an impression which is confirmed by historians who compare his observations with those of his contemporaries. James Froude concludes his series of lectures in 1893–94 by saying to his students, 'I believe that you will best see what it [the most exciting period of modern history] really was if you will look at it through the eyes of Erasmus.'[18] More recently, James Tracy credits Erasmus with being 'a reliable source', 'well-informed' and with understanding of 'what was happening before his eyes'.[19] Erasmus himself, it is also worth noting, regards no books as having 'more to offer' than 'the works of those who have transmitted to posterity a true account of events public and private'.[20]

Erasmus in Opposition to Realism

Erasmus perceives the conflicts of his time realistically, but he rejects a response which, according to Otto von Gierke, Martin Wight and Hedley Bull, the realists would have given. While his whole work testifies to this refusal, one of his writings provides an especially good example both of his familiarity with the realist way of thinking and his rejection of it.[21] The writing in question is *Julius Exclusus e Coelis*, a satire which appeared

1973), p. 309. Subsequent ages have identified this event as the end of the Italian renaissance.

17 Erasmus to Bartholemeus Latomus, 24 August 1535, in R. L. DeMolen (ed.), *Erasmus* (London: Edward Arnold, 1973), p. 182.

18 J. A. Froude, *Life and Letters of Erasmus: Lectures Delivered at Oxford 1893–49* (New York: Charles Scribner's Sons, 1927), p. 420; see also Froude's 'Preface'.

19 J. D. Tracy, *The Politics of Erasmus: A Pacifist Intellectual and His Political Milieu* (Toronto: University of Toronto Press, 1978), pp. 103, 105, 125, 129.

20 Erasmus to Dukes Frederick and George of Saxony, 5 June 1517, in *Collected Works of Erasmus*, vol. 4, *The Correspondence of Erasmus: Letters 446 to 593, 1516 to 1517*, transl. R. A. B. Mynors and D. F. S. Thomson, annotated J. K. McConica (Toronto: University of Toronto Press, 1977), p. 375.

21 Machiavelli's *The Prince* existed in manuscript form from 1513; it was printed only in 1532. There is no mention in Erasmus's works that he saw either version. This, however, does not necessarily mean that he did not see it or that, as C. R. Thompson suggests, he would not have understood it if he had seen it. C. R. Thompson, 'Erasmus

anonymously in 1514, about a year after the death of Pope Julius II.[22] It is presented in the form of a dialogue between Julius, knocking at the gate of heaven and demanding to be admitted, and Saint Peter, refusing to admit him.

In the course of the dialogue Julius reminds Peter of his deeds on earth. Had he not restored Bologna, after it had been occupied by the Bentivogli, to the Roman See? Had he not defeated the Venetians, previously not conquered by anyone? Had he not nearly succeeded in 'trapping' the Duke of Ferrara after harrying him in war for a long time? He also drove the French out of Italy, and intended to do the same with the Spaniards 'if death had not snatched' him from the earth. And he disposed of a schismatic council by 'faking a counter-council'. In brief, his 'authority', or perhaps his 'cunning', had been such that 'today there are no Christian kings whom I have not provoked to arms, rending, tearing, and shattering all the treaties by which they had been closely bound together'.[23] And when he died, he made sure that the wars which he had 'stirred up' everywhere would not come to an end, and that the money put aside for that purpose would be secure. Without money, Julius submits, 'nothing goes well, either sacred or profane'.

Saint Peter takes up each point in turn. Why, he demands to know, did Julius occupy Bologna? Had it broken away from the faith? Was Bentivoglio a bad administrator? Had he taken over the administration

as Internationalist and Cosmopolitan', *Archiv fuer Reformationsgeschichte*, vol. 46, 1955, p. 194. Machiavelli's name, as Thompson mentions on the same page, appears in a letter by John Angelus Odonus of March 1535 to Erasmus. See P. S. Allen, H. M. Allen and H.W. Garrod (eds), *Opus Epistolarum Des. Erasmi Roterodami* [The Letters of Desiderius Erasmus of Rotterdam], vol. 11, *1534–36* (Oxford: Clarendon Press, 1947), p. 93.

22 'But the majority of his contemporaries and most modern scholars attribute the dialogue to the pen of Erasmus', M. J. Heath writes in his 'Introductory Note' to 'Julius Excluded from Heaven: A Dialogue', in *Collected Works of Erasmus*, vol. 27, *Literary and Educational Writings* 5, ed. A. H. T. Levi (Toronto: University of Toronto Press, 1986), p. 156, adding that 'external circumstances' as well as 'the contents of the dialogue point very clearly towards Erasmus as its author', p. 157. Earlier scholars to attribute the work to Erasmus include, for example, Nichols, *The Epistles of Erasmus*, vol. 2, 1904, pp. 448–49; P. S. Allen (ed.), *Opus Epistolarum Des. Erasmi Roterodami*, vol. 2, *1514–17* (Oxford: Clarendon Press, 1910), pp. 418–20; D. Erasmus, *The Julius Exclusus of Erasmus* (hereafter *Julius Exclusus*) transl. P. Pascal, intro. and critical notes J. K. Sowards (Bloomington, IN: Indiana University Press, 1968), pp. 14–23, 97–98. However, the issue has not been fully resolved. German historian Peter Fabisch has recently disputed Erasmus's authorship, which in turn is reaffirmed by Werner von Koppenfels, translator of a new German edition. P. Fabisch, *Julius Exclusus e Coelis: Motive und Tendenzen gallikanischer und bibelhumanistischer Papstkritik im Umfeld des Erasmus* [Motives and Tendencies of Gallican and Biblical Humanist Papal Criticism in Erasmus's Milieu] (Münster: Aschendorff Verlag, 2008); Erasmus, *Papst Julius vor der Himmelstür: Julius exclusus e coelis* [Pope Julius Before the Door of Heaven: Julius Excluded from Heaven], transl. and annotated W. von Koppelfels (Mainz: Dieterich'sche Verlagsbuchhandlung, 2011).

23 Erasmus, *Julius Exclusus*, p. 53.

without the consent of the citizens? Did the citizens dislike him as a prince? Julius answers each question in the negative. His reasons had been different: Bentivoglio administered Bologna in such a way that 'from the immense sum he collected from the citizens, only a few thousand found their way to our treasury'. Furthermore, the occupation of that city was 'expedient' for his plans at that time.

Saint Peter next inquires about the Venetians. Julius does not hesitate with his reply: they behaved 'like Greeks', they 'made sport' of him. They bestowed priesthoods without consulting anybody; they referred none of their trials to the appropriate courts; they purchased no dispensations. In brief, they caused the Roman See an 'intolerable loss'.[24]

Next, Saint Peter wishes to know why the pope had been hostile to the Duke of Ferrara. Julius's main reason was that the Duke's realm should be joined to his own, because of its 'strategic location'. But why, Saint Peter asks a little later, did you turn against the French and their king? Julius replies that it would take a long time to tell the whole story, but the crux of it is that:

> I never really loved the French ... No Italian really loves barbarians[25] ... But I ... used them as friends for just so long as I needed their services, since up to that point one may take advantage of barbarians.[26]

Saint Peter moves on to the next point. How did Julius manage to provoke the greatest kings to grave wars, especially when, as a means to that end, he had to break so many alliances? Julius has no problem in answering this question:

> This was my major concern, to become thoroughly acquainted with the animating spirit, character, emotions, wealth, and strivings of all nations, and especially of all princes: who was at peace with whom, who had fallen out with whom; and then to make use of all these things for our own purposes.[27]

Having revealed his general approach, Julius goes into the details. It was easy to rouse the French against the Venetians; he then made 'common cause' with them, and the emperor also joined. At the same time he began to incite the Spanish against the French, as it was not desirable that the latter should become too strong;[28] he also made it look as if the Venetians were 'back in favor'; then he alienated the emperor from the French; and he made use of his knowledge that the English have an

[24] Ibid., pp. 52, 58–59.
[25] That is, people born outside Italy.
[26] Erasmus, *Julius Exclusus*, pp. 71–72.
[27] Ibid., pp. 76, 77.
[28] This passage suggests that Erasmus might include 'balance of power politics' in the realist approach to international politics. See ibid., pp. 77–78.

'instinctive hatred' of the French, as well as of the Scots. In this way he managed to involve these princes in 'the gravest war of all'. In addition, he approached all the other kings as well, for he knew that if they were parties to the conflict, too, 'no one else would be at peace'.

There is another point about which Saint Peter wishes to know more, and that is the Council which Julius had managed to evade. Had he not been bound by oath to convoke a general council? Had he not been elected pope on that condition? Julius agrees: that is correct, but he released himself from that oath when it seemed best. 'Who would hesitate to swear to anything at all, when it is a question of a kingdom?' Julius then was the kind of person people said he was? Saint Peter asked. The response came without hesitation: 'What does that matter? I was Pope.' And the Pope, God's representative on earth, cannot be criticized by any human being, not even a general council. Saint Peter pursues the question further: A 'criminal and pestilent Pope' can then not be removed at all? 'Who's to remove the man at the top?' Julius does not doubt his absolute power. But why did he then try to avoid a general council? Julius replies:

> Why don't you ask monarchs why they hate a senate and general assemblies? The fact is, when so many outstanding men gather together, the royal dignity is overshadowed to a certain extent ... [H]ardly any council has ever turned out so well that the supreme Pontiff has not experienced some loss to his majesty, and departed less supreme.

So, all that matters then is that 'the royal majesty' of the pope should be secure, rather than 'the general interest' of Christendom? Julius is in no doubt: 'Each man looks out for his own interest; we take care of our business.'[29]

Julius's values were not those of Saint Peter: he is not admitted. Arguably, the dialogue presents a caricature of realist thought, but its satire highlights the central ethical issue that divides the 'hard' realists from theorists of international society, and it makes Erasmus's position clear.[30]

Erasmus in Opposition to Universalism

Erasmus sees the conflicts of his time realistically, but his response does not consist in advocating the abolition of the existing political plurality and the establishment, in its place, of a universal state or ruler as a

[29] Ibid., pp. 60–65.

[30] See the comparison 'Erasmus and Machiavelli', in H. Muenkler, *Im Namen des Staates: Die Begruendung der Staatsraison in der Fruehen Neuzeit* [In the Name of the State: Origins of Reason of State in Early Modern Times] (Frankfurt am Main: Fischer Verlag, 1987), pp. 46–64.

way of overcoming them – an approach which had highly placed supporters at the time. Wight refers to the 'revolutionists' of that period as in fact counter-revolutionary, seeking to revive a medieval *Respublica Christiana*, which had 'a degree of constitutional unity out of any comparison greater than the constitutional unity of the society of states since then'.[31] Erasmus, as his writings amply demonstrate, rejects universalism and what he perceives as so many steps in its direction: territorial expansionism or what has come to be referred to as imperialism.[32]

As early as 1495, when he was a student of theology in Paris and invited by the well-known French historian Robert Gaguin to fill a blank page at the end of his history of France, Erasmus voices opposition to policies of *agrandissement*:

> Our early forbears used to pay godlike honours to those of their countrymen who had either won imperial power or increased the boundaries of the commonwealth ... Yet it is a much nobler act to spread the fame of one's ancestors from the rising to the setting sun than to extend the boundaries of one's territory.[33]

In 1502 he contributed a preface to 'one of the most strident contemporary statements of universal monarchy': *De Precellentia Potestatis Imperatorie* [On the Excellence of Imperial Power] by Jacobus Anthonisz, the vicar general of the Bishop of Cambrai.[34] While not withholding all praise from this 'compendium of legal and theological opinions', Erasmus does not hesitate to liken the author to a 'busy-bee' which flies everywhere and collects honey wherever it can find it. 'I would', he writes, 'that you had exercised more choice and also a little restraint.'[35]

Two years later, in 1504, Erasmus delivered 'The Panegyric' at Brussels on the safe return from Spain of the Duke of Burgundy. In the course of his public address he says: 'The best form of political government is not the one which extends the boundaries of its empire by war-like actions,

[31] M. Wight, *International Theory: The Three Traditions*, ed. G. Wight and B. Porter (Leicester: Leicester University Press for the Royal Institute of International Affairs, London, 1991), p. 9.

[32] Erasmus was not alone among his contemporaries in perceiving a connection between expansionism and universalism. See, for example, R. Menéndez Pidal, 'Formación del Fundamental Pensamiento Político de Carlos V' [Formation of the Basic Political Ideas of Charles V], in P. Rassow and F. Schalk (eds), *Karl V: Der Kaiser und seine Zeit* [Charles V: The Emperor and His Times] (Koeln and Graz: Boehlau Verlag, 1960), esp. p. 158.

[33] Erasmus to Robert Gaguin, October 1495, in *Collected Works of Erasmus*, vol. 1, *The Correspondence of Erasmus: Letters 1 to 141, 1484 to 1500*, transl. R. A. B. Mynors and D. F. S. Thomson, annotated W. K. Ferguson (Toronto: University of Toronto Press, 1974), p. 91.

[34] J. M. Headley, 'Gattinara, Erasmus and the Imperial Configurations of Humanism', *Archiv fuer Reformationsgeschichte*, vol. 71, 1980, p. 83n.

[35] Tracy, *The Politics of Erasmus*, p. 17.

but the one which comes closest to the image of the celestial city.'[36] His letter to Antoon van Bergen in 1514 includes a passage about the building up of empires:

If we would find something to call glorious, it is far more glorious to found states than to destroy them ... What expenditure of blood it cost to build the Roman empire, and how soon its collapse began![37]

Three years later, in 1517, Erasmus dedicated to the Dukes of Saxony his edition of *De Vita Caesarum* [The Lives of the Caesars], historical biographies of the Roman emperors from Julius Caesar to Domitian, by the Roman historian Gaius Suetonius Tranquillis. In his preface Erasmus asks whether the Roman Empire, 'that ancient empire' whose authority was 'founded and consecrated by impiety, murder, parricide, incest and tyranny', should be restored as it once was? 'For my part', he answers,

I do not think any intelligent man would desire this, even if wishes could put it back: so far is it from seeming right to defend and revive an institution which for many centuries now has been largely outdated and non-existent, at the price of a great upheaval in human affairs and very great loss of Christian lives.

Monarchy, Erasmus elaborates, is the best form of government if he who exercises it surpasses every other human being by as much goodness and wisdom as he does in power, but he doubts that one could be so fortunate to get such a ruler, and if one were, he does not think it likely that any mortal's mind would be capable of such extensive rule. But suppose it were. When would such a ruler find out what was happening among far-distant subjects? But suppose he discovered. When would he be in a position to help? A 'great emperor', Erasmus concludes, who does no more than levying taxes, is not a 'true emperor'.[38]

In the same year, 1517, Erasmus dedicated a revised edition of the history of Alexander the Great by Quintus Curtius Rufus to the Duke of Bavaria. In the letter accompanying the gift he expresses his views against the ideal of a ruler which the author sets before his readers in the person of Alexander the Great:

For my own part, I have no more liking for the Alexander of the Greek historians, than I have for Homer's Achilles. Both the one and the other present the worst example of what a sovereign should be, even if some good qualities may seem to be mingled with so many faults. It was forsooth well worth while, that Africa,

[36] Erasmus, 'Le Panegyrique de Philippe Le Beau' [The Panegyric of Philip the Fair], 1504, in Margolin, *Guerre et Paix dans la Pensée d'Érasme*, p. 43.

[37] Erasmus to Antoon van Bergen, 14 March 1514, p. 281.

[38] Erasmus to Dukes Frederick and George of Saxony, 5 June 1517, in *Collected Works of Erasmus*, vol. 4, pp. 378, 381–82.

Europe and Asia should be thrown into confusion, and so many thousands of human beings slaughtered, to please one young madman, whose ambition this solid globe would have failed to satisfy![39]

In March 1527, when the imperial forces were fighting a winning battle against the allied forces of Francis I and the Pope in Italy, the chancellor of Charles V, Mercurino Gattinara, wrote from Valladolid in Spain to Erasmus:

I have recently discovered Dante's *De Monarchia*, a suppressed book as I am told by those who aspire unduly to a universal monarchy[40] ... As it may serve the cause of the Emperor, I would like to see it published ... Nobody in our time is better suited to be entrusted with this work. It is up to you to decide whether it is convenient to publish the work or to leave it unpublished.[41]

As P. S. Allen and H. M. Allen, editors of Erasmus's letters in Latin, comment, 'The proposal here made is interesting, as marking an attempt to commit Erasmus definitely to the Imperial side.'[42] He decided not to publish *De Monarchia*.[43] Two months later he wrote to the Polish King Sigismund I: 'Just as certain ships are too big to be navigated, in the same way it is extremely difficult to successfully administer an empire which is too extended.'[44]

About two years later, in March 1529, Erasmus responded in a letter to Alfonso Valdes, Gattinara's 'loyal secretary', to 'the stupid argument' put forward by the Spanish Franciscan Luis de Carvajal in a tract entitled *Apologia Monasticae Religionis Diluens Nugas Erasmi* [A Defence of Monasticism in Refutation of the Nonsense Written by Erasmus]. The whole 'chicanery' of these people, Erasmus writes, is directed at the word 'new': 'The Emperor wants a new, universal monarchy' ... [A]s if there ever had been, apart from God, a universal monarch.' Even today, part of the world continues to be unknown, and the known part has never obeyed one ruler. But listen to 'that good man', he invites Valdes: Proposition One, 'What the sun is in the heaven, the Emperor

39 Erasmus to Duke Ernest of Baviara, 4 November 1517, in Nichols, *The Epistles of Erasmus*, vol. 3, p. 130.

40 The Latin text reads: 'Nactus sum his diebus libellum Dantis, cui titulum fecit Monarchia, suppres(s)um, vt audio, ab his qui eam vsurpare contendunt.' See P. S. Allen and H. M. Allen (eds), *Opus Epistolarum Des. Erasmi Roterodami*, vol. 6, *1525–1527* (Oxford: Clarendon Press, 1926), p. 470.

41 Mercurino Gattinara to Erasmus, 12 March 1527, in A. Renoudet, *Études Érasmiennes: 1521–1529* [Studies of Erasmus: 1521–1529] (Paris: E. Droz, 1939), p. 96.

42 Allen and Allen (eds), *Opus Epistolarum*, vol. 6, p. 470.

43 As Renoudet remarks, *De Monarchia* was not published until 1559. Renoudet, *Études Érasmiennes*, p. 97.

44 Erasmus to Sigismund I, 15 May 1527, in Margolin, *Guerre et Paix dans la Pensée d'Érasme*, pp. 301–02.

is on earth.' This comparison would be justifiable only if one man were capable of giving his attention to every nation on earth. Two, 'Aristotle places monarchy ahead of aristocracy.' Yes, if it were possible to find a man who excelled every other in virtue and wisdom; but when Aristotle speaks of monarchy, he does not have in mind the world, but independent states such as Crete, Sparta, and Athens. Three, Carvajal quotes Homer saying that one leader is better than many. True, but Horner refers to a military leader, and even then he accords him absolute power only in combat. Finally, Carvajal holds that Christ himself approves the imperial authority: 'Give to Caesar what is Caesar's ...'. Yes, but '[i]f Christ had taught in Savoy ... he would have said: Give to the Duke what is the Duke's.'[45]

Not long afterwards Johann Rinck, a lawyer from Cologne, requested Erasmus's opinion on the question of whether or not to make war against the Turks. Erasmus's response was the *Consultatio* of March 1530. The passage which is of interest in the context of this section reads as follows:

> Most of us ... dread the name of World Empire ... a title at which others seem to be aiming ... A unified empire would be best if we could have a sovereign made in the image of God, but, men being what they are, there is more safety in kingdoms of moderate power united in a Christian League.[46]

Erasmus, as his writings reveal, is a constant and consistent opponent of universalism: neither the road to it nor the destination itself hold any promise of generating less conflict than the existing political plurality.[47]

[45] Erasmus to Alphonse Valdes, 21 March 1529, in Gerlo (ed.), *La Correspondance d'Érasme*, vol. 8, pp. 121–22.

[46] The passage here quoted is from F. Hinsley, *Power and the Pursuit of Peace: Theory and Practice in the History of Relations between States* (Cambridge: Cambridge University Press, 1963), p. 18. But Hinsley does not refer directly to the treatise, and the passage is not to be found in Margolin, *Guerre et Paix dans la Pensée d'Érasme*, pp. 328–74, nor Gerlo (ed.), *La Correspondance d'Érasme*, vol. 8, pp. 489–93. It is in A. G. Weiler (ed.), *Opera Omnia Desiderii Erasmi Roterodami*, V–III, vol. 15 (Amsterdam: North Holland Publishing Co., 1986), pp. 80–81.

[47] The opposite conclusion is formulated by Geldner: '[A]bove all, universalism influenced Erasmus: with him, as with the Stoics, it deprived the individual state of its basis and demanded the world state which should encompass all peoples.' He offers no evidence to support this conclusion. See F. Geldner, *Die Staatsauffassung und Fuerstenlehre des Erasmus von Rotterdam* [Erasmus of Rotterdam: His Conception of the State and Theory of the Prince] (Berlin: Emil Ebering, 1930), pp. 137, 168, 172. On the other hand, one meets with the statement that Erasmus considers 'the establishment of a Christian universal monarchy' as 'impossible and also not desirable'. See Geldner, *Die Staatsauffassung*, p. 97. And for the latter, as this section has shown, there is ample evidence in Erasmus's writings. Bruce Mansfield, in reviewing the literature on Erasmus's political thought, comes to the same conclusion. Mansfield, *Erasmus in the Twentieth Century*, pp. 24–6.

Erasmus Presents a Model of the Perfect Temporal Christian Prince

In opposition to both realism and universalism, Erasmus puts forward the idea of Christian princes being linked in concord to one another. References to this idea can be found in many of his writings, for example, in the *Adage* 'War Is Sweet to Those Who Do Not Know It', in the treatise *The Education of a Christian Prince*, and in letters to the Dukes of Saxony and the French King Francis I.[48] It is an idea which includes both political plurality and that which links. This section and the next focus on the former, presenting Erasmus's ideas of the temporal Christian prince and of the spiritual Christian prince respectively, while the later sections are concerned with that which makes for concord among Christian princes.

Erasmus gives expression to his idea of the temporal Christian prince by means of a model, intended to instruct the young prince and to remind 'good rulers' of what they ought to do.[49] The inspiration for adopting such a course comes from classical Antiquity. The ancients, Erasmus explains, did not praise their rulers in order to flatter them; they praised them because they understood that, proud and impatient as they often were, they would not 'tolerate either the authority of a mentor or the censure of a critic':

> So, out of regard for the nation's well-being, they altered course, and reached the same goal by a less obvious route. In the guise of a panegyric they presented the prince with a kind of model of the perfect ruler, depicted in a painting as it were, in order that he might measure himself upon the pattern thus offered and privately acknowledge how far he fell below the standard of the prince they lauded.[50]

The three prime qualities of the Christian prince are wisdom, goodness, and power.[51] Wisdom, according to Erasmus, is an attribute in itself, and it tells a prince how to rule 'beneficently'. 'But there is only

[48] Erasmus, 'War Is Sweet to Those Who Do Not Know It' (1515), in M. M. Phillips, *The Adages of Erasmus: A Study with Translations* (Cambridge: Cambridge University Press, 1964), pp. 322–23; D. Erasmus, *The Education of a Christian Prince*, transl. and intro. L. K. Born (New York: Columbia University Press, 1936), p. 238; Erasmus to Dukes Frederick and George of Saxony, 5 June 1517, in *Collected Works of Erasmus*, vol. 4, p. 382; Erasmus to François I, 16 June 1526, in Gerlo (ed.), *La Correspondance d'Érasme*, vol. 6, 1977, p. 432.

[49] Erasmus to Adolph of Burgundy, ca. March 1499, in *Collected Works of Erasmus*, vol. 1, p. 182.

[50] Ibid.

[51] Erasmus, *The Education of a Christian Prince*, p. 158. See also Erasmus, 'The Sileni of Alcibiades' (1515), in Phillips, *The Adages of Erasmus*, p. 280. The word 'silenus', as Erasmus explains, was used by the Greeks 'either with reference to a thing which in appearance … seems ridiculous and contemptible, but on closer and deeper examination

one means of deliberating on a question, and that is wisdom.'[52] Of goodness, Erasmus says: 'Nothing is really "good" unless associated with moral integrity.' Goodness is acting in a true Christian spirit. A prince's goodness makes him want 'to help all', 'to fill as many needs as possible for everyone'.[53] Wisdom and goodness are closely linked in the Christian prince, '[f]or true wisdom consists not only in the knowledge of truth, but in the love and eager striving for what is good'.[54] Power is the quality which makes the prince the supreme ruler of his realm. Supreme, however, does not mean absolute. Above him, there is the law:

> In meetings of the council, one shall listen to the most noble and the old; but in such a way that the decision is with the king … who cannot be compelled or passed over by anyone. The king obeys only the law, and the law corresponds to the idea of honesty.[55]

The power of the Christian prince is limited in a second way. His subjects are not only free men; they also are Christians, that is 'people who are twice free'. '[A]mong Christians', Erasmus insists, 'supreme rule means administration of the state, and not dominion.'[56] Wisdom, goodness and power belong together, for 'power, unless it is allied to wisdom and goodness, is tyranny and not power'. 'Power without goodness', the idea recurs, 'is unmitigated tyranny; without wisdom it brings chaos, not domain.'[57]

The Christian prince employs wisdom, goodness and power for the good of his country. 'The cardinal principle of a good prince', Erasmus is in no doubt, 'should be not only to preserve the present prosperity of the state but to pass it on more prosperous than when he received it.' And prosperity, he is equally certain, does not only mean material

proves to be admirable, or else with reference to a person whose looks and dress do not correspond at all to what he conceals in his soul' (p. 269).

52 Erasmus, *The Education of a Christian Prince*, pp. 133, 174.

53 Ibid., pp. 148, 157, 158.

54 Erasmus, 'Kings and Fools Are Born, Not Made' (1515), in Phillips, *The Adages of Erasmus*, p. 217.

55 D. Erasmus, *Enchiridion: Handbuechlein eines christlichen Streiters* [Enchiridion: The Handbook of a Christian Soldier], transl. and ed. W. Welzig (Graz and Koeln: Hermann Boehlaus Nachf., 1961), p. 38. See also Erasmus, 'The Fabulous Feast' (1524), in Thompson (transl.), *The Colloquies of Erasmus*, p. 260.

56 Erasmus, 'Kings and Fools Are Born, Not Made', p. 221. See also Erasmus, *The Education of a Christian Prince*, pp. 233, 236; and Erasmus, 'The Complaint of Peace' (1517), in J. P. Dolan, *The Essential Erasmus: Selected and Translated with Introduction and Commentary* (New York and Scarborough, Ontario: Meridian/The New American Library, 1964), p. 194.

57 Erasmus, 'The Sileni of Alcibiades', p. 280; Erasmus, *The Education of a Christian Prince*, p. 158.

wealth; it also includes physical health and, most importantly, spiritual well-being.[58]

In order to attain these ends, the Christian prince has to see not only how 'things that are evil can be avoided or removed' but also how 'good conditions can be gained, developed, and strengthened'.[59] The guiding ideas in this endeavour are justice and cooperation, and the Christian prince follows their inspiration, within his own realm and beyond it.

As far as his own realm is concerned, the Christian prince knows that:

> The most felicitous condition exists when [he] is obeyed by everyone, [he] himself obeys the laws, and the laws go back to the fundamental principles of equity and honesty, with no other aim than the advancement of the commonwealth.[60]

And equity, as Erasmus explains, does not consist in bestowing upon everybody 'the same reward, the same rights, the same honor'; this, he declares, is sometimes 'a mark of the greatest unfairness'.[61]

The Christian prince also knows, and this is a second, more complex image inspired by the ideas of justice and cooperation, that it is for the good of his country if the various elements of society can be made to check and balance one another in such a way as to achieve an 'eternal truce':

> [E]ach part of the body politic would retain its rightful authority, the people would be given their due, the councillors and magistrates would be paid the respect proper to their learning, to law and to justice; the bishops and priests would receive the honour due to them. Nor would the monks be denied what is due to them. The harmonious discord of all these, this variety tending to one and the same end, would serve the commonwealth.[62]

More specifically, the Christian prince knows and loves his country and its people, and seeks to win its love in turn – a task made easier if it is his fatherland, too, for 'friendship is created and confirmed most when the source of good will is nature itself'. He makes it his concern that his country's young people are given a proper education, for citizens who have been acquainted with 'the best principles' will follow 'the right course' of their own accord, and there will be less need for either many laws or punishment. He burdens his people with as few taxes as possible, and least of all the poor. Thrift, Erasmus notes, 'is a great source of revenue'. The Christian prince's laws are not only equitable, but also written

[58] Erasmus, *The Education of a Christian Prince*, p. 212.
[59] Ibid., p. 187.
[60] Ibid., p. 221.
[61] Ibid., p. 212.
[62] Erasmus, 'Make Haste Slowly' (1508), in Phillips, *The Adages of Erasmus*, p. 183. See also Erasmus, *The Education of a Christian Prince*, pp. 173, 180–81.

in a 'clear language', with as few 'complexities' as possible, and familiar to the people. His magistrates are not only wise but also incorruptible.[63]

The ideas of justice and cooperation are the Christian prince's guide not only within his realm, but also beyond it. For purposes of analysis, however, it seems best to present the latter aspect not at this point, but to leave it for inclusion in a later section.

Erasmus's Christian prince is an idea. It is also a reality, as his letter of 1527 to King Sigismund of Poland shows, and this reality, for purposes of instruction, may be transmitted without separating the external from the internal aspect:

> [T]hree qualities seem to me to be especially necessary for the man who means to appease human movements of such·magnitude:[64] piety, an elevated soul, and wisdom. The term 'piety' embraces two virtues, love of one's country and religious ardour ... Have you not deployed all your vigilance, all your zeal and all your care to look after the interests of your kingdom, to preserve them, to make them fruitful, to enhance them and to consolidate them ... Besides, the integrity of your whole being manifests the fact that the Christian religion is not a minor concern for you ...
>
> In the inevitable wars which you have often fought with as much success as with valour, against the Vlachs, the Tatars, the Muscovites and the Prussians, you have testified to a really royal elevation of soul. But the signs of a still rarer sublimity were there when you preferred to conclude a truce with the Muscovites who so often have made war on you, rather than to subject by (force of) arms to your rule an area of an extreme affluence, when this would have been easy for you, and the unanimous pressure of the notables urged you to do so ...
>
> However, I think that the same facts reveal the exceptional wisdom which you possess.[65]

To use Erasmus's own classificatory system, the letter to the King of Poland is a panegyric reminding a good ruler of what he is doing.

Erasmus Presents a Model of the Perfect Spiritual Christian Prince

The prince of the Christian church possesses the same three cardinal qualities as the temporal Christian prince, that is, wisdom, goodness, and power. '[Y]our goodness', Erasmus writes to Pope Leo X in 1515, 'makes

[63] Erasmus, *The Education of a Prince*, pp. 207, 212–13, 217, 234, 235–37.

[64] The Latin text reads: '[T]ria potissimum requiri videntur in eo qui tantos rerum humanarum motus sit compositurus'. See P. S. Allen and H. M. Allen (eds), *Opus Epistolarum Des. Erasmi Roterodami*, vol. 7, *1527–1528* (Oxford: Clarendon Press, 1928), p. 61.

[65] Erasmus to Sigismund I, 15 May 1527, pp. 297–301.

you wish to be of service, your singular wisdom shows you how to aid humanity, and your supreme position as pontiff makes this possible.'[66]

While the prime attributes are the same, the aims in the pursuit of which they are employed are different. For the temporal Christian prince, as the preceding section has shown, there is nothing more important than to enhance his country's prosperity, whereas the spiritual Christian prince delights 'in upholding the rule, the glory and the justice of Christ'; he longs 'for nothing other than the glory of Christ and the salvation of all mankind'.[67]

In the pursuit of his aims, the spiritual Christian prince travels along a road which is different from that followed by the temporal Christian prince. The great importance which Erasmus attaches to this point is reflected in many of his works, for example, in the *Adage* 'The Sileni of Alcibiades':

> I wish the Popes to have the greatest riches – but let it be the pearl of the Gospel, the heavenly treasure ... I wish them to be fully armed, but with the arms of the Apostle ... I wish them to be fierce warriors, but against the real enemies of the Church, simony, pride, lust, ambition, anger, irreligion ... Which models are more suitable for imitation by the vicar of Christ – the Juliuses, Alexanders, Croesus, and Xerxes, nothing but robbers on the grand scale, or Christ himself?[68]

Again, when he addresses the French King Francis I,

> [T]he evangelical pastors possess the evangelical sword which has been given to them by Christ, in order to eliminate human vices, and to remove human passions. The kings possess their proper sword, which Christ, too, has given to them in order to frighten the wicked and to honour the good ... There are two kinds of swords, just as there are two ways of exercising sovereignty.

A king, Erasmus submits, does not possess 'greater majesty' than when he sits in the courts of justice, administering justice, or when he attends the meetings of council, looking after the interests of the state. A bishop, on the other hand, manifests the 'dignity of his office' no more truly than when he teaches the philosophy of Christ from the height of a pulpit.[69]

The spiritual Christian prince uses his wisdom, goodness and power as prescribed by his aims, and does not get 'immersed in the kingdom

66 Erasmus to Leo X, 21 May 1515, in *Collected Works of Erasmus*, vol. 3, *The Correspondence of Erasmus: Letters 298 to 445, 1514 to 1516*, transl. R. A. B. Mynors and D. F. S. Thomson, annotated J. K. McConica (Toronto: University of Toronto Press, 1976), p. 102.

67 Erasmus to François I, 1 December 1523, in Margolin, *Guerre et Paix dans la Pensée d'Érasme*, p. 277; Erasmus, 'A Fish Diet' (1526), in Thompson (transl.), *The Colloquies of Erasmus*, pp. 326–27.

68 Erasmus, 'The Sileni of Alcibiades', pp. 286–88.

69 Erasmus to François I, 1 December 1523, p. 270.

of this world'. Leaving 'worldly things to the world',[70] he is in a position to meet the demands made by the office of arbitrator and mediator. It is appropriate for the pope, for cardinals, bishops and abbots, Erasmus writes in 1514 to Antoon van Bergen to work for the settlement of disputes among princes. This is, he insists, how 'they should wield their authority and reveal the power they possess'. But let the world experience the power of the pope – his addressee this time is the French King Francis I, and the year is 1523 – 'as being beneficial for the reconciliation of kings and the maintenance of their concord'.[71]

Erasmus's prescription is clear: the spiritual Christian prince is in charge of one form of administration, and the temporal Christian prince of another; and the two ought to be kept separate. Where they intersect, as happens in cases of arbitration and mediation on the part of the spiritual Christian prince, the latter does not threaten political plurality, but acts as its defender.

The World as It Ought to Be: The Idea of Harmonious Discord

Concord or harmony, it is Erasmus's view, is discernible in the world as a whole. 'In this universe, composed of such different elements', he writes in 'War Is Sweet to Those Who Do not Know It', 'there is a harmony'.[72] He finds it, as was shown above, in the state in which 'the various elements of society' so balance and control one another that they achieve an 'eternal truce'. Why should it not be operative among Christian princes and the peoples committed to their care?

Wise and good Christian princes, Erasmus suggests, follow the idea of justice not only within their respective realms but also beyond them – in their relations with one another and with non-Christian princes. '[I]t is the part of a Christian prince to regard no one as an outsider unless he is a nonbeliever, and even on them he should inflict no harm.'[73]

'Inflicting no harm', in relation to non-Christians, means that Christian princes do not attack them; they do not take their riches; they do not subject them to their political rule; they do not force them to become

[70] Erasmus, 'The Sileni of Alcibiades', pp. 290, 293.

[71] Erasmus to Antoon van Bergen, 14 March 1514, p. 281; Erasmus to François I, 1 December 1523, p. 267. See also Erasmus to Willibald Pirckheimer, 8 February 1524, in Gerlo (ed.), *La Correspondance d'Érasme*, vol. 5, 1976, p. 500.

[72] Erasmus, 'War Is Sweet to Those Who Do Not Know It', p. 329. See also D. Erasmus, 'The Antibarbarians', transl. and annotated M. M. Phillips, in *Collected Works of Erasmus*, vol. 23, *Literary and Educational Writings 1*, ed. C. R. Thompson (Toronto: University of Toronto Press, 1978), pp. 59–61.

[73] Erasmus, *The Education of a Christian Prince*, p. 220.

Christians; and they keep promises made to them.[74] It means, in other words, that they respect their separateness and independence. 'Inflicting no harm', in relation to one another, has the same meaning. As Erasmus formulates it: 'Let us not do anything by force, and certainly do unto others what we would wish them to do unto us.'[75] Irrespective of whether it concerns non-Christians or Christians, '[a] good prince should never go to war at all unless, after trying every other means, he cannot possibly avoid it'. In such a case, Erasmus adds, the good prince endeavours to wage the war 'with as little calamity to his own people' as possible, and to conclude it as soon as possible.[76]

While the idea of justice applies equally to Christians and non-Christians, the idea of cooperation does not. Good and wise Christian princes, Erasmus submits, are not 'too closely allied' to those who have a different religion.[77] These they neither attack nor do they have them as allies.

The idea of cooperation which guides Christian princes prescribes that they preserve peace with one another:

> A good and wise prince will make an effort to preserve peace with everyone but especially with his neighbors; for if they are wrought up they can do a great deal of harm, while if they are friendly they are a big help, and without their mutual business relations the state could not even exist.[78]

It invites them, in times of peace, to collaborate in strengthening and beautifying their realms: 'To make beneficial arrangements together for these things, and to compare all their plans for these ends is the one thing really worthy of Christian princes.'[79] It urges them, when war has broken out, to 'take counsel together' in order to re-establish peace:

> I will only urge princes of Christian faith to put aside all feigned excuses and all false pretexts ... to work for the ending of that madness for war ... that among those whom so many ties unite there may arise a peace and concord ... [I]f, after

74 Ibid., pp. 240, 256; Erasmus to Sigismund I, 15 May 1527, p. 299; Erasmus, 'A Valued Discussion on War Against the Turks', in Margolin, *Guerre et Paix la Pensée d'Érasme*, pp. 350, 351, 354. Erasmus's displeasure with Christian conduct in relation to the Turks finds ready expression in this treatise. 'Through our dissension, our ambition, our perfidy' (such as violating an oath or poisoning the enemy's prince) 'we have always opened the path to the most serious disasters' (p. 350).

75 Erasmus, 'On Mending the Peace of the Church' (1533), in Dolan, *The Essential Erasmus*, p. 386.

76 Erasmus, *The Education of a Christian Prince*, p. 249. See also below, the section 'The Question of War'.

77 Ibid., p. 240.

78 Ibid., p. 239.

79 Ibid., p. 248.

common counsel, we should carry out our common task … each one would be more prosperous.[80]

It encourages them to offer help if one of them is 'in distress':

[I]t is not sufficient that all those who support the Christian cause heave lamentations; it is also necessary to help fellow-peoples in distress: for, unless we consider these misfortunes as being common to all of us … it is to be feared that in reality they will become our common lot.[81]

While justice supports separateness and independence, cooperation circumscribes both.

The aim which wise and good princes set for themselves – securing the good of their country – is an end in itself, and it serves another end. 'If each [prince] does his best to embellish his own possessions', Erasmus writes, 'then all will be flourishing everywhere…. [I]f one of them does wrong, it is to the detriment not of one family but of the whole world.'[82] The idea that whatever happens in one Christian country is of significance to the whole of Christendom is persistent in Erasmus's writings. For example, it reappears in *The Education of a Christian Prince*, it occurs in his preface to 'Of How to Write Letters', and it is included in his discussion of the question of war against the Turks.[83]

That which links one Christian to another also links one Christian prince to another Christian prince. 'Among all Christian princes', Erasmus writes, 'there is at once a very firm and holy bond.' '[A]mong good and wise princes', it comes back like an echo, 'there is an established friendship.' The concord which unites Christian princes among themselves is not based on 'many painstaking contracts', and certainly not on marriage alliances, for even though 'common opinion' regards such alliances as the 'adamantine bonds of public harmony', they are, as a matter of fact, the cause of 'the greatest upheavals [in] human affairs'.[84] The concord which is operative among wise and good Christian princes

[80] Ibid., pp. 256–57.

[81] Erasmus, 'A Valued Discussion on War Against the Turks', p. 340.

[82] Erasmus, 'You Have Obtained Sparta, Adorn It' (1515), in Phillips, *The Adages of Erasmus*, pp. 302, 308. When Erasmus uses the term 'the whole world', he usually means the Christian world. On this point, see also J. Beumer, *Erasmus der Europaeer: Die Beziehungen des Rotterdamers zu den Humanisten seiner Zeit unter den verschiedenen Nationen Europas* [Erasmus the European: The Relations of the Man from Rotterdam to the Humanists of His Time from among the Various Nations of Europe] (Werl, Westfalia: Dietrich Coelde, 1969), p. 10.

[83] Erasmus, *The Education of a Christian Prince*, p. 248; Erasmus to Nicholas Beraldus, 25 May 1522, in Margolin, *Guerre et Paix dans la Pensée d'Érasme*, p. 264; Erasmus, 'A Valued Discussion on War Against the Turks', pp. 339–40.

[84] Erasmus, *The Education of a Christian Prince*, pp. 238, 241–43. See also Erasmus, 'The Complaint of Peace', p. 194.

is traceable to one source, and Erasmus places this source at the centre of three circles:

Christ ... is the centre surrounded by various circles. The centre must not be removed from its position. For, in accordance with it, all human actions are to be judged. Those who are nearest to Christ, the priests, bishops, cardinals and popes whose duty it is to follow Him wherever He goes, are to uphold that purest sphere and, as much as possible, transmit it to those next to them. The second circle is formed by the temporal princes whose arms and laws serve Christ in their own way, be it that they defeat the enemy in necessary and just wars and protect public tranquillity, be it that by lawful punishments they keep evil-doers within bounds ... In the third circle finally ... there are the ordinary people; although they form the grossest part ... they nevertheless belong to Christ.[85]

The image of the three circles is Erasmus's illustration of how divine law as expressed in the teachings and life of Christ is transmitted from the centre of the 'community which is our religion' to the periphery, becoming less pure as it travels outward. It also shows that divine law is the source from which the Christian princes derive the principles informing their actions. Divine law – and Erasmus makes it clear that it is a law which 'neither ought to be judged nor can it be abolished' – is the Christian princes' standard and guide.[86]

The three circles are a description of Christianity. They leave out all those who do not share its spirit – that is, the non-Christians are excluded. These outsiders, however, are potential insiders:

I have no doubt whatever that Christianity, now confined within narrow limits, would happily spread if the barbarous nations realized they were called not to human servitude but to gospel freedom; sought out not for the purpose of plunder but for the fellowship of happiness and holiness. When they have united with us and found in us truly Christian behaviour, they will contribute voluntarily more than any force could wring from them.[87]

Sharing the philosophy of Christ removes the boundary which separates outsiders from insiders. In other words, while Erasmus's international society is limited to the Christian world, it is not exclusive, but its expansion can take place only through example and persuasion, not through conquest.

[85] Erasmus to Paul Volz, 14 August 1518, in C. Kisch, *Erasmus und die Jurisprudenz seiner Zeit* [Erasmus and the Jurisprudence of His Time] (Basel: Helbing & Lichtenhahn, 1960), pp. 126–28. See the slightly different version in J. C. Olin (ed.), *Christian Humanism and the Reformation: Selected Writings of Erasmus, with the Life of Erasmus by Beatus Rhenanus* (New York: Fordham University Press, 1980), pp. 118–21. Erasmus's image of the 'Three Circles' finds a mention mainly in German sources.

[86] Erasmus, 'A Fish Diet', p. 339.

[87] Ibid., pp. 324–25.

Law as a Link

Erasmus's writings contain a number of ideas suggesting ways of bringing the world as it was more into accord with his normative vision. The remainder of this chapter is devoted to a discussion of these ideas.

One way of narrowing the gap consists in reforming existing laws, at two levels. First, the laws that give expression to the philosophy of Christ need to be purified and simplified;[88] and second, human laws should be revised and emended according to the idea of justice as derived from the philosophy of Christ.

The philosophy of Christ, Erasmus holds, is no longer as pure and simple as when it subdued 'both the pride of the philosophers and the unconquered scepters of the princes'.[89] With the passage of time, it has become corrupted, not only through mistakes committed by 'unskilled' or 'inattentive' copyists, and 'ignorant' or 'lazy' translators, but also through the inclusion of many a human decree. As a result, it no longer provides the standard by which everything else is judged, or, as he puts it, 'matters of the greatest importance depend not on the law of Christ but on the definitions of scholastics and the power of some bishop'. If the philosophy of Christ is to be 'true', 'authentic' and 'efficacious' again, it is necessary to return to its sources, to read and compare the early manuscripts, to re-edit them and to make them accessible by translating them into 'all the languages', Latin as well as the vernaculars. Furthermore, it is necessary that the Church refrain from issuing a new decree 'every day'.[90] The attempt to regulate too many aspects of human life is responsible for much of the dissension within Christendom, and it deters non-Christians from joining the community of the Christian religion. As Erasmus writes in the *Colloquy* 'A Fish Diet',

> Nowadays we see the whole world shaken by reason of these deadly disputes. If these and ones like them were got rid of, we could both live in greater peace, not bothering about ceremonies, but straining only after those things Christ taught, and other races would more readily embrace a religion joined with freedom.[91]

[88] For statements of the philosophy of Christ see, for example, Erasmus, *Enchiridion*; 'The Paraclesis', Erasmus's preface to the Greek and Latin edition of the New Testament, and 'Letter to Paul Volz', both in Olin (ed.), *Christian Humanism and the Reformation*, pp. 92–106, 107–33. See also note 3 to this chapter.

[89] Erasmus to Paul Volz, 14 August 1518, in Olin (ed.), *Christian Humanism and the Reformation*, p. 113.

[90] Erasmus to Martin Dorp, May 1515, in Olin (ed.), *Christian Humanism and the Reformation*, pp. 73, 84–90; Erasmus, 'The Paraclesis', pp. 96–97.

[91] Erasmus, 'A Fish Diet', p. 324.

And he meets the argument that '[i]t is easy to prescribe in general' when what is needed is advice on 'specific matters', and 'particular cases', with the following counter-argument: human affairs are so numerous and varied that it is impossible to respond with certainty regarding each one of them; there is such 'a variety of circumstances' that, unless one knows them all, one cannot even respond with certainty; finally, even if one thinks that one has certainty on one's side, there are others who think likewise, but their answer is not necessarily in agreement with one's own. Hence, those who are 'the more sensible' will not say: 'Do this', 'avoid that', but rather: 'In my opinion this is the safer course, this I think is tolerable.'[92]

It is Erasmus's view that many human laws and practices sanctioned by law fall far short of the standard set by divine law – they are not equitable[93] – and he submits a number of examples in support of his view. One concerns the effects of deceased foreigners. These effects, he notes, are usually taken over by the prefect in the king's name – a practice which goes back to a good intention: 'To prevent those who had no right to the stranger's property from claiming it', and to keep it safely 'until the rightful heirs appeared'. Now, however, it is the case that 'the property of a foreigner reverts to the treasury whether there be heirs or not'.[94]

Another example relates to the imposition of import and export duties. It all began, Erasmus tells his readers, as an excellent plan. Officials, whose task it is to supervise imports and exports with the particular purpose of guaranteeing safe passage, were stationed along the boundaries of the various kingdoms. If anything was stolen, the prince in whose territory the theft occurred saw to it that the merchant suffered no loss and the thief was punished. As 'a matter of courtesy', perhaps, 'merchants started to give a small fee'. Now, however, 'everywhere the traveler is stopped for his custom fee, the stranger is bothered by it, the merchants are fleeced', and there is no suggestion of offering any protection to anybody, even though 'the tax mounts from day to day'.[95]

A third example concerns goods surviving from a shipwreck. Erasmus notes that originally the law prescribed that only goods which were not properly claimed by anyone became the property of the state where they

[92] Erasmus to Paul Volz, 14 August 1518, in Olin (ed.), *Christian Humanism and the Reformation*, p. 117.

[93] For Erasmus's understanding of 'equitable', see, for example, Erasmus to Nicolas Everard, 26 July 1524, in Gerlo (ed.), *La Correspondance d'Érasme*, vol. 5, pp. 635–36; and Erasmus to Alphonse Valdes, 21 March 1529, in Gerlo (ed.), *La Correspondance d'Érasme*, vol. 8, pp. 121, 121n, 128.

[94] Erasmus, *The Education of a Christian Prince*, p. 229.

[95] Ibid., pp. 229–30.

were found. Now, however, 'the prefect, more unrelenting than the sea itself, seizes upon whatever is lost by any cause at sea as if it were his own':

There are many provisions like these among many nations which are no less unjust than injustice itself. It is not the purpose of this treatise to change any particular state. These practices are common to substantially all states, and they have been condemned by the judgment of everyone. I have brought them up for purposes of instruction.

It is for princes to change them.[96]

In suggesting to princes that they improve the laws that obtain among them, Erasmus takes up a position which accords with what Richard Tuck says of humanists in general, and of humanist lawyers in particular. 'What was important to them', he observes, 'was not natural law but humanly constructed law; not natural rights but civil remedies.'[97] Erasmus refers in passing to the law of nature, but he does not put it to any use.[98] Law has only a minor place in his thinking on international society; he does not engage in the discussion of the law of nature and the law of nations which preoccupied the jurists – not surprisingly, since this was at that point a debate among the scholastics. His larger concern is to bring law more into accord with the philosophy of Christ, and his discussion of practical improvements in implementing human laws is persuasive but not systematic.

Learning as a Link

Erasmus places more emphasis on a second way of achieving greater correspondence between the world as it was and the world as it ought to be – the advancement of learning. Christian princes are not as wise and good as they ought to be. Greater learning will make them wiser and better.

One meets with this idea on numerous occasions, for example, in the *Adage* 'Make Haste Slowly' (1508):

[W]e spend our time on the rubbish written by all and sundry, and in the meantime the noble old systems of thought are lying neglected with the authors who expounded them, and ruin threatens the authority of senate, council, school,

[96] Ibid., pp. 229–31.
[97] R. Tuck, *Natural Rights Theories: Their Origin and Development* (Cambridge: Cambridge University Press, 1979), pp. 33, 34.
[98] '[T]he precepts of Christ do not abrogate the law of nature', Bainton records Erasmus as saying. Bainton, *Erasmus of Christendom*, p. 145. 'But grace, the grace of the Gospel, is more efficacious than (the precepts of the law of nature)', Erasmus submits to the reader in 'War Is Sweet to Those Who Do Not Know It', p. 338.

legal expert or theologian. If things go on as they have begun, the result will be that supreme power will be concentrated in the hands of a few, and we shall have as barbaric a tyranny among us as there is among the Turks.[99]

Or, to give another example, in the *Adage* 'Kings and Fools Are Born, not Made' (1515):

[I]f we may not choose a suitable person to be our ruler, it is important to try to make that person suitable whom fate has given us ... It seems to me that he should have attached to him, while still an infant, some skilful educator ... Let him instil into this childish mind, as yet blank and malleable, opinions worthy of a prince; arm it with the best principles of conduct, show it the difference between a true prince and a tyrant.[100]

The two passages just quoted hint at the kind of learning that Erasmus wants to see propagated: '[T]he noble old systems of thought', 'the best principles of conduct', both refer to the same product – the ideas contained in the literature of Antiquity, sacred and profane, uncontaminated by the passage of time. He revives these ideas partly by incorporating them as sources in his own writings, partly by publishing them in their original versions. In this way, Ambrose and Aristotle, Chrysostom and Cicero, Jerome and Origen, Plato and Plutarch, Seneca and Vergil, and the New Testament – to name just a few – come to life again, and for him there is no inherent conflict between the Christian and non-Christian writings of Antiquity. As he puts it in the *Colloquy* 'The Godly Feast' (1522),

Sacred Scripture is of course the basic authority in everything; yet I sometimes run across ancient sayings or pagan writings ... so purely and reverently and admirably expressed that I can't help believing their authors' hearts were moved by some divine power. And perhaps the spirit and the company of saints includes many not in our calendar.[101]

The ideas contained in the literature inherited from Antiquity are the subject matter destined to narrow the gap between practice and principle,

[99] Erasmus, 'Make Haste Slowly', p. 183.

[100] Erasmus, 'Kings and Fools Are Born, not Made', pp. 220–21. Suggested first readings include the Proverbs of Solomon, *Ecclesiasticus*, the Book of Wisdom, the Gospels, the *Apophthegmata* of Plutarch and his *Morals*; also his *Lives*; then Seneca, the *Politics* of Aristotle, and the *Offices* of Cicero. And last but not least Plato, 'the most venerable source of such things – in my opinion at least'. See Erasmus, *The Education of a Christian Prince*, pp. 199–201.

[101] Erasmus, 'The Godly Feast' (1522), in Thompson (transl.), *The Colloquies of Erasmus*, p. 65. See also Erasmus, 'The Antibarbarians', pp. 59–61. As Kisch explains, the idea of *Logos* (which identifies the word of God with Christ) taken from ancient Christian theology made it possible for the humanists to hold that the workings of Christ did not commence with the Christian era, but that 'his wisdom pervaded the world from the beginning'. Kisch, *Erasmus und die Jurisprudenz seiner Zeit*, p. 150.

and Erasmus not only publishes as much of it as he is able to but also directs most of it to the attention of the princes of his day, and those near them, by dedicating each writing to one of them. The list of dedications compiled by the editors of *Opus Epistolarum* is long;[102] a few examples must suffice to make the point:

Philip of Burgundy, Bishop of Utrecht and 'one of the pillars of Margaret's government in the Netherlands': *The Complaint of Peace* (1517); Prince Charles (Charles V): *The Education of a Christian Prince* (1516); Henry VIII, King of England: Plutarch's *On Distinguishing between a Flatterer and a Friend* (1517); Pope Leo X: *The New Testament* (1516); Ferdinand, Archduke of Austria and brother of Charles V: *Paraphrase on the Gospel of St John* (1523); Francis I, King of France: *Paraphrase on St Mark* (1523); Christopher of Schydlowyetz, a Polish statesman whose 'energies were devoted to the maintenance of peace':[103] *Lingua* (1525), a treatise on the power of the human tongue for good and evil; Alonso Fonseca, Archbishop of Toledo, who 'took a leading part in the government of Spain during the absence of Charles V': *The Works of Augustine* (1529).

The dedications usually include a message in accord with the gift. For example, he writes to Henry VIII in 1517:

Another chief merit is this, that among so many affairs in which your kingdom, and indeed the whole world, is concerned, you scarcely let a day pass but you bestow some time upon reading, and delight in converse with those ancient sages, who are anything but flatterers; while you choose especially those books, from which you may rise a better and a wiser man, and more useful to your country.[104]

And to Francis I in 1523:

Indeed, I had dedicated Matthew to Charles, my Prince; John, whom I interpreted immediately after Matthew, to Ferdinand, Charles' brother; and Luke, whom I tackled in the third place, to the King of England; Mark seemed rightly left to you so that the four volumes of the gospel were consecrated to the four most important monarchs of the world. May it please Heaven that the text of the gospel unite your names in a harmony similar to that which the spirit of the gospel ought to bind your hearts.[105]

[102] B. Flower and E. Rosenbaum (compil.), *Opus Epistolarum Des. Erasmi Roterodami*, vol. 12, *Indices* (Oxford: Oxford University Press, 1958), pp. 78–80.

[103] P. S. Allen and H. M. Allen (eds), *Opus Epistolarum Des. Erasmi Roterodami*, vol. 3, *1517–1519* (Oxford: Clarendon Press, 1913), p. 14; Allen and Allen (eds), *Opus Epistolarum*, vol. 6, pp. 134, 410.

[104] Erasmus to Henry VIII, 9 September 1517, in Nichols, *The Epistles of Erasmus*, vol. 3, p. 45.

[105] Erasmus to François I, 1 December 1523, p. 267. Both Margolin and Mesnard interpret this act as signifying the realization of the first society of nations. See Margolin, *Guerre et Paix dans la Pensée d'Érasme*, p. 6, and P. Mesnard, *L'Essor de la philosophie politique au XVIe Siècle* [The Flourishing of Political Philosophy in the Sixteenth Century] (Paris: J. Vrin, 1951), p. 116.

The ideas of Antiquity, chosen to promote harmony in discord, are distributed not only within Christendom but also beyond it. Erasmus offers this information in 1508 when he writes in the *Adage* 'Make Haste Slowly' that the symbol of the anchor and dolphin cannot have enjoyed greater prestige, when it passed from hand to hand on the imperial coinage, than now when it is dispatched into the world beyond Christendom 'on all kinds of books, in both languages, recognized, owned and praised by all to whom liberal studies are holy'.[106]

The world needed learning in order to become more as it ought to be, but learning also needed the world in order to survive and prosper. As Erasmus sees it, and notes in a letter to a friend in 1500, it is a question of obtaining 'from whatever source' what is necessary in order to be able to live a scholar's life, or else having to abandon studies.[107] A letter written thirty years later testifies to the success he has had in gaining patrons not only for himself – he now has a 'room full of letters from men of learning, nobles, princes and cardinals' and a 'chest full of gold and silver plate, cups, clocks, and rings' – but also for learning in general. 'Compare the world as it was thirty years ago', he writes, and look at it now. 'Then, not a prince would spend a farthing on his son's education; now every one of them has a paid tutor in his family.'[108]

Stefan Zweig describes the success of learning in winning social and financial support in the following way:

> Everyone wanted to become a citizen, a cosmopolitan, in this realm of learning; emperors and popes, princes and priests, artists and statesmen, young men and women competed to be educated in the arts and *Wissenschaften*; Latin became their common brotherly language.[109]

When Erasmus refers to 'this realm of learning', he sometimes uses the term *res publica literaria*, the Republic of Letters.[110] He is even credited with having coined the term. He speaks of 'our commerce' when he refers to the exchange of ideas which takes place amongst the members of the Republic of Letters. He comments on its fortunes in peace and war, noting that peace is favourable to the advancement of learning while war

[106] The famous printing house Aldus of Venice adopted the symbol of the anchor and dolphin as its trademark.

[107] Erasmus to Jacob Batt, ca. 12 December 1500, in *Collected Works of Erasmus*, vol. 1, p. 303.

[108] Erasmus to Mexia, 30 March 1530, in Froude, *Life and Letters of Erasmus*, pp. 377–78. See also Erasmus to Antoon van Bergen, 14 January 1518, in Nichols, *The Epistles of Erasmus*, vol. 3, p. 224.

[109] S. Zweig, *Triumph und Tragik des Erasmus von Rotterdam* [Triumph and Tragedy of Erasmus of Rotterdam] (Wien: Herbert Reichner, 1935), p. 16. There is no satisfactory English translation for *Wissenschaften*, as they comprise all branches of knowledge.

[110] See, for example, Erasmus, 'The Antibarbarians', pp. 42, 43.

obstructs it, although he also observes that it is possible for princes to be at war while scholars are at peace and communicate with one another. The Republic of Letters has the aim of advancing 'the cause of enlightenment'; it has its own language and its own values.[111] One finds all this in his writings, but he does not say, as Zweig does, that

> The humanists are as determined to rule the world in the name of reason, as the princes are in the name of authority, and the Church in the name of Christ. Their dream aims at an oligarchy, a government of the aristocracy of learning.[112]

According to Erasmus, it is the product of the Republic of Letters which is the element providing for more harmony in discord, not its practitioners.

Moderation as a Link

Avoiding extremes or, to put it positively, observing moderation is another suggestion on the part of Erasmus to move practice in the direction of principle, and he advocates this idea – J. A. K. Thomson speaks of Erasmus's passion for moderation[113] – whenever he meets with its opposite. 'It is amazing', he writes in a letter of 1515, 'how there is no middle course'.[114]

This finding may be documented with the help of a few examples relating to religion and politics, within Christendom and beyond it.

One set of examples consists of Erasmus's advice to the princes within Christendom to resolve their conflicts by arbitration and mediation. '[W]hat need is there', he asks in 1515, 'to fly to arms at once?'

> The world has so many earnest and learned bishops, so many venerable abbots, so many aged peers with the wisdom of long experience, so many councils, so many conclaves set up by our ancestors, not without reason. Why do we not use their arbitration to settle these childish disputes between princes?[115]

He includes the advice in almost identical wording in *The Education of a Christian Prince*, dedicated to Prince Charles in 1516, and submits it to the French King in 1523:

[111] See, for example, Erasmus to Nicholas Beraldus, 25 May 1522, p. 264; Erasmus to Guolfangus Fabritius Capito, 26 February 1517, in Nichols, *The Epistles of Erasmus*, vol. 2, p. 506; Erasmus to Thomas More, ca. 10 July 1517, in Nichols, *The Epistles of Erasmus*, vol. 2, p. 576.

[112] Zweig, *Triumph und Tragik des Erasmus von Rotterdam*, p. 114.

[113] J. A. K. Thomson, 'Desiderius Erasmus', in F. J. C. Hearnshaw (ed.), *The Social and Political Ideas of Some Great Thinkers of the Renaissance and the Reformation* (New York: Barnes & Noble, 1949), p. 156.

[114] Erasmus to Martin Dorp, May 1515, p. 80. Here Erasmus reacts to the attitude shown by theologians to the 'new' learning.

[115] Erasmus, 'War Is Sweet to Those Who Do Not Know It', p. 343.

As far as I am concerned, Excellent King, I like to persuade myself that, given your character, that of the Emperor Charles, and of the King of England, you all would have, without any doubt, followed good advice for a long time if a counsellor could have been found, who was free in his moderation at the same time as moderate in his freedom.[116]

And he praises the Polish King in 1527 for supporting the cause of moderation by intervening, with the help of diplomacy, in a dispute between two neighbouring princes 'in an attempt to avoid war until all other means susceptible to prevent it had been tried'.[117]

A second set of examples concerns the conflict which developed within Christendom with the appearance of Luther. Erasmus prescribes moderation as an approach to the solution of this conflict, as many of his writings bear witness. To quote from a letter written prior to the Diet of Worms (1521) called together to decide on Luther's fate,

The question is not what Luther deserves, but what is best for the peace of the world. The persons who are to prosecute, the remedies which are to be applied, must be carefully chosen ... Force never answers in such cases, and other means must be found ... Luther was advised to be more moderate ... His prosecutors were cautioned too ... The fear is that, if Luther's books are burnt and Luther executed, things will only grow worse ... Luther's conduct and the causes which led to it ought to be referred to a small committee of good learned men who will be above suspicion.[118]

To quote from another letter written nine years later, when the Diet of Augsburg was meeting and news emanating from there did not sound favourable to the cause of moderation, pope and emperor were reported to be 'urging extremities', and 'the reforming leaders' made it no secret that 'they were in earnest on their side':

If the Emperor is only putting on a brag, well and good; if he means war in earnest, I am sorry to be a bird of ill omen, but I am in consternation at the thought of it ... The question is not what the sectarians deserve, but what course with

[116] Erasmus, *The Education of a Christian Prince*, pp. 252–53; Erasmus to François I, 1 December 1523, pp. 274–75.

[117] Erasmus to Sigismund I, 15 May 1527, p. 300. Arbitration and mediation are the ideas which secured Erasmus a place in J. Ter Meulen's and P. J. J. Diermanse's study, *Der Gedanke der Internationalen Organisation: 1300–1800* [The Idea of International Organization: 1300–1800] (The Hague: Martinus Nijhoff, 1968), pp. 124–27.

[118] Erasmus to Conrad Peutinger, 9 November 1520, in Froude, *Life and Letters of Erasmus*, p. 268. For a discussion of Erasmus's attempt at translating his idea of moderation into practice during the weeks preceding the Diet of Worms, see P. Kalkhoff, 'Die Vermittlungspolitik des Erasmus und sein Anteil an den Flugschriften der ersten Reformationszeit' [The Politics of Mediation of Erasmus and His Share in the Pamphlets of the First Period of the Reformation], *Archiv fuer Reformationsgeschichte*, vols 1–2, 1903–05.

them is expedient for Europe. Toleration may be a misfortune, yet a less [sic] misfortune than war.[119]

And in the treatise 'On Mending the Peace of the Church', published in 1533, Erasmus reminds those on whom the affairs of men depend that '[p]ower that is lacking in discretion falls to the ground with its own weight', adding that the 'gods carry tempered power to greater heights', and suggesting that 'with moderate advice and calm minds' the task of establishing peace in the Church may be accomplished.[120]

A third set of examples is given by Erasmus's advocacy of moderation on the part of Christendom in its approach to the non-Christian world. The case which concerns him in particular is the Turkish question.

In 1515, at a time when there was peace between Christendom and the Turkish empire, the latter having renewed its treaties with Hungary and Venice, Erasmus writes:

To me it does not even seem recommendable [sic] that we should now be preparing war against the Turks ... What is taken by the sword is lost by the sword. Are you anxious to win the Turks for Christ? Let us not display our wealth, our armies, our strength. Let them see in us not only the name, but the unmistakable marks of a Christian ... Why do we not rather acknowledge them, give them encouragement and gently try to reform them?[121]

Fifteen years later Christendom and the Turkish empire were no longer at peace, and Turkish troops were moving in the direction of Vienna, but Erasmus's *Consultatio* of 1530 on the question of war against the Turks still argues for moderation, even though it does not reject war: 'It would be highly desirable', he writes, to win the territories of the Turkish empire in the same way in which the Apostles won 'the nations of the earth' for Christ; to overcome the enemy with 'a behaviour and a soul worthy of the Gospel'; to send 'heralds of integrity' who seek all advantage for Christ, and none for themselves; and to permit those who do not immediately accept the Christian religion 'to live for some time under their own laws, until they slowly become one with us'. This is how Christian rulers 'progressively abolished paganism' in former times.[122]

Whether within Christendom or beyond it, moderation is more easily exercised if a distinction is drawn between essentials and non-essentials. Erasmus expresses this idea on numerous occasions. For example,

[119] Erasmus to Campeggio, 18 August 1530, in Froude, *Life and Letters of Erasmus*, pp. 383–84.
[120] Erasmus, 'On Mending the Peace of the Church', p. 388.
[121] Erasmus, 'War Is Sweet to Those Who Do Not Know It', pp. 344–47.
[122] Erasmus, 'A Valued Discussion on War Against the Turks', pp. 373–74.

concerning the world within Christendom he observes in a letter of 1523 to John Carondelet, Councillor to Margaret of Austria:

The perfection of our religion consists in peace and harmony. And this can hardly be established unless we define as few things as possible and leave each man free to form his own decisions on many questions.[123]

And he chooses almost the same wording when he presents the idea in relation to the world beyond Christendom.[124]

It is mainly in the context of religion that Erasmus advances this idea, but in the following passage he expresses it in the context of politics:

If any portion of a treaty appears to have been broken, we should not at once conclude that the whole pact is invalidated, lest we seem to have pounced upon an excuse for breaking off friendly relations. On the contrary, we should rather strive to patch up the breach with the least trouble possible. It is advantageous sometimes even to overlook some points, since not even among private individuals do agreements long remain in effect, if they carry out everything to the letter, as the saying goes.[125]

The foregoing examples reflect Erasmus's belief that moderation, whether it finds expression in arbitration and mediation, toleration, persuasion or restraint in general, reduces not only the incidence of conflict but also its severity, thus making the world as it was more like the world as it ought to be.

The Question of War

It is mainly in the context of the question of war that Erasmus has been mentioned in the literature of international relations. The passionate eloquence of his denunciations of war has led many commentators to term him a pacifist, and international relations scholars have tended to follow in their footsteps. F. H. Hinsley writes:

Pacifists like Erasmus in the early sixteenth century and like the Quakers in the seventeenth century were untypical of the age in abandoning the medieval distinction between just and unjust wars on the ground that all war was incompatible with reason and morality.[126]

[123] Erasmus to John Carondelet, 5 January 1523, in J. Hillerbrand (ed.), *Erasmus and His Age: Selected Letters of Desiderius Erasmus* (New York: Harper & Row, 1970), p. 168. See also Erasmus to Pope Paul III, 23 January 1535, in Hillerbrand, *Erasmus and His Age*, pp. 283–84.

[124] Erasmus, 'War Is Sweet to Those Who Do Not Know It', p. 348.

[125] Erasmus, *The Education of a Christian Prince*, p. 239.

[126] Hinsley, *Power and the Pursuit of Peace*, p. 16.

Likewise Michael Howard: 'Erasmus did not concede, indeed, that there could be any circumstances under which war would be justified.'[127]

However, he was not a pacifist in the strict sense, which has also been termed the modern sense: one who rejects all justification of war, and refuses all participation.[128] His attitude towards war may rather be identified as: not to approve of war but to accept it in case of necessity. Such an attitude directs attention to the existence in his thought of another way of bringing practice more into accord with principle.

Erasmus expresses his ideas about war against a climate of opinion which accepts it readily. As he observes,

> War is now such an accepted thing that people are astonished to find anyone who does not like it; and such a respectable thing that it is wicked (I nearly said heretical) to disapprove of the thing.[129]

Erasmus does not approve of war. '[E]ven when it is waged with perfect justification', he writes, 'no man who is truly good approves it.'[130] His reasons for not approving it include moral as well as practical considerations. War is fundamentally contrary to the spirit of Christ's teaching: love of one's neighbour, forgiveness – and peace. The ready acceptance of war among Christians is especially repugnant:

> Who ever heard of a hundred thousand animals rushing together to butcher each other, which men do everywhere ... What depths of hell have hatched this monstrosity for us?[131]

War is immensely destructive, both physically and morally; it inflicts the greatest suffering on those who least deserve it, the common people. The costs almost invariably outweigh the value of any possible gains, and the outcome is never certain.[132]

For Erasmus, not to approve of war means to avoid it if possible:

[127] M. Howard, *War and the Liberal Conscience* (London: Temple Smith, 1978), p. 16. There have been a few writers, mainly not specialists in international relations, who have qualified these general statements. For example, Thomson, 'Desiderius Erasmus', p. 162: 'Erasmus was not in the complete sense a pacifist, for he believed that some things would justify a war'; and E. von Koerber, *Die Staatstheorie des Erasmus von Rotterdam* [The Theory of the State of Erasmus of Rotterdam] (Berlin: Duncker & Humblot, 1967), p. 97. For a more extensive study, see J. A. Fernández, 'Erasmus on the Just War', *Journal of the History of Ideas*, vol. 34, no. 2, 1973; but this author leaves out evidence which would not only strengthen his argument, but also render it more balanced.

[128] Y. S. Choue (ed.), *World Encyclopedia of Peace*, 2nd edn, vol. IV (New York: Oceana Publications, 1999), p. 114.

[129] Erasmus, 'War Is Sweet to Those Who Do Not Know It', p. 310.

[130] Erasmus to Antoon van Bergen, 14 March 1514, p. 280.

[131] Erasmus, 'War Is Sweet to Those Who Do Not Know It', pp. 315–16.

[132] See, for example, ibid., pp. 312–14, 339–43; Erasmus, 'The Complaint of Peace', pp. 194–95; and Erasmus, *The Education of a Christian Prince*, pp. 250, 253–54.

If there is anything in mortal affairs which should be approached with hesitancy, or rather which ought to be avoided in every possible way, guarded against and shunned, that thing is war.[133]

In his view, as we have seen, there are better ways of trying to resolve a conflict, for example, arbitration and mediation. 'The pagan warriors, before they took to arms, took to parley.' A wise and good prince, he insists, never goes to war 'unless, after trying every other means, he cannot possibly avoid it'.[134]

However, as two of the above passages already imply, Erasmus does not rule out war altogether. The sword was taken away from Peter, he writes to Francis I in 1523, but it was not taken away from the princes. 'What is the significance of the sword', he asks in 1516, if it does not mean that a country ought to be safe under its prince's protection – 'safe both from outside enemies and those within?'[135] 'I do not condemn war absolutely', he affirms in 1526;[136] and in 1530 he says in his discussion of the question of war against the Turks: 'There are in fact people who think that the right to make war is forbidden to Christians in an absolute way – an opinion which I consider to be too absurd to have to refute it.'[137] There is a case, he holds, when war may have to be resorted to, and that case is necessity: 'It is possible that a good prince will, one day, go to war, but then an extreme necessity will have pushed him into this position, after he has tried everything in vain.'[138]

What, in Erasmus's eyes, is necessity, and what is it not? The answer, contained in many statements scattered over his writings, is clear: ambition, anger, greed for riches, thirst for glory, desire for power, hatred, envy, an old title, or some selfish treaty – none of these constitutes necessity, even though most wars, both within Christendom and with non-Christians, have arisen from one of these 'trivial, stupid or wicked reasons'.[139] Necessity, however, does present itself when it is a question of having to defend one's country and religion against an aggressor.[140]

133 Erasmus, 'War Is Sweet to Those Who Do Not Know It', p. 309.

134 Ibid., p. 333; Erasmus, *The Education of a Christian Prince*, p. 249.

135 Erasmus to François I, 1 December 1523, p. 269; Erasmus, *The Education of a Christian Prince*, p. 187.

136 Erasmus to the Sorbonne, 1526, in Bainton, *Erasmus of Christendom*, p. 244.

137 Erasmus, 'A Valued Discussion on War Against the Turks', p. 351.

138 Erasmus to François I, 1 December 1523, p. 269.

139 Erasmus, 'The Complaint of Peace', pp. 188–92; Erasmus, 'War Is Sweet to Those Who Do Not Know It', pp. 336, 341, 343, 348–50; and Erasmus, *The Education of a Christian Prince*, pp. 251–52.

140 See, for example, Erasmus to François I, 1 December 1523, pp. 268–69; Erasmus, 'War Is Sweet to Those Who Do Not Know It', p. 348; Erasmus, 'The Complaint of Peace', p. 195.

There is a suggestion, both in *Julius Exclusus* and in 'War Is Sweet to Those Who Do not Know It', that a war which is fought in order to remove a tyrant may be regarded as having necessity on its side, but this idea does not recur and is not elaborated in any way.[141]

Erasmus is scornful of the classical and the scholastic traditions of the just war. '"Just" indeed – this means any war declared in any way against anybody by any prince ... Who does not think his own cause just?' And: '[Roman law] regards war as praiseworthy if it is just. "Just" is defined as what has been ordered by the prince, even if he be a child or a fool.'[142] However, there is an occasional hint that, despite all his reservations, his thinking on the possibility of justifying war follows the same lines:

> War is not to be condemned entirely, if it is undertaken for a just reason, which means in defence of public tranquillity, under circumstances which make it unavoidable; if it is undertaken by piously thinking princes and with the consent of those for whom it is waged; if it is announced in the generally recognized way and is conducted in a just and moderate manner, which means as few bloody losses and sacrifices as possible for those who have not caused the war, and if the war is concluded as soon as possible.[143]

Erasmus's writings suggest a further condition which ought to be met if a war is to be just – a condition which he does not include explicitly in the statement above, but which he expresses elsewhere: 'If you cannot defend your realm without violating justice, without wanton loss of human life, without great loss to religion, give up and yield to the importunities of the age!'[144] In other words, it is his view that a war ceases to be just if it risks destroying the society in whose defence it is fought.[145]

Not only does Erasmus distinguish between just and unjust wars but, as his theory of the three circles reveals, the former has a well-defined place in his thought: 'The second circle is formed by the temporal princes whose arms and laws serve Christ in their own way, be it that they defeat the enemy in just wars.'[146] As he himself points out, in not ruling out war

141 Erasmus, *Julius Exclusus*, pp. 57–58; Erasmus, 'War Is Sweet to Those Who Do Not Know It', p. 341.
142 Erasmus, 'War Is Sweet to Those Who Do Not Know It', pp. 331, 337.
143 Erasmus, 'Paraphrase on St Luke', in Koerber, *Die Staatstheorie des Erasmus von Rotterdam*, p. 99.
144 Erasmus, *The Education of a Christian Prince*, p. 155.
145 This idea appears, for example, in the context of the war between Francis I and Charles V (see Erasmus to François I, 1 December 1523, p. 268) and of the conflict between Christian states and the Turkish empire. (See Erasmus, 'A Valued Discussion on War Against the Turks', p. 373.)
146 See note 85 to this chapter.

altogether, he takes up a position which differentiates him from those who 'deny that Christians should wage any war' and those who 'blow the trumpet to summon men to war for any and every cause'.[147]

Some Reflections in Conclusion

Erasmus wrote and published five hundred years ago, yet his works continue to be readily available – in old editions and in new ones, in their original language and in translation. His language is straightforward, he has a good sense of the apt title, yet his thought remains somewhat elusive for the modern reader. He is not a systematic thinker. He needs space when writing; he uses many words where others limit themselves to a few. He attempts to persuade with the help of eloquence rather than dialectics. Ideas relating to different spheres of human experience – religion, philosophy, morality, law, government, society, national and international politics, to mention a few – are closely interwoven, and difficult to separate; only the emphasis changes, highlighting different ideas at different times and in different contexts.

Erasmus's way of presenting his ideas may be unpalatable to the twentieth-century specialist – it certainly does not invite the formulation of theory – and it is easy to miss a particular idea in a particular work. However, as one continues to explore his writings, definite impressions begin to form, for his ideas return, in different configurations, but consistently and continuously, and in the end one is tempted to compare his method with that of a printmaker who uses many plates, each one by itself partial, perhaps unimpressive, to create a print – a picture which is complete, and perhaps telling.

In opposition to both realism and universalism Erasmus puts forward a third way. Central to it is the idea of political plurality, and he joins to it the idea of that which links and circumscribes. Political plurality, in his case, means a plurality of Christian princes, but it also means a plurality of Christian peoples or states, for 'a prince cannot exist without a state'.[148] He places the emphasis on princes rather than peoples, not because the latter are unimportant, but because princes are responsible for their peoples. Princes, with their peoples, are the 'discordant elements' within Christendom, but he does not focus on that which differentiates them, but rather on that which they have, or ought to have, in equal

[147] Erasmus to Paul Volz, 14 August 1518, in Olin (ed.), *Christian Humanism and the Reformation*, pp. 123–24; Erasmus, 'A Valued Discussion on War Against the Turks', pp. 350–52.

[148] Erasmus, *The Education of a Christian Prince*, p. 233.

measure – wisdom, goodness and power, and also checks and balances in their internal affairs. And the spiritual Christian prince does not aim at overthrowing political plurality, but acts in its support.

That which links and keeps within bounds Christian princes and their peoples – or, to use the language of this chapter, that which promotes harmony in discord – is the Christian religion or philosophy of Christ, reinforced and complemented by learning, hints of a positive law of nations, moderation and an attitude towards war which rejects it unless, all other measures having failed, it proves unavoidable. The idea of the just war is not entirely absent, but he does not associate himself with classical or scholastic just war doctrine.

In the course of the twentieth century, Erasmus's political thought, hitherto neglected or even disparaged, has come to receive more attention; indeed, Mansfield's survey of the literature devotes a chapter to it. It is not, like his role in religious conflicts of the time or the question of his influence, an area of major controversy. Except for the question of war, his thinking on international relations is still neglected, but Mansfield's few comments tend to support the present interpretation, in particular on Erasmus's rejection of universalism and the qualifications to his pacifism.[149] There are differences of opinion on whether he disregarded political institutions, but the most contested issue is his supposed lack of political realism. Mansfield finds the counter-arguments more convincing: the shrewdness of his political observations, his keen awareness of social and political ills, including abuses of power, and the practical influence of his thinking on the duties of the ruler in the German states.[150] Along these lines, the present chapter has drawn attention to his use of the form of the panegyric as a way of circumventing the vanity of monarchs, and there are indications that he was well aware of the limits of what could be achieved through moral appeals. Moreover, some of his comments – for example, on the acceptance of the culture of war, on the effects of the spread of learning or on inherent weaknesses of the monarchical system – raise issues of the kind taken up in the contemporary sub-discipline of political sociology.

At the outset of the modern states system Erasmus presents, in the language of classical humanism, a remarkably clear account of the essentials of the idea of international society. For a few brief years he may have hoped that the young monarchs – Charles V, Francis I, and Henry VIII – would act in ways that would bring this idea closer to realization. Such

[149] Mansfield, *Erasmus in the Twentieth Century*, pp. 24–27.
[150] Ibid., pp. 34–39.

hopes were disappointed, and before long, doctrinal schisms and wars in the name of religion were to negate the idea, in practice, for more than a century. Wight and Bull, of course, were well aware of this phenomenon, having lived through such a period in the twentieth century. The idea itself, however, was not extinguished, as will be seen in the chapters to follow.

3 Francisco de Vitoria

The second thinker to be included in this study is the Spanish Dominican Francisco de Vitoria (1480?–1546).

Otto von Gierke, as well as Martin Wight and Hedley Bull, mention him in their respective accounts of the three ways of thinking about international relations but list him under different headings. Gierke attaches him to the universalists and gives a source upon which he bases his decision; Wight and Bull group him with the representatives of the *via media*, Wight offering a source and Bull omitting to do so.[1]

The reference given by Gierke turns out, on closer examination, to be rather unilluminating. It reads: 'Rel. III, nos. 12 and 15', followed by the sentence that Vitoria speaks 'of a human *respublica* which comprises all states as members, and in which majority decisions hold'.[2] Without the title of Vitoria's treatise it is difficult to identify this source, as not all the editions of Vitoria's *relectiones*[3] follow the same order of presentation. For example, the 1694 edition which is the basis for the well-known publication of 1917 in *The Classics of International Law* gives as the third *relectio* 'On Civil Power'.[4] Its items 12 and 15, however, do not relate to the point in question. In fact, a perusal of all thirteen *relectiones* as published by the Dominican Teófilo Urdánoz in 1960[5] leads to the

[1] O. von Gierke, *Das Deutsche Genossenschaftsrecht*, vol. 4 (Graz: Akademische Druck und Verlagsanstalt, 1954), p. 362; M. Wight, 'Why Is There No International Theory?' in H. Butterfield and M. Wight (eds), *Diplomatic Investigations: Essays in the Theory of International Politics* (London: George Allen & Unwin, 1969), p. 22; M. Wight, 'Western Values in International Relations', in Butterfield and Wight (eds), *Diplomatic Investigations*, p. 96; H. Bull, *The Anarchical Society: A Study of Order in World Politics* (London: Macmillan, 1977), p. 28.

[2] Gierke, *Das Deutsche Genossenschaftsrecht*, vol. 4, p. 362.

[3] Translated: re-readings. A *relectio* was a dissertation on a question treated in the ordinary lectures.

[4] E. Nys (ed.), *Francisci de Victoria De Indis et De Iure Belli Relectiones* [Relectiones on the Indians and the Law of War by Franciscus de Victoria], The Classics of International Law (Washington, DC: Carnegie Institution, 1917, reprinted New York: Oceana Publications, 1964), p. 104.

[5] T. Urdánoz (ed.), *Obras de Francisco de Vitoria: Relecciones Teológicas* [Works by Francisco de Vitoria: Theological Relectiones] (Madrid: Autores Cristianos, 1960).

conclusion that items 12 and 15, wherever they appear, are not relevant to the question. And the sentence which Gierke adds in his footnote does not explain his decision. Wight offers a reference to the *relectiones* 'On Civil Power' and 'On the Indians', but the ideas which they identify – 'the world as a whole, being in a way one single State' and 'natural society and fellowship' – could also belong to the universalist pattern of thought. Rather than giving evidence to justify their respective decisions, Gierke, Wight and Bull may be said to withhold it.

The present reading supports Wight and Bull: it places Vitoria squarely within the *via media*. However, differing interpretations persist. Annabel Brett associates him with universalism:

> Vitoria saw the *ius gentium* as a law neither between individual men, nor between sovereign states, but between all human beings as forming one community: 'The whole world, which is in a sense a commonwealth, has the power to enact laws which are just and convenient to all men; and these make up the law of nations.'[6]

Antony Anghie introduces yet another interpretation: Vitoria's project was to provide a new doctrine to legitimize Spain's imperial conquests.[7] These interpretations are discussed in the conclusion to the chapter. But this introductory section will refer to some general problems posed by the interpretation of Vitoria's writings, which go some way towards explaining why they are open to such radically different readings.

One problem for today's readers is that the scholastic mode of reasoning readily lends itself to different interpretations. The scholastics followed a rigorous form of argumentation based on Aristotle's syllogistic logic, eschewing all forms of rhetorical persuasion. This followed a uniform pattern, setting out the question, the proposed answer, argument and counter-argument, making much of distinctions and qualifications, but the overall import may not be clear – seemingly more a debate than a conclusive argument. Vitoria made frequent use of conditional arguments (if 'x', then 'y') without necessarily committing himself to the truth or otherwise of 'x'. Others engage in elaborate reasoning which comes across as casuistry, coherent but unpersuasive.

Scholasticism is usually defined in terms of this mode of argumentation rather than as a body of doctrine, and had long seen contending doctrines, notably Thomism (the thought of St Thomas Aquinas), Scotism (following the Franciscan Duns Scotus) and nominalism (looking to

[6] A. S. Brett, *Changes of State: Nature and the Limits of the City in Early Modern Natural Law* (Princeton, NJ: Princeton University Press, 2011), p. 13.

[7] A. Anghie, *Imperialism, Sovereignty and the Making of International Law* (Cambridge: Cambridge University Press, 2004), pp. 13–31.

William of Ockham). It was the subtle disputes between these schools, or sometimes within them, over seemingly inconsequential issues, which brought scholasticism into disrepute and prompted the scorn of the humanists. The Dominican Order, which Vitoria joined at a young age, was committed to Thomism, but this was by no means predominant at the turn of the sixteenth century; rather, nominalism was the more widely taught, in particular in Paris.[8]

Vitoria was the most eminent Spanish theologian of his day, at a time when theology could claim to be relevant to every branch of knowledge. He was an exceptionally influential teacher, his students occupying most of the chairs in theology in Spain in the next generation. Thus he is seen as the founder of the Salamanca School or 'second scholasticism' – not a new theological doctrine, but a literature applying Thomist theology to address the great public issues of the day. Of special interest here are Vitoria's views on the moral and political questions raised by the transition from medieval Europe to a new states system yet to be defined, and by the Spanish conquests in America.

The paucity of information on Vitoria's life may well present the greatest problem for interpreting his thought. The person behind the austere prose is scarcely known. There is no satisfactory biography.[9] His date of birth is often given as ca. 1485, but some place it as late as 1492. It was earlier assumed that he was born in Vitoria, in the basque province of Alava, and then moved to Burgos, but this is now taken to have been his birthplace. Here he entered a Dominican monastery, probably in 1506; whether as a child or a young adult remains unclear. Very little is known of his family, except that his parents came from well-established families, his mother's ancestry may have been Jewish, and his (probably) elder brother, Diego, was also a Dominican monk and a fierce critic of Erasmus.

[8] For scholasticism in this period, see Q. Skinner, *The Foundations of Modern Political Thought*, vol. 2, *The Age of Reformation* (Cambridge: Cambridge University Press, 1978), pp. 135–73. For an account of the teaching of scholasticism in the University of Paris a few years earlier, see R. J. Schoeck, *Erasmus of Europe*, vol. I, *The Making of a Humanist, 1467–1500* (Edinburgh: Edinburgh University Press, 1990), pp. 162–82, 196–205. For the different schools, see D. Knowles, *The Evolution of Medieval Political Thought* (London: Longmans, 1962), pp. 251–68, 301–36.

[9] See the comment in A. Pagden and J. Lawrance (eds), *Francisco de Vitoria: Political Writings* (Cambridge: Cambridge University Press, 1991), p. xxxi. The account in C. Norena, *Studies in Spanish Renaissance Thought* (The Hague: Nijhoff, 1975), pp. 36–68 is informative, but some details may be overstated. For short accounts, see B. Hamilton, *Political Thought in Sixteenth-Century Spain: A Study of the Political Ideas of Vitoria, De Soto, Suárez and Molina* (Oxford: Clarendon Press, 1963), pp. 171–76; N. Campagna, *Francisco de Vitoria: Leben und Werk* [Francisco de Vitoria: Life and Work] (Zurich and Munster: LIT Verlag, 2010), pp. 26–34.

The outline of his scholarly career is clearer. The Dominicans must have soon recognized his intellectual potential, sending him unusually early to the University of Paris in 1509 or 1510, where he followed the usual practice of first studying the humanities before proceeding to theology. The theological faculty was not highly regarded, but his main teacher, the Dominican Thomist, Peter Crockaert, was an exception. Vitoria subsequently became his assistant with respect to his publications, notably an edition of Aquinas's *Summa Theologica*. He himself began teaching in Paris, and was awarded his doctorate in theology in 1522.

Humanism had become more prominent in Paris than during Erasmus's years there, and humanist influences have been discerned in Vitoria's writings: the range of classical authors whom he cites, certain of his expressions, and indeed his opting for moral and political issues rather than scholastic dialectic may have been a response to humanism. He is reported to have defended Erasmus against student critics, but it is scarcely plausible that his admiration for Erasmus was 'unqualified'; it is more in accord with what is known of his character that 'he followed the new trends with moderation and a critical spirit'.[10]

In 1523 he was appointed Professor of Theology at the Dominican College of San Gregorio in Valladolid, and three years later, in 1526, he was one of the two candidates nominated by the Order for election to the Prima Chair in Theology in the University of Salamanca, regarded as the leading chair, to which he was elected – by the students! – and where he remained until his death in 1546. He attracted overflow audiences to his main course, an extended commentary on Aquinas. He was required to give a public lecture each year on a question arising in the course – a *relectio*.[11] Instead of the usual practice of taking up an intricate doctrinal question, as we have seen, he made his statements on the most sensitive issues of the day, albeit refraining from wider publication.

[10] The Spanish humanist, Juan Luis Vives, describing Vitoria in a letter to Erasmus, wrote of his 'worshipping admiration' (Norena, *Spanish Renaissance Thought*, p. 47). Mesnard terms Vitoria 'a friend and disciple of Erasmus' (P. Mesnard, *L'Essor de la philosophie politique au XVIe Siècle* (Paris: J. Vrin, 1951), p. 455). The more qualified assessment is that of T. Urdánoz, 'Introducción Biográfica', in Urdánoz (ed.), *Obras de Francisco de Vitoria*, p. 15.

[11] J. Soder quotes the Spanish historiographer E. de Hinojosa, who wrote towards the end of the nineteenth century: 'I do not know anybody who would have chosen as the topic of his lectures such delicate and burning questions of the day as did the famous Dominican ... Usually only the typical "school questions" were discussed'. J. Soder, *Die Idee der Voelkergemeinschaft: Francisco de Vitoria und die Philosophischen Grundlagen des Voelkerrechts* [The Idea of the Community of Nations: Francisco de Vitoria and the Philosophical Bases of the Law of Nations] (Frankfurt am Main/Berlin: Alfred Metzner, 1955), pp. 19, 22.

He did not play a major role in public life, but his advice was widely sought on all manner of issues. A chronicler of the Convent of Estoban, where he lived, recorded:

From all the kingdoms and remotest provinces theologians, jurists, knights, merchants, royal councillors, consulted him, and all depended on his verdict as on an oracle.[12]

It was not uncommon for the monarch to consult theologians on matters with theological implications, and the Emperor Charles V consulted Vitoria on a number of occasions, even after his lecture 'On the American Indians' questioning the legitimacy of Spain's imperial conquests. Charles's initial reaction had been explosive, but did not go beyond demanding that all copies be confiscated. He even invited Vitoria to be a delegate to the Council of Trent in 1546, but Vitoria, close to death, had to decline: his next journey would be to the afterlife.[13]

One episode of particular interest for this study – because it concerns Vitoria's view of Erasmus – throws a good deal of light on the manner in which Vitoria participated in public discussion, even though his role was open to different interpretations. This is the *junta* of Valladolid in 1527, which was summoned by the Chief Inquisitor to determine whether Erasmus's works, in particular the *Enchiridion*, should be condemned as heretical. On one view, 'his opinion was moderate'; on another, 'his judgement is one of the most severe'.[14] Marcel Bataillon's detailed account of the proceedings makes it clear that, while he was sharply critical of some of Erasmus's formulations – which, he urged, should be corrected or 'expurgated' – he rejected the charge of heresy: Erasmus's work as a whole showed that he was a good Catholic. In a conference deeply divided between partisans and enemies of Erasmus, Vitoria was a leading spokesman for a judicious balance.[15] The outcome was inconclusive: the *junta* was adjourned due to an epidemic, and never resumed: a temporary success for the Erasmians.

But little is known beyond the bare externals of Vitoria's life. For example, nothing is known of his relations with his brother, who is

[12] Urdánoz, 'Introducción biográfica', p. 38. For additional comments by contemporaries, see E. Nys, 'Introduction,' in Nys (ed.), *Francisci de Victoria De Indis*.

[13] Hamilton, *Political Thought in Sixteenth-Century Spain*, p. 176.

[14] M. Barbier, 'Introduction', in M. Barbier (ed.), *Francisco de Vitoria: Leçons sur les Indiens et sur le Droit de Guerre* [Francisco de Vitoria: Lectures on the Indians and on the Law of War] (Geneva: Droz, 1966), p. xii; Urdánoz, 'Introducción Biográfica', p. 34.

[15] M. Bataillon, *Érasme et l'Espagne* [Erasmus and Spain], vol. I, nouvelle edn (Paris: Droz, 1991, first published 1937), pp. 253–99, especially pp. 269, 273, 275–76, 283; Norena, *Spanish Renaissance Thought*, pp. 49–50. Norena's account of Vitoria's written submission supports Bataillon's interpretation.

mentioned in a letter which Erasmus wrote to him in 1527, on the advice of the Spanish humanist, Juan Luis Vives, requesting that he intercede to restrain his brother's polemics, but no reaction is recorded, and it is not known whether he received the letter.[16]

Only a handful of Vitoria's letters survive, and these provide a tantalising insight into a few of his attitudes, notably the strength of his feeling on the Spanish treatment of the 'Indians':

> I must tell you, after a lifetime of studies and long experience, that no business shocks me or embarrasses me more than the corrupt profits and affairs of the Indies. Their very mention freezes the blood in my veins.[17]

He clearly had admirers and disciples, but nothing is known of his relations with colleagues more generally, or whether he had highly placed enemies in the University or in the Church. The suspicion that he may have had is raised by the University's treatment of his papers and their projected publication. The University set up a committee to determine what was to be published, but nothing emerged from its labours, and there is a suggestion that the University decided to make no money available for publication. It is known that there was an original manuscript, either in Vitoria's hand or authorized by him, but this was allowed to disappear.[18]

An edition of the *relectiones*, not authorized by the University, edited by Jacopo Boyer, was published in Lyon in 1557; a second, edited by Alonso Muñoz, in Salamanca in 1565. Boyer had many complaints about the state of the manuscript, and Muñoz made disparaging comments on Boyer's edition, even though his revisions were marginal.[19] All translations before the mid-twentieth century were based on these editions until research on the manuscripts in various archives by Beltrán de Heredia established that a direct copy of the original still existed, and thus the first editions must have been based on less reliable copies. This direct copy is translated into English for the first time in the Cambridge text on Vitoria's political writings.[20] Not all specialists are prepared to rely so heavily on this single manuscript: Urdános, for example, finds many imperfections in it, and bases his edition on comparison with other

[16] Norena, *Spanish Renaissance Thought*, pp. 47–49.

[17] Francisco de Vitoria, Letter to Miguel de Arcos, 8 November (probably 1534), in Pagden and Lawrance (eds), *Francisco de Vitoria*, p. 331.

[18] Pagden and Lawrance (eds), *Francisco de Vitoria*, pp. xxxiii–xxxiv; also Campagna, *Francisco de Vitoria*, p. 33.

[19] H. F. Wright, 'Prefatory Remarks Concerning the Text,' in Nys (ed.), *Francisci de Victoria De Indis*, pp. 194–95.

[20] Pagden and Lawrance (eds), *Francisco de Vitoria*, pp. xxxiii–xxxviii.

early manuscript copies[21] – but the differences relate to points of detail, and thus are not of major consequence for the interpretation of Vitoria's thought. Nonetheless, since it may be assumed that Vitoria chose his words carefully, the fate of the original manuscript represents a significant loss for subsequent scholarship.

Vitoria's ideas are presented in the same sequence as those of Erasmus, but in this and the following chapters the number and headings of the sections vary, reflecting differences in the thought of the authors.

Vitoria and the Events of His Time

This section, like its counterpart in the preceding chapter, notes some of the political events and conflicts of the time – the emphasis is again on conflict rather than cooperation – and explores the question whether Vitoria, like Erasmus before him, may be regarded as a realistic observer.

During the first half of the sixteenth century, the conflicts in Europe were uppermost in the concerns of Spain's rulers. Since these conflicts were outlined in the previous chapter, they may be noted briefly, from the Spanish perspective.

The initiative for the conclusion of the alliance of Italian powers against the French in 1495 came from Ferdinand, King of Aragon. The French attempt to take up their claim to Naples was unsuccessful, and Naples became Spanish in 1504. In 1508 Ferdinand joined the side of the French in the League of Cambrai against Venice. The Holy League of 1511 re-established the old adversaryship between the Spanish and the French, and in 1512 Ferdinand helped Pope Julius II to return the Medici to Florence.

The French throne changed its occupant in 1515, the Spanish thrones in 1516, and the Imperial throne followed in 1519. The new rulers (Francis I and Charles I/V) continued the Italian policies of their predecessors, and war resumed in 1521. In 1530 Pope Clement VII crowned Charles with the Imperial crown and the crown of Italy at Bologna. R. Trevor Davies observes: 'Charles, mainly by the help of his Spanish kingdoms, had now reached the height of his power.'[22] The meeting at Bologna of emperor and pope is also seen as the moment when 'Spain definitely became antagonistic to the humanistic movement'.[23]

In 1532 Charles I (V) led six thousand Spanish soldiers to Central Europe to fight the Turks. In 1536 Francis I and the emperor were at

[21] Urdánoz (ed.), *Obras de Francisco de Vitoria*, p. 99.

[22] R.T. Davies, *The Golden Century of Spain: 1501–1621* (London: Macmillan, 1961), p. 92.

[23] C. Phillipson, 'Franciscus a Victoria (1480–1546): International Law and War', *Journal of the Society of Comparative Legislation*, New Series, vol. 15, 1915, p. 176.

war over the Duchy of Milan. It ended in a truce mediated by Pope Paul III, but hostilities resumed in 1541. Henry VIII became Charles's ally, and Francis I was supported by Suleiman the Magnificent. A peace was signed in 1544. Francis died three years later; meanwhile Charles went on to achieve military successes against the Lutherans but failed in his ambition to put an end to the Reformation, or at least fatally weaken it.

The Spanish conquest of America raised issues that were central to Vitoria's concerns. The developments there may therefore be presented in greater detail. The discovery of the New World in 1492 by the Genoese Christopher Columbus was followed, in 1493, by Pope Alexander VI's famous donation: the Bull *Inter Cetera*[24] appointed the Spanish kings and their successors 'the lords of the islands and mainland discovered or to be discovered'.[25] The papal grant did not mention coercion or war, but, as Benno Biermann points out, 'everywhere the advancing Spaniard employed force, subjugated the Indians, and treated them as rebels if they offered resistance'.[26]

The first discussion of 'the basis for Spanish rule in America and the right of Spaniards to profit from Indian labor' took place in Spain in 1503. It resulted in the decision that 'the Indians should serve the Spaniards and that this was in accordance with law, human and divine'.[27] The Dominican Antonio de Montesinos is credited with raising the first public protest in America. In 1511 he asked on the island of Hispaniola:

> Tell me, by what right or justice do you keep these Indians in such a cruel and horrible servitude? On what authority have you waged a detestable war against these people, who dwelt quietly and peacefully on their own land?[28]

One answer consisted in the Laws of Burgos – a comprehensive code of legislation, essentially ratifying existing practice – promulgated in Spain in 1512/1513; another came by way of two treatises – *Concerning the Rule*

[24] Elton notes that '[p]apal decrees are called Bulls after the lead seal (bulla) attached to them, and are named after their initial words'. G. R. Elton, *Reformation Europe: 1517–1559* (Glasgow: Fontana/Collins, 1977), p. 22n. For a meaningful translation one would need more than the two words *inter cetera* with which the Bull begins.

[25] L. Hanke, *Bartolomé de Las Casas: An Interpretation of His Life and Writings* (The Hague: Martinus Nijhoff, 1951), p. 36. The Spanish kings asked for this Bull in order to resolve differences with and protests from the Portuguese. By the Treaty of Tordesillas of 1494, the two powers agreed to demarcate a line 370 miles to the east of the Azores. Urdánoz (ed.), *Obras de Francisco de Vitoria*, p. 528.

[26] B. M. Biermann, 'Bartolomé de Las Casas and Verapaz', in J. Friede and B. Keen (eds), *Bartolomé de Las Casas in History: Toward an Understanding of the Man and His Work* (DeKalb, IL: Northern Illinois University Press, 1971), p. 443.

[27] L. Hanke, *The Spanish Struggle for Justice in the Conquest of America* (Boston, MA: Little Brown & Co., 1965), p. 25–26.

[28] Hanke, *Bartolomé de Las Casas*, p. 17.

of the King of Spain over the Indies by Matias de Paz (1512) and *On the Ocean Isles* by Juan Lopez de Palacios Rubios (1512) – both of which agreed that the just title of Spain to the Indies rested on Pope Alexander VI's grant; a third answer was the *reguerimiento* (requirement), a document composed by Palacios Rubios in 1513, which required the Indians to acknowledge the Church as the ruler of the world and in its place the Spanish kings, and to allow the Christian religion to be preached.[29]

The conquest spread and the debate about its justice continued. In 1519 Bartolomé de Las Casas confronted Charles, King and Emperor, at an audience in Barcelona with the following words: 'I am one of the first who passed over to the Indies, and I have been there many years. In those years I have seen with my own eyes the greatest cruelties done.'[30] The Council of the Indies was established in 1524, but the nature of the conquest did not change.[31]

The papal Bull *Sublimis Deus*, appearing in 1537, signalled a new approach. Pope Paul III decreed that 'the said Indians ... though they be outside the faith of Christ, must not be deprived of their liberty or ownership of their possessions'. He further ruled that the Indians 'must be invited to receive the said faith of Christ with the preaching of the word of God and with the examples of a good life'.[32] The New Laws – an attempt to limit Spanish rights over the Indians – were promulgated in 1542, only to be partly revoked three years later.[33]

In subsequent years there was no change in either Spanish conduct in America or the intensity with which it was debated. A *junta* summoned by Charles I (V) met at Valladolid in 1550–51 'to inquire into and establish the manner and the laws by which our Holy Catholic faith can be preached and promulgated in that New World', and to examine 'in what form those peoples may remain subject to His Majesty the Emperor without injury to his royal conscience, according to the Bull of

[29] R. A. Williams, Jr, *The American Indian in Western Legal Thought* (New York: Oxford University Press, 1990), pp. 88–93.

[30] M. M. Martínez, 'Las Casas on the Conquest of America', in Friede and Keen (eds), *Bartolomé de Las Casas*, p. 335.

[31] The Council of the Indies was the principal governing body resident in Spain to advise the monarch on matters relating to the New World. It consisted of a president and eight councillors. J. H. Elliott, *Imperial Spain: 1469–1716* (London: Edward Arnold, 1963), p. 161. A typical report from the New World in the 1530s reads: 'This whole land is in turmoil and the Indians greatly aroused because of the cruelties and maltreatment of the Christians. Wherever they go their feet scorch the grass and the ground over which they pass. Their hands are bloody with slaying'. J. Comas, 'Historical Reality and the Detractors of Father Las Casas', in Friede and Keen (eds), *Bartolomé de Las Casas*, p. 491.

[32] Martínez, 'Las Casas on the Conquest of America', p. 316.

[33] Hanke, *The Spanish Struggle for Justice*, pp. 83–105.

Pope Alexander'. The protagonists were Las Casas and Juan Gines de Sepulveda. The debate ended inconclusively.[34]

Vitoria's formal writings, his *lectiones* and *relectiones*, refer to the conflicts of his time, but they do not often reveal how realistic an observer he is. References to Spanish involvement in European affairs take the following form:

If Spain declares war on France for reasons which are otherwise just, and even if the war is useful to the kingdom of Spain, if the waging of the war causes great harm and loss to Christendom – for example if the Turks are enabled in the meantime to occupy Christian countries – then hostilities should be suspended.[35]

The conquest of America figures prominently in his formal writings, but again the argument often takes the formula 'if then'. For example:

If any barbarians are converted to Christ, and their princes try to call them back to their idolatry by force or fear, the Spaniards may on these grounds, if no other means are possible, wage war on them.[36]

Vitoria's conditional arguments may point to a general familiarity with the situations referred to, but do not reveal the extent of his knowledge and understanding of what is actually the case.

However, there are instances in Vitoria's formal writings which may be read as well-informed appraisals of what is the case. To give two examples:

[The Indians] are not in point of fact madmen, but have judgment like other men … they have some order in their affairs; they have properly organized cities, proper marriages, magistrates and overlords [*domini*], laws, industries and commerce, all of which require the use of reason.[37]

Or:

It is not sufficiently clear to me that the Christian faith has up to now been announced and set before the barbarians in such a way as to oblige them to believe it … I hear only of provocations, savage crimes, and multitudes of unholy acts.[38]

A much clearer picture emerges when one turns to Vitoria's informal writings, his letters. Not many have survived, and not all of these are

[34] M. Giménez Fernández, 'Fray Bartolomé de Las Casas: A Biographical Sketch', in Friede and Keen (eds), *Bartolomé de Las Casas*, p. 109. Sepúlveda, the imperial chronicler, was a learned Latinist who, as far as his political views were concerned, would qualify as universalist.

[35] Vitoria, 'On Civil Power', in Pagden and Lawrance (eds), *Francisco de Vitoria*, pp. 21–22.

[36] Vitoria, 'On the American Indians', in Pagden and Lawrance (eds), *Francisco de Vitoria*, p. 286.

[37] Ibid., p. 250.

[38] Ibid., p. 271.

intact, but they project a man who is in touch with events and discerning when assessing a situation.

There are, for example, his two letters to the Constable of Castile, probably written in 1536, in one of which he writes on the situation in Europe:

> The whole affair is crooked, but if I could find a way to effect a meeting between His Majesty and the King of France in my view it would be a much greater achievement than the battle of Tunis ... tell me, good men all: are our wars for the good of Spain, or France, or Italy, or Germany? Or are they for their universal destruction, and for the increase of Moordom and heresy?[39]

Regarding the situation in America, in the letter to Miguel de Arcos, cited earlier, he writes:

> I do not understand the justice of that war ... but as far as I understand from eyewitnesses who were personally present during the recent battle with Atahuallpa, neither he nor any of his people had ever done the slightest injury to the Christians, nor given them the least grounds for making war on them.[40]

Vitoria's concern is not the particular events but their larger consequences and the moral issues that they raise. The indications are that his judgements are well informed and judicious. The comment of the chronicler of San Estoban, cited earlier, suggests that this was also the view of his contemporaries.

Vitoria's Position within the Three Traditions of Thought

The study of Vitoria's writings indicates that it is his thought as a whole rather than any particular work or idea which excludes him from universalism and realism, and identifies him as a thinker of the *via media*. For this reason, it seems preferable not to try to delimit his position in this section, but to permit it to crystallize in the course of the chapter as a whole and, at this stage, to offer no more than a few introductory observations.

As far as the realist way of thinking is concerned, there is no mention of Machiavelli or other thinkers in what Edward Keene terms the 'reason of state' political discourse.[41] In contrast to Erasmus, its rejection is not one of his concerns. However, he does occasionally refer to a

[39] Vitoria to Pedro Fernandez de Velasco, 19 November 1536, in Pagden and Lawrance (eds), *Francisco de Vitoria*, pp. 337–38.
[40] Vitoria to Miguel de Arcos, 8 November 1534, p. 332.
[41] E. Keene, *International Political Thought: A Historical Introduction* (Cambridge: Polity Press, 2005), pp. 106–18.

specific proposition associated with realism: for example, he denies that 'the enlargement of empire' could be a just cause of war.[42]

On the other hand, as will be seen in various contexts, universalism is a major concern. Here, by way of introducing his thought on the topic, it suffices to present one example: the proposition that there is no universal temporal ruler now, nor was there in the past. Vitoria advances it in his *relectio* 'On the American Indians' against those who claim that the Spaniards, when they first travelled to the New World, took with them a right to occupy the lands of the Indians; and he uses it in the *relectio* 'On the Power of the Church', as part of his attempt to define the extent of spiritual power. In the former, he develops his ideas in relation to both emperor and pope; in the latter, he limits himself to discussing papal claims.[43]

To abstract from a complex argument: Vitoria sets out with the statement that '[t]he Emperor is not master of the whole world', and the proofs which he offers come from natural law, divine law, and human law. His main authority regarding natural law is St Thomas: '[I]n natural law all are free other than from the dominion of fathers or husbands ... therefore no-one can be emperor of the world in natural law.'[44] Regarding divine law, he looks back into history and, supported by numerous references to the Scriptures, concludes that 'no one before Christ obtained an empire by divine law' and the same is true of the time which followed 'our Lord's coming'. He dismisses the relevance of human law in the following way:

> [I]t is established that in this case, too, the emperor is not master of the whole world, because if he were, it would be solely by the authority of some enactment [*lex*], and there is no enactment. Even if there were, it would have no force, since an enactment presupposes the necessary jurisdiction.[45]

And, without appealing to any specific authorities, he concludes this line of reasoning by saying:

> Nor does the emperor have universal dominion by legitimate succession, gift, exchange, purchase, just war, election, or any other legal title, as is established. Therefore the emperor has never been master of the whole world.[46]

As regards the Pope, he argues, similarly, that he 'cannot have any dominion except by natural, divine or human law. It is certain that he does not

42 Vitoria, 'On the Law of War', in Pagden and Lawrance (eds), *Francisco de Vitoria*, p. 303.
43 Vitoria, 'On the American Indians', pp. 252–64; Vitoria, 'I On the Power of the Church', in Pagden and Lawrance (eds), *Francisco de Vitoria*, pp. 83–85.
44 Vitoria, 'On the American Indians', p. 254.
45 Ibid., pp. 255, 257.
46 Ibid., pp. 257–58.

have it by natural or human law. As for divine law, no authority is forthcoming.'[47] He states that 'the pope has temporal power only in so far as it concerns spiritual matters' and that he 'has no temporal power over these barbarians or any other unbelievers'.[48] The pope, then, has no greater claim than the emperor to universal authority.

Vitoria totally rejects universalist claims, whether on behalf of emperor or pope, as justification of Spanish rule in America.

The Perfect Temporal Community

Vitoria's concept of the perfect temporal community is especially significant, since it is his basic premise for his alternative to universalism. He offers two approaches to this idea. One is direct and swift, inspired by Aristotle:

> The commonwealth is, properly speaking, a perfect community ... A perfect community or commonwealth is one which is complete in itself, that is, one which is not part of another commonwealth, but has its own laws, its own independent policy, and its own magistrates.[49]

As examples, he cites the kingdom of Castile, the kingdom of Aragon and the Republic of Venice, adding that 'it does not matter if various independent kingdoms and commonwealths are subject to a single prince'. Elsewhere he quotes a similar definition of Tommaso de Vio, Cardinal Cajetan, adding that '[t]his holds true, moreover, regardless whether or not [that group] has a superior'.[50] The example he gives is the Duke of Milan who is subject to the emperor. '[N]evertheless, [the state of Milan is] perfect and does not share its being with any other state.'[51]

The other approach is more winding, and awkward, consisting of several steps, but is also more instructive of Vitoria's thinking.[52] It follows authorities such as Aristotle, the Scriptures, Cicero, St Augustine and St Thomas.

47 Ibid., p. 260.

48 Ibid., p. 262.

49 Vitoria, 'On the Law of War', p. 301.

50 Vitoria, 'On War', transl. G. L. Williams, in J. B. Scott, *The Spanish Origin of International Law: Francisco de Vitoria and His Law of Nations* (Oxford and London: Clarendon Press and Humphrey Milford, 1934), p. cxvii. Vitoria never explains his concept of the 'superior lord', but gives examples: the emperor is superior to certain kings. The superior lord has certain rights, but rather than discussing these he speaks of those that he does not have. For example, the perfect temporal community can wage war without the authorization of the emperor ('On the Law of War', p. 301). See also the requirement to rule in accordance with existing laws, discussed later in the chapter.

51 Vitoria, 'On War', p. cxvii.

52 For Vitoria, it is a way of arriving at a definition of civil power, following Aristotle's assumption that one knows a thing if one knows its causes.

The first step consists in proving that: '[T]he primitive origin of human cities and commonwealths was not a human invention or contrivance … but a device implanted by Nature in man for his own safety and survival.'[53] Vitoria arrives there by arguing that man needs society, not only because nature has made him frail and needy, but also because it has given him reason and virtue:

In the case of [the] will, whose ornaments are justice and amity, what a deformed and lame thing it would be outside the fellowship of men. Justice can only be exercised in a multitude and amity.[54]

He maintains that of all human partnerships, civil society best fulfills men's needs – 'the most natural community'.[55]

In the second part of his argument, he is concerned to show that society for its continued existence needs a force or power to maintain and direct it.[56] As he puts it,

If all members of society were equal and subject to no higher power each man would pull in his own direction as opinion or whim directed, and the commonwealth would necessarily be torn apart.[57]

Third, given that society has its origin in natural law, of which God is the author, it follows that the power without which society cannot continue to exist must also derive from that source. This is the proposition which he advances as the third step in his argument:

If … public power is founded upon natural law, and if natural law acknowledges God as its only author, then it is evident that public power is from God, and cannot be overridden by conditions imposed by men or by any positive law.[58]

In the fourth part, Vitoria gives the power which is necessary for the continued existence of society its home. It resides, he says, in society itself. His proof runs as follows:

[S]ince in the absence of any divine law or human elective franchise there is no convincing reason why one man should have power more than another, it is necessary that the power be vested in the community, which must be able to provide for itself.[59]

Here, then, the idea of the perfect community is encountered again. This time it means that a community or state is perfect if the force or

53 Vitoria, 'On Civil Power', p. 9.
54 Ibid., p. 8.
55 Ibid., pp. 8–9.
56 Vitoria defines 'public power' as 'the authority or right of government over the civil commonwealth'. Ibid., p. 18.
57 Vitoria, 'On Civil Power', p. 9.
58 Ibid., p. 10.
59 Ibid., p. 11.

power which directs it inheres in the community or state itself. And there is no need for the community to be unanimous, 'the act of the greater part' being 'the act of the whole'. But it does not have the authority to dispense with government altogether: '[E]ven if all the members of the commonwealth were to agree ... their agreement would be null and void as contrary to natural law.'[60]

However, the community itself (the 'multitude') cannot exercise this power directly; it must be entrusted to 'certain men', either to one or to a number.[61] At one point he allows that the community 'may adopt whatever constitution it prefers, even if this is not the best constitution', but the emphasis is on his arguments for the superiority of monarchy.[62] One version of the text states that the safest form of government is the mixed constitution, but this idea is not further developed.[63]

He who is entrusted with the administration of a perfect community is obliged to procure the temporal good of the community. Vitoria offers no definition or description of the temporal good, but his writings leave no doubt that the most basic value or purpose to be secured by the prince is the life or survival of the community. The state must be guarded against injury from its own citizens or from aliens. This means that, in the internal context, the prince is entitled to punish transgressors of the law and, as far as external relations are concerned, he has the right to go to war – to defend the community and to avenge a wrong received. 'It is necessary for the proper administration of human affairs that this authority should be granted to the commonwealth.'[64]

There is equally no doubt that the most elevated value or purpose of the perfect community is 'natural felicity' or 'human well-being'. For the prince, this goal means that, within his own realm, the exercise of virtue must be made possible; and, beyond his community, the prince is entitled to intervene in other communities if innocent people suffer there.[65]

[60] Ibid., p. 19.
[61] Ibid., p. 14.
[62] Ibid., pp. 19–20, 32.
[63] This proposition was omitted in the earlier translations, but is included in Urdánoz's Latin text (*Obras de Francisco de Vitoria*, p. 167). Pagden and Lawrance have a different version (*Francisco de Vitoria*, p. 21 and note 45, and comment p. xix).
[64] Vitoria, 'On the Law of War', p. 300; Vitoria, 'De la Temperancia' [On Temperance], in L. Pereña (ed.), *Francisco de Vitoria: Escritos Políticos* (Buenos Aires: Ediciones Depalma, 1967), p. 267. Survival is so important that Vitoria, who normally insists that faith is always to be kept with the enemy, relaxes this condition in circumstances where 'to do so would be in the highest degree detrimental to the state, with the result that it would perish; for in that case it would not be just ... to have kept faith'. Vitoria, 'On War', p. cxxx.
[65] Vitoria, 'De la Temperancia', pp. 259–62. Intervention is discussed later in the chapter.

Vitoria explicitly rejects the idea that virtue can be exercised only in the Christian context.[66]

Between life and survival on the one hand and natural felicity or human well-being on the other, there exist other values. Vitoria especially mentions peace and unity. It is important for the prince to ensure harmony amongst the citizens and if conflict cannot be avoided, that it be resolved peacefully. '[U]nity is such a great good that, without it, the community cannot subsist.' Yet there are limits to peace and unity. 'Sometimes, it is necessary to disturb the tranquillity of the state'. When it is faced with the rule of a tyrant, 'the concord of its citizens may be fatal'.[67] Another example at this level of values is the imposition of religious uniformity. The coexistence of different religions within one community, he holds, may cause less strain than enforced unanimity.[68]

The prince's obligation to pursue the temporal good of the community is no other than his obligation to be just in the exercise of power, and just means to be mindful not only of what is lawful but also of what creates and conserves felicity. In less abstract language, Vitoria holds that the prince must rule in accordance with existing laws, for '[t]he law must consider the common good'.[69] It is for this reason that a prince who has been entrusted with the administration of more than one perfect temporal community is obliged to rule each one according to its own laws. G. R. Elton's comment is relevant here, namely: 'The point about the rule of law was not that it made puppets of kings but that it prevented strong kingship from deteriorating into despotism.'[70]

The perfect temporal community is not only an old institution – according to Vitoria 'After Noah, the world was certainly divided into various countries and kingdoms'; it also is ubiquitous. Using St Paul

[66] See his *relectio* 'De la Obligación de Convertirse a Dios al Llegar al Uso de Razón' [On the Obligation to Convert to God when Attaining to the Use of Reason], in Urdánoz (ed.), *Obras de Francisco de Vitoria*, p. 1342.

[67] Vitoria, 'De la Sedición o de la Guerra Civil' [On Sedition or Civil War], in Pereña (ed.), *Francisco de Vitoria*, pp. 290, 292. Vitoria distinguishes two kinds of tyrant: (1) a ruler who is not entitled to the territory he occupies – it is not his state but he seizes it; and (2) a legitimate ruler, but one who governs the state to his own advantage. 'Es lícito con autoridad privada matar al tirano?' [Is it lawful to kill the tyrant on private authority?] (p. 323).

[68] Vitoria may have been inclined to favour religious conformity, as Hamilton suggests, but when discussing this point, he insists on considering what is advisable as well as what is lawful. See Hamilton, *Political Thought in Sixteenth-Century Spain*, p. 113.

[69] An idea borrowed from Aristotle. See Vitoria, 'De la Temperancia', pp. 261, 269.

[70] Elton, *Reformation Europe*, pp. 302–03. Elliott refers to this state of affairs as the 'patrimonial concept' and mentions that it was practiced by Castile and Aragon in Vitoria's times: 'The union of the crowns did not imply that their legal and constitutional systems should be brought in line … Each state remained in its own compartment, governed by its traditional laws.' Elliott, *Imperial Spain*, p. 66. He also attributes it to the empire of Charles V (pp. 157–58).

as his authority, he asserts: '[A]mongst the unbelievers there is complete temporal and civil authority.'[71] '[T]here can be no doubt', the idea returns, 'that the heathen have legitimate rulers and masters.' For him, there is no doubt. A plurality of political entities is not only a fact but an extremely pleasing fact. Reminding his audience of Cicero's reference to Scipio's words, he says: 'Nothing is more acceptable to the deity who created everything in the world than the assemblies and councils of men duly banded together which we call cities [*civitates*].'[72]

In addition to its temporal power, the perfect community has spiritual power over itself, and this by natural law.[73] It is an aspect which Vitoria does not discuss in a general way, perhaps because he believes that, although spiritual power has been possessed by all perfect communities at all times, perfect spiritual power has come into existence only with Christ and now exists only where there are Christians – an idea which underlies his thinking about the perfect spiritual community.

The Perfect Spiritual Community

All those perfect temporal communities which have adopted the Christian religion and all Christians who live in non-Christian communities form a community in their turn. Vitoria variously refers to this community as the Christian church, the Christian community or the Christian state. 'Christendom is in some sense a single commonwealth and a single body.'[74] It is perfect because it is complete in itself. It is spiritual because the end which it pursues – ultimate or eternal felicity – is spiritual. He posits its existence when he discusses Christian spiritual power and its relation to Christian temporal power. His argument, which he sees as 'steering a middle course between the disputants'[75] – enlists support mainly from the Scriptures, Aristotle, Pope Innocent III, St Thomas, Torquemada and Cajetan.

Spiritual power, Vitoria declares, is as old as temporal power and has existed since the beginning. Proof of this is man's nature: man consists of body and soul; therefore, it is natural for him to worship God not only with his soul but also with material and external acts. And, as in the case of temporal power, it is necessary to give it direction. He pursues the

71 Vitoria, 'On the American Indians', p. 255; Vitoria, 'De la Potestad de la Iglesia' [On the Power of the Church] (One), in L. Getino (transl.), *Francisco de Vitoria: Derecho Natural y de Gentes* [Francisco de Vitoria: Natural Law and the Law of Nations], intro. E. de Hinojosa (Buenos Aires: Erneсé Editores, 1946), p. 51.

72 Vitoria, 'On Civil Power', pp. 10, 18.

73 Vitoria, 'De la Temperancia', p. 259.

74 Vitoria, 'On Civil Power', p. 31.

75 Vitoria, 'I On the Power of the Church', p. 83.

fortunes of spiritual power through the ages of natural law and written law to arrive at the conclusion:

> [P]roperly and perfectly spiritual authority, which is that of the keys of the kingdom of heaven, never existed ... before the advent of our lord and redeemer Jesus Christ.[76]

The power to open or close the heavens, to give or refuse to give eternal life, is 'more excellent' than any other spiritual power. It is true, he says, that the Indians have priests, but they are 'certainly false ones'; it also is true that the Turks have a religion – he calls it a sect – but it consists of no more than 'tales and mere trifles'.[77]

Not only is Christian spiritual power 'more excellent' than the spiritual power which resides in non-Christian perfect communities; it also is 'more eminent' than the temporal power which exists in Christian perfect temporal communities.

> [T]he purpose of spiritual power far exceeds that of temporal power, in the measure that perfect bliss and ultimate felicity excel all human or earthly happiness.[78]

But temporal power is not equipped to secure ultimate felicity. A separate power is required to administer spiritual life.

> But the temporal rulers have no expertise in divine law, which ought to be the guideline of ecclesiastical power. Therefore the supreme heads of the Church ought to be different people from their secular lords.[79]

He accords no equality to the two powers in question. The inferior, temporal power is separate from the superior, spiritual power, and yet the former is linked to the latter in a certain way: civil and spiritual power are not like two separate states, for example, the French and the English. The truth rather is that,

> [I]n the Christian commonwealth, all offices, purposes and powers are subordinated and interconnected ... temporal things exist for spiritual ones, and depend on them.[80]

The relationship is one of dependence and subordination, and it holds even if it proves detrimental to temporal power.

[76] Ibid., p. 77.

[77] Vitoria, 'De la Temperancia', p. 260; Vitoria, 'Es lícito mantener relacion con infieles?' [Is it Lawful to Maintain Relations with Infidels?], in L. Pereña and J. M. Pérez Prendes (eds), *Francisco de Vitoria: Relectio de Indis o Libertad de los Indios* (Madrid: Consejo Superior de Investigaciones Científicas, 1967), p. 131.

[78] Vitoria, 'I On the Power of the Church', p. 82.

[79] Ibid., p. 52.

[80] Ibid., p. 91.

Spiritual power does not reside in the whole community in the way in which temporal power does, but 'the Pope is the supreme ruler of all ecclesiastical power'.[81] Not being a temporal prince, the pope has no power in purely temporal matters. For example, he is not entitled to set up or depose temporal princes, to judge in disputes between temporal princes or to intervene in questions of law relating to temporal matters.[82] However, if spiritual interests are at stake, the pope has 'a plenitude of temporal power' over all Christian princes, kings, and the emperor.

[T]he spiritual commonwealth ought to be perfect and hence self-sufficient. Just as the temporal commonwealth is ... if the spiritual power cannot preserve itself and its commonwealth in safety and well-being in any other way, it may do everything necessary for this purpose by its own authority. Otherwise its power would be crippled and insufficient for its own purpose.[83]

That is, if it were necessary for the defence of the faith – Vitoria insists on this condition – the pope has, by virtue of his spiritual power, the right to do all the things which temporal princes do and more. He could, for example, require the King of Spain to go to war against the Saracens and oblige Christians to elect a single monarch if this should be necessary for 'the defence of the Faith'.[84] He may entrust the spreading of the Christian religion to one Christian ruler rather than to another; permit trade with a non-Christian country to one Christian people rather than to another; or give a Christian prince to a pagan people converted to Christianity.[85] The temporal power of the pope in case of necessity is extensive, but it does not include the right to dissolve Christian perfect temporal communities.

Vitoria raises the question whether the temporal power of the Church 'to preserve and protect itself' should be exercised directly or only indirectly, and this leads him to clarify his understanding of necessity. The pope 'should first avail himself of his spiritual power', that is to say, he should use persuasion and command before resorting to the direct exercise of temporal power, for he 'ought not and may not usurp the civil power without necessary cause':

For a thing to pertain to the pope's province, it is not sufficient that it be necessary for spiritual ends; his intervention must also be a case of necessity. That is to say, the limit is set not by the extent of the power of the pope's office, but by the limitations of civil power.[86]

[81] Ibid., p. 82. At this point he states this as an assumption ('supposition'); it is discussed in the second *relectio* on the power of the Church.
[82] Ibid., pp. 86–89.
[83] Vitoria, 'I On the Power of the Church', pp. 93–94.
[84] Ibid., p. 93; Vitoria, 'On Civil Power', p. 31.
[85] Vitoria, 'On the American Indians', pp. 284, 287.
[86] Vitoria, 'I On the Power of the Church', pp. 93–94.

Thus, the perfect spiritual community which he delimits by describing Christian spiritual power and its relation to Christian temporal power is based on a dual obligation: on the part of Christian temporal power to further and, if necessary, to serve the interests of Christian spiritual power – on the part of Christian spiritual power to respect the separateness of Christian temporal power and to limit interference with it to cases of necessity. In view of these rights of the spiritual power, the perfect temporal community falls far short of the sovereign state, as this came to be understood. In practice, however, in the actual political circumstances of the sixteenth century, the papal power to assume overriding control appears purely notional: the effective power of the pope would have depended on persuasion through the exercise of spiritual authority.

The World as a Community of Perfect Communities

Vitoria's writings contain the idea of a third community, that of the whole world. It does not become clearly visible when one looks at the general statements he makes about it. These indeed tend to mystify rather than explain it. For example, as discussed earlier, in 'On Civil Power' he asserts: 'The whole world, being in a sense a commonwealth, has the power to enact laws which are just and convenient to all men.' In 'On the Law of War' he refers to 'the purpose and good of the whole world', which can be secured only if commonwealths and princes have the authority to constrain tyrants and other wrong-doers.[87] This latter is the crucial point: it is the temporal communities and their rulers who have rights and obligations; the world as a whole is no actor. Vitoria's third community, upon which he never confers the attribute of being perfect, takes on shape only when one examines his thought on the laws which direct relations within it and the rights and obligations which derive from these laws.

Laws

According to Vitoria, the world as a whole is made up of perfect temporal communities or, as he puts it, 'any commonwealth is part of the world as a whole',[88] and intercommunication within it, that is amongst its component parts, in peace and in war, is based on two laws: natural law and the law of nations. Natural law governs all spheres of life; the law of nations relates only to relations among temporal communities.

[87] Vitoria, 'On Civil Power', p. 40; Vitoria, 'On the Law of War', pp. 298–301.
[88] Vitoria, 'On Civil Power', p. 21.

There appears to be no single source where Vitoria fully spells out his concept of natural law – 'the law of reason by which all human beings are naturally governed'.[89] It is derived from God, but not as His commands; rather, humans are created with reason, through which they may ascertain what is right, just and obligatory, and what is prohibited. Although he refers to the natural light of reason, it becomes clear that the process of acquiring the knowledge of this 'necessary' law is far from automatic.

He postulates that the necessary has degrees and, in agreement with St Thomas, he distinguishes three such degrees:

1. All that which by natural light is evidently known to all as just and in accordance with right reason, and its opposite as unjust, is called natural law.
2. All that which one infers and deduces with sound logic from naturally evident principles, is also natural law.
3. All that which one deduces by means of a moral conclusion, morally known, is very probably natural law.[90]

Urdánoz illuminates Vitoria's rather cryptic language by referring to the first level or degree as 'first principles' of natural law; to the second level as 'precepts derived from these principles by direct and evident conclusion'; and to the third level as 'indirect conclusions from the natural principles by way of a more distant sequence'.[91]

Vitoria's threefold division suggests that not all of natural law may be equally easily knowable. He allows for the possibility that not all know it and that, when it is not known, it may be difficult to prove. From 'On Temperance':

> [F]urthermore, one ... cannot demonstrate with evidence all the things which belong to natural law, at least to every one.[92]

From 'On the American Indians':

> [I]t is not every sin against the law of nature that can be clearly shown to be such, at any rate to every one ... We certainly possess clearer proofs whereby to demonstrate that the law of Christ is from God and is true than to demonstrate that ... things which are ... forbidden by natural law are to be shunned.[93]

[89] Brett, *Changes of State*, p. 12.
[90] Vitoria, 'Cuestión sobre el Derecho de Gentes' [Question Regarding the Law of Nations], in Pereña (ed.), *Francisco de Vitoria*, pp. 301–02.
[91] Urdánoz (ed.), *Obras de Francisco de Vitoria*, pp. 553–54.
[92] Vitoria, 'De la Temperancia', in Pereña (ed.), *Francisco de Vitoria*, p. 260.
[93] Vitoria, 'On the American Indians', pp. 274–75.

It is possible, Vitoria submits, that ignorance of the law of nature is invincible; consequently, it also is possible that war may be just on both sides. His reasoning is this: on one side there may be 'right' and on the other 'invincible ignorance'.[94]

Turning to his definition of the law of nations, one meets with ambiguity. Like Aquinas before him, he is inconsistent on the question of whether it falls within natural law or positive law. In a *lectio*, part of which is entitled 'On the Law of Nations and Natural Law', he treats it as positive law: it is not an absolute good, but derives only 'from agreement among men ... from the common consensus of all peoples and nations'. He goes on to ask whether it is a sin to violate the law of nations, given that 'it is of the positive law', and his answer is that 'it is always illicit to violate the *ius gentium*, because it is contrary to the common consensus'. He also asks whether the law of nations can be abrogated, and his reply is: never the whole of it, but only in part, for 'it is impossible that the consensus of the whole world could be obtained for the abrogation of the law of nations'.[95]

The most frequently cited passage on the law of nations as positive law does not bring greater clarity:

> The law of nations [*ius gentium*] does not have the force merely of pacts or agreements between men, but has the validity of a positive enactment [*lex*]. The whole world, which is in a sense a commonwealth, has the power to enact laws which are just and convenient to all men; and these make up the law of nations. From this it follows that those who break the law of nations, whether in peace or in war, are committing mortal crimes.[96]

However, in his *relectio* 'On the American Indians', Vitoria offers a very different definition: the law of nations either is or derives from natural law, as defined by the jurist: 'What natural reason has established among all nations is called the law of nations.'[97] Consequently its derivation

[94] Ibid., p. 282. This is the main exception to his general rule that a war cannot be just on both sides.

[95] Vitoria, 'On the Law of Nations and Natural Law', transl. F. Crane Macken, in Scott, *The Spanish Origin of International Law*, Appendix E, pp. cxi–cxii.

[96] Vitoria, 'On Civil Power', p. 40.

[97] Vitoria, 'On the American Indians', p. 278; In this definition, taken from Justinia, Vitoria replaces the word *homines* (men) with *gentes* (peoples or nations). Noted by A. Nussbaum, *A Concise History of the Law of Nations*, rev. edn (New York: Macmillan, 1954), pp. 80–81. Brett, *Changes of State*, p. 13. See J. A. C. Thomas, *The Institutes of Justinian: Text, Translation and Commentary* (Amsterdam: North-Holland, 1975), p. 4. The earlier jurist, Gaius, is sometimes given as Vitoria's source; for his formulation, see Brett, *Changes of State*, p. 12, note 6.

from natural law 'is manifestly sufficient to enable it to enforce binding rights'. But he soon expresses a doubt:

> But even on the occasions when it is not derived from natural law the consent of the greater part of the world is enough to make it binding, especially when it is for the good of all men.[98]

Vitoria offers no explanation of these constant changes of position, but perhaps it is to be found in the *lectio* referred to, when he dismisses the dispute as one of words, 'concerning the name rather than the thing', the important point being a moral one on which he never changes his position: it is always illicit to violate a law – be it of divine or human origin.[99]

Rights and Obligations

The law of nations – whether it be positive or natural law – is the source of the rights and obligations which Vitoria ascribes to all perfect temporal communities, Christian and non-Christian alike, in their relations with one another. His ideas on this subject are contained mainly in two of his *relectiones*, 'On the American Indians' and 'On the Law of War', but they are not confined to these. In the former, to be discussed in this section, he formulates his argument in relation to the encounter of a Christian people, the Spaniards, with non-Christian peoples, the Indians of the New World, but he makes it clear that it applies equally to Christian perfect temporal communities in relation to one another; in 'On the Law of War', to be discussed in the next section, the setting for his ideas is the world of Christian perfect temporal communities, but again it is evident from his argument that the world beyond it is included on equal terms.

In 'On the American Indians' Vitoria presents some of the rights in question in the negative form, and enlists for support of his argument sources such as the Scriptures, St Thomas, Torquemada and Cajetan. For example:

- Having first established that the Indians have true dominion, both publicly and privately, he argues that the Spaniards have no right to deprive them of it on the grounds that the emperor, their king, is lord

[98] Vitoria, 'On the American Indians', p. 281.

[99] Vitoria, 'On the Law of Nations and Natural Law', p. cxii. Brett offers a different reading on this point, which may, nonetheless, be regarded as complimenting the above. She emphasizes the 'close proximity' of the two concepts in Vitoria's thinking: the general consensus, the law of nations, is 'a result of natural reasoning processes'. A. Brett, 'Francisco de Vitoria (1483–1546) and Francisco Suárez (1548–1617)', in B. Fassbender and A. Peters (eds), *The Oxford Handbook of the History of International Law* (Oxford: Oxford University Press, 2013), pp. 1087–88.

of the world, for the emperor never had lordship over the whole world and does not have it now.

- Since the Indians have true dominion, the pope has no right to declare the King of Spain sovereign over them on the grounds that he is temporal lord of the world. The pope has no temporal power over the Indians or other unbelievers, for he has no spiritual power over them.
- Since the lands of the New World have true owners, there is no right of discovery on the part of the Spaniards. 'This title', Vitoria holds, 'gives no support to a seizure of the aborigines any more than it would if they had discovered us.'
- The Indians may refuse to accept the Christian religion; the Spaniards have no right to compel them to accept it.
- Although the Indians commit many sins against nature, some very serious, the Spaniards have no right, even with the authorization of the pope, to compel them to desist from these or to punish them.[100]

The above negative rights which he ascribes to Christian and non-Christian perfect communities alike correspond to the obligation, on the part of these same communities, to respect one another's separateness and independence. As he sees it, the division of the world, inherited from a distant past, is by the mutual agreement of peoples, and it is proper that it should be defended.[101]

Vitoria also identifies positive rights, and in support of his reading of the laws in question he cites mainly the Scriptures.

- He argues that the Spaniards have a right 'to travel and dwell in those countries'; the obligation on their part is 'to do no harm' to the Indians; the latter's obligation, in turn, is to honour the Spaniards' right. He interprets this right extremely broadly:

  > [I]t would not be lawful for the French to prohibit Spaniards from travelling or even living in France, or *vice versa* ... therefore it is not lawful for the barbarians either ... running water and the open sea, rivers, and ports are the common property, and by the law of nations [*ius gentium*] ships from any nation country may lawfully put in anywhere.[102]

- The Spaniards have a right to trade with the Indians; their obligation is to do no harm; and the Indians must accept the Spaniards' right:

  > [I]t is certain that the barbarians can no more prohibit Spaniards from carrying on trade with them, than Christians can prohibit from doing the same.[103]

100 Vitoria, 'On the American Indians', pp. 252–58, 258–64, 264–65, 265–72, 272–75.
101 Ibid., p. 255.
102 Ibid., pp. 278–79.
103 Ibid., p. 280.

- The Spaniards 'have the right to preach and announce' the Christian religion to the Indians, and the latter may not hinder them, for:

  [I]f they have the right to travel and trade among them, then they must be able to teach them the truth if they are willing to listen.[104]

- The Spaniards have a right to defend innocent people from tyrannical rulers and tyrannical laws; but the Indians sacrifice innocent people for human sacrifice or for cannibalistic purposes; hence the latter can be compelled to abstain from such 'nefarious custom or rite', and it is of no relevance that 'all the barbarians consent to these kinds of rites and sacrifices or that they refuse to accept the Spaniards as their liberators', for 'herein they are not of such legal independence'.[105]

It is not surprising that Vitoria's positive rights have been interpreted as his doctrine to legitimize Spanish imperialism, the fine words on community and fellowship being no more than casuistry obscuring his real intent.[106] However, it is difficult to accept that this was his intention. All the rights in question are subject to the condition that the Spaniards do no harm to the Indians; but, as we have seen, Vitoria was keenly aware of the harm that they were inflicting. And his conclusion is not a defence, even a qualified one, of the Spanish empire; rather, he considers the possibility that none of the just titles prove to be applicable, and points to the example of the Portugese, who carry on a profitable trade in the East without occupying the lands in question.[107] Further issues raised here are taken up in the chapter's conclusion.

Vitoria's view of the international community, then, may be summed up as follows. To the principle of separateness and independence, the principle of 'natural society and fellowship' has been joined. Their coexistence makes for the plurality, equality and community which Vitoria ascribes to the world as a whole. As he understands it, it is not the intention of peoples, by that division, to do away with mutual communication.[108] The world as a whole is mankind. It has been given a law – natural law. Mankind is divided into perfect temporal communities. They, too, have been given a law – the law of nations as natural law, and they themselves are the source of a law – the law of nations as positive law. The right to enforce them and punish violations of them is held by perfect temporal communities and their rulers – and this is by natural law, the law of nations and the authority of the world as a whole.

[104] Ibid., p. 284.
[105] Ibid., p. 287–88.
[106] Anghie, *Imperialism, Sovereignty and the Making of International Law*, pp. 13–31; Williams, *The American Indian in Western Legal Thought*, pp. 97–108.
[107] Vitoria, 'On the American Indians', pp. 291–92.
[108] Ibid., p. 278.

The Question of War

Vitoria's main concerns are the just war and lawful conduct in war. The first is discussed here, the second in the next section.

There are two kinds of war, he states at the outset, and both may be just. The first is defensive war. As he sees it, any defensive war is just – it is lawful to resist 'force with force' – and any community, irrespective of whether or not it enjoys the attribute of being perfect, may resort to it. For him, the right of self-defence is obvious – natural law attests to its justice, and so does the written law, the Gospel, St Augustine and St Thomas – and he devotes little space to it.[109]

It is the second kind, offensive war, which absorbs his attention, for it is his view that the avoidance of 'disorder in the world' may require a more effective means than defensive war. 'The peace and security of the commonwealth' and the happiness of the world may not be secured 'if war could only be waged to repel unjust invaders ... and never to carry the conflict into the enemies' camp.'[110] But a wrong must have been committed: he is not endorsing preventive war on the mere suspicion of an attack. 'The sole and only just cause for waging war is when harm has been inflicted.'[111] Offensive war is justified only within this larger, essentially defensive context. He categorically rejects as a just cause religious differences, the enlargement of empire or 'the personal glory or convenience of the prince'.[112]

The right to declare and make war – that is, the right to commence a war – is reserved to the perfect temporal community or its ruler, for, as Vitoria sees it, if everybody had the right to be 'the judge of his own cause', the world would be ungovernable. In fact, he considers this right to be one of the basic elements of the state's self-sufficiency. It must have the authority not only to defend itself but also to avenge and punish injuries done to itself and its members. He also sees it as a right conferred by the world as a whole:

> If the commonwealth has these powers ... there can be no doubt that the whole world has the same powers against any harmful and evil men. And these powers can only be exercised through the princes of commonwealths.[113]

[109] Vitoria, 'On the Law of War', p. 297.
[110] Ibid., p. 298.
[111] Ibid., p. 303.
[112] Ibid., pp. 302–03.
[113] Ibid., pp. 305–06. This passage lends support to the present, pluralist interpretation of Vitoria. The commonwealth has these powers, by natural law. By inference, the whole world must also have them. For the universalist, although the world is only 'in a sense' a commonwealth, its rights or powers, are somehow prior to those of the commonwealths.

Vitoria is well aware that the practical application of his principles presents serious problems. 'In moral matters it is difficult to hit on the true and just course of action.'[114] Princes normally believe that their cause is just, but a war cannot be just on both sides. If it were, all the belligerents would be innocent parties, and none could lawfully be killed. His advice is that the prince must proceed with extreme care, listen to the arguments of the opponent and the advice of 'wise men' before taking a decision with such serious consequences.[115]

In the case of the American Indians, he is prepared to make a partial exception. There may be justice on both sides, where there is 'invincible ignorance' on the part of the Indians, or where they have understandable fears. Assuming the Spaniards come with peaceful intent, the Indians may not believe this and, fearing their military power, may attack in self-defence – a just cause. Then the Spaniards may lawfully defend themselves, but in this case they should refrain from further acts of war: in view of their understandable fears, the Indians are in effect innocent parties.[116]

In 'On Civil Power' he makes an important qualification: even if it is justified in other respects, 'no war is legitimate if it is shown to be more harmful than useful to the commonwealth', and furthermore, since it is part of the world as a whole, and a Christian country is part of the Christian commonwealth, a (Christian) commonwealth may not justly go to war if this would be injurious to the world as a whole or to Christendom, however advantageous it might otherwise appear to be.[117]

The interests of Christendom also enter into Vitoria's account of what justifies going to war. There is a right, and even an obligation, to assist Christians maltreated by a non-Christian ruler; this would, for example, justify war against the 'Indians', which could even extend to changing the ruler. In this context, Vitoria expresses a rare personal opinion:

> I myself have no doubt that force and arms were necessary for the Spaniards to continue in those parts; my fear is that the affair may have gone beyond the permissible bounds of justice and religion.[118]

Vitoria distinguishes between a wrong done to the prince's own community and a wrong done to others. In the case of allies and friends he sees no problem. In agreement with Cajetan, he asserts:

[114] Ibid., p. 307, note 24. This sentence was not in the original manuscript, but was in the first printed edition. It appears to capture Vitoria's underlying premise: to make explicit his 'unspoken assumption'.

[115] Ibid., pp. 306–07.

[116] Vitoria, 'On the American Indians', p. 282.

[117] Vitoria, 'On Civil Power', pp. 21–22.

[118] Vitoria, 'On the American Indians', p. 286.

There can be no doubt that fighting on behalf of allies and friends is a just cause of war ... equally, a commonwealth may call upon foreigners to punish its enemies and fight external malefactors.[119]

The right to go to war in response to a wrong done to others applies also in the absence of a link such as friendship or alliance. Vitoria permits intervention in a number of cases, provided there is no doubt regarding the wrong done and injustices greater than the one to be rectified do not result. For example, a prince has the right to intervene in another community if that community is ruled by a tyrant – a prince who does not rule in accordance with the existing laws – and the community as a result is 'suffering unjustly'. '[T]he people in question are an innocent people, and ... princes may and can defend the world, lest injury be inflicted upon it.'[120] Also, if the laws of a community are tyrannical – that is, if they 'work wrong to innocent folk' – he allows intervention by an outside prince. Examples refer to the Turks, whose laws permit exposing unwanted children, and to some Indian peoples who act in accordance with their own laws when innocent human beings are killed for cannibalistic purposes: 'The barbarians are all our neighbours, and therefore anyone, and especially princes, may defend them from such tyranny and oppression.'[121] He raises the question of intervention in the case where a people seem to be 'unsuited to setting up or administering a commonwealth both legitimate and ordered in human and civil terms', but is not prepared to give a categorical answer.[122]

Vitoria's examples of intervention have one criterion in common: the suffering of innocent peoples.

In principle, then, Vitoria's category 'just offensive war' covers a wide range of cases. In practice, however, when his qualifications are taken into account, in particular the need for certainty as to the justice of the cause, and that the costs should not exceed the gain, his doctrine becomes quite restrictive. Indeed, his first conclusion to the *relectio* 'On the Law of War' sounds remarkably Erasmian; princes 'should strive above all to avoid all provocations and causes of war'. Deliberately to seek war 'is a mark of utter monstrousness ... The prince should only accede to the necessity of war when he is dragged reluctantly but inevitably into it.'[123] The two had quite different purposes, Erasmus seeking to transform the culture of ready acceptance of war, Vitoria to delimit the conditions under which it is justified. But their practical recommendations are very similar.

119 Ibid., p. 289.
120 Vitoria, 'On War', pp. cxvii, cxviii.
121 Vitoria, 'On the American Indians', p. 288.
122 Ibid., p. 290.
123 Vitoria, 'On the Law of War', pp. 326–27.

Moderation

The idea of moderation, not postulated by the initial hypothesis derived from Gierke, Wight and Bull, but consistent with it, is ever present in Vitoria's writings, especially on three topics: administering a perfect temporal community; spreading the Christian religion; and waging a just war.

Administering a Perfect Temporal Community

Apart from his condemnation of tyranny, Vitoria does not in a general way link moderation to the internal context; his concern is rather with a particular situation, that of a Christian prince ruling over a non-Christian community.

In the fragment of his *relectio* 'On Temperance' he argues that, when a Christian prince acquires the rule over a non-Christian community, he must not burden it more heavily than his Christian community by, for example, imposing higher taxes, taking away liberty or subjecting it to other oppressive measures. The reason he gives is this: the non-Christian community is not part of the Christian community; neither does it subordinate itself to it. Hence, in order to avoid acting 'unfaithfully', the prince must have regard for what is good for his new community, not only the Christians.[124]

He also argues that the Christian religion is to be introduced only gradually into the newly acquired community. As he explains,

> It would not be a tolerable law if immediately an edict were passed which required that nobody, on penalty of death, must worship Mohamed or the idols, or that all adore Christ; or that the same be ordered under penalty of exile or confiscation of their belongings.[125]

Rather, the first step should consist in persuading the non-Christian community by teaching and instruction of the truth of the Christian religion and the falsehood of the old laws and rites.[126] A law ordering the destruction of idols or of the Moslem religion should be considered only at a later stage, and even then it should not threaten death or exile but choose 'a much milder approach'.[127]

124 Vitoria, 'De la Temperancia', pp. 267–68.

125 Ibid., p. 269.

126 Las Casas also attached great importance to this point. Giménez Fernández reports that Las Casas 'sought (March 1541) and obtained (1 December 1541) from the theologians of the University of Salamanca (headed by Fray Francisco de Vitoria) a *parecer* or opinion approving his thesis that the baptism of Indians had to be preceded by adequate instruction in the truths of the Christian religion'. Giménez Fernández, 'Fray Bartolomé de Las Casas', p. 94.

127 Vitoria, 'De la Temperancia', p. 269.

In a *lectio* which discusses the question 'Whether one can force the infidels to convert (to Christianity)', Vitoria presents the case of Christians and non-Christians living together in one community under the rule of a Christian prince. He argues that, while in itself it is lawful to do so, St Paul has pointed out that 'there are many things which are lawful but not advisable'. The prince would never know for certain whether the Christian faith has 'really been received'; a wrong impression would be created, that force has always been used in the conversion to Christianity; and he thinks that many Moslems forced to convert never became good Christians.[128]

In the same tract he also raises the question of whether the prince may treat his non-Christian subjects more harshly than his Christian subjects by imposing higher burdens, and the answer is that, while it may be lawful, it may not be advisable. It would amount to coercion to convert.[129]

Spreading the Christian Religion

Preaching the Christian religion in realms that are not under the rule of Christian princes is, according to Vitoria, a right on the part of Christians, but it is linked to the obligation not to use force when exercising it.

His most extensive example in support of his view is the conversion of the Indians in America. The Indians, he argues, are not bound to believe immediately and 'merely by not believing a simple announcement' that Christianity is the true religion. Following Cajetan, he writes: 'It is foolhardy and imprudent of anyone to believe a thing without being sure it comes from a trustworthy source, especially in matters to do with salvation.'[130] 'Peaceful persuasion' is the way to attract the Indians, but if they continue to reject Christianity, Vitoria insists that this does not entitle the Christians to resort to war, for 'war is no argument for the truth of the Christian faith'.[131]

The resort to war becomes lawful if the Indians deny the Christians their right to preach. In such a case, the latter may do 'all the things which are lawfully permitted in other just wars', but 'always observe reasonable

[128] Vitoria, 'Si se puede obligor', in Pereña and Pérez Prendes (eds), *Francisco de Vitoria*, pp. 121, 122.

[129] Ibid., p. 125.

[130] Vitoria, 'On the American Indians', p. 269. See also Vitoria, 'De la Obligación de Convertirse a Dios', p. 1368.

[131] Vitoria, 'On the American Indians', pp. 271–72.

limits and do not go further than necessary'. However, he again draws attention to the possibility that what is lawful may not be advisable:

It may happen that the resulting war with its massacres and pillage, obstructs the conversion of the barbarians instead of encouraging it. The most important consideration is to avoid placing obstructions in the way of the Gospel.

If so, 'this method of evangelization must be abandoned'.[132]

Waging a Just War

Vitoria's two writings, his *lectio* 'On War' and his *relectio* 'On the Law of War', devote numerous pages to the idea of moderation in war. In the words of Ernest Nys, 'In treating of the cruel topic of the law of war, he asserted principles which bore the imprint of moderation and humanity.'[133]

Vitoria states his general position as follows:

Once war has been declared for a just cause, the prince should press his campaign not for the destruction of his opponent but for the pursuit of the justice for which he fights and the defence of his homeland, so that by fighting he may eventually establish peace and security.[134]

He arrives at his general position after examining a number of particular questions. For example, he asks whether it is lawful to kill the innocent, that is, those presumed to be innocent: children, women, peasants, clerics, members of religious orders and foreigners who happen to be in the country of the enemy. His answer is that in itself it never is lawful. It may become lawful through the force of circumstances, that is 'if it would otherwise be impossible to wage war against the guilty, thereby preventing the just side from fighting', but the obligation is to see to it that 'the evil effects of the war do not outweigh the possible benefits'.[135]

Another question which he raises is whether it is lawful to kill all the guilty. His reply is: 'In the actual conflict of battle' – yes; after the war – yes in principle, but when the nature of the wrong done by the enemy is taken into account, it may be found that it would not be right to do so. His authority is Cicero: 'We should punish wrong-doers only so far as justice and humanity permit.'[136]

To give a third example: Vitoria enquires into the lawfulness of deposing the princes of the enemy and installing new ones or of placing the

132 Ibid., p. 286.
133 Nys, 'Introduction', p. 69.
134 Vitoria, 'On the Law of War', p. 327.
135 Ibid., p. 315.
136 Ibid., p. 321.

foreign community under one's own rule. His findings are that this would often be 'altogether too savage and inhumane'. He restricts it to cases where 'the number or atrocity of the injuries and harm done by the enemy' call for it, or especially 'when security and peace cannot otherwise be ensured'.[137]

For the most part, his advice concerning moderation in war does not differentiate between Christian and non-Christian adversaries. There are, however, some instances where he does suggest a different response depending on whether or not the enemy is Christian. For example, 'it is not to be doubted that we may lawfully enslave the women and children of the Saracens', but 'it is not lawful to enslave fellow Christians, at any rate during the course of the war'.[138] Likewise, in wars against the infidel, one may kill all the enemy combatants if security cannot otherwise be ensured, but 'in wars against fellow-Christians I do not think that it is permissible'.[139]

Vitoria's instances of differential treatment are, on the whole, limited to the Old World; however, there is a passage in the *relectio* 'On the American Indians', in the form of a conditional statement, which reads that if the Indians act like 'treacherous foes', all the rights of war may be exercised, but 'with moderation and in proportion to the actual offence'.[140]

Thinking about moderation, then, Vitoria invites his audience to consider what is lawful but also to take account of what is advisable. The advisable, when linked to the lawful, for most of the time makes for more moderation; only in cases of persistent enmity, it makes for less.

Conclusion

Vitoria did not see himself as a theorist of international relations, or for that matter of international law. He wrote as a theologian, spelling out the practical implications of his moral principles in these domains. However, underlying the relevant writings is a set of general assumptions about international relations which amounts to a theory, not in the contemporary sense but a conception of the kind Wight employs to characterize his three traditions. And these assumptions place Vitoria squarely within what Wight terms the *via media* tradition.

The central elements of his conception are the states (the perfect temporal communities) and the international society – the community of these temporal communities – which pursue their interests subject to

137 Ibid., p. 326.
138 Ibid., p. 318.
139 Ibid., p. 321.
140 Vitoria, 'On the American Indians', p. 283.

generally accepted rules – natural law and the law of nations – which provide criteria to determine the legitimacy of their actions. These temporal communities are not yet quite the sovereign states of later theorists, thanks to what may be seen as residual medieval concepts. The emperor remains in some sense the superior of many of the kings and princes, but his powers as overlord are not spelled out, while the limits of his authority are clear: most crucially, it is the kings and princes who decide whether or not the state is to engage in war.

The perfect spiritual community represents, in principle, a more significant restriction on state sovereignty. And Christendom retained a certain political significance, as seen, for example, in the Spanish monarch's readiness to consult theologians on the legitimacy of one or other course of action. The pope's spiritual power was accepted, and this could have practical political consequences. However, the far-reaching powers which Vitoria ascribes to him *in extremis* to override the power of the temporal ruler are lacking in credibility in the political circumstances of the day. In practice, if not in theory, the perfect temporal communities amounted to sovereign states.

But Vitoria's writings are not concerned with practice, as such, but rather to set out a system of norms which determine the legitimacy of practices. In contrast to Erasmus, he does not address the question of how the world may be brought into closer accord with his normative ideal. The political-sociological dimension in Erasmus's thinking is absent. Nor do his writings express anything of Erasmus's keen awareness of the readiness with which high principles may be abused to legitimize unacceptable ends. He may well have been a shrewd political observer, but such observations did not have a place in his theoretical framework.

In comparison with Erasmus, Vitoria's thought appears one-dimensional. If Erasmus's image of international society may be likened to a multi-layered print, Vitoria's could be seen as an abstract sketch, lacking the colourful detail of Erasmus's oeuvre. But it is a powerful sketch, illustrating the strengths of abstraction: to capture the essentials in a complex situation or set of issues – or, more plausibly, a telling image of the essentials – on one view, the essence of theorizing. The abstract theorist may perceive some connections which elude the multi-dimensional printmaker. For example, Vitoria's thinking on the just war brings in the issue of international order which is absent, or at least not explicit, in Erasmus's reflections on the topic.

It was noted earlier that the present reading of Vitoria differs from certain other recent interpretations, notably the universalist and the imperialist. Brett's universalist thesis starts from the premise that for Vitoria, the *ius gentium* was not among sovereign states but among all human beings, forming one community. She goes on to the well-known passage referring to the whole world as 'in a sense a commonwealth', with the power to enact laws – the law of nations. The world may be divided among different peoples, but retains its essential juridical unity. The *ius gentium* legitimizes both the separation and the rules which limit the state's right to exclude outsiders. His view, she suggests, may be likened to the contemporary idea of cosmopolitanism.[141]

Her brief presentation addresses central issues for the interpretation of Vitoria. It does not amount to universalism as defined by Gierke, Wight and Bull: the plurality of states being replaced by a world government or dissolved into a world community. The plurality remains, but is subordinated to 'the whole world', the quasi-commonwealth, which is entitled to legislate for it. However, her premise that Vitoria saw the law of nations as between all human beings forming a world community is highly questionable, given that Vitoria defines it as holding between peoples, and elsewhere refers to the consensus of peoples. The present interpretation was unable to find substance in the notion of the world commonwealth as the key to explaining the nature of the community of temporal communities. Rather, it may be suggested, Vitoria invokes it in the way contemporary leaders invoke the international community, in order to lend greater authority to what is being claimed.

The present interpretation, on the other hand, begins with the legitimacy of the temporal community, derived from natural law. And its close association with natural law also provides the most convincing support for the legitimacy of the law of nations – more so than the fictional legislative power of the quasi-world commonwealth. Thus political plurality and the law of nations are at the same level of legitimacy. It is evident that Vitoria's texts are especially open to differing interpretations. One important test of any interpretation is its capacity to take account of the whole of the relevant text; the present interpretation has sought to satisfy this criterion.

This same criterion also arises in relation to the recent imperialist readings of Vitoria, which scarcely refer to the many conditions which Vitoria attaches to Spanish rights vis-à-vis the American Indians and to the justification of war. Thus Robert Williams's reference to Vitoria's 'discourse of conquest' is, to say the least, a vast overstatement – but his reading shows that a skilful advocate could construct such a discourse by linking together a series of Vitoria's stated rights, out of context and not subject to his qualifications.[142]

[141] Brett, *Changes of State*, pp. 13–14.
[142] Williams, *The American Indian*, pp. 96–108; 'discourse of conquest', p. 106.

Anghie's interpretation is more nuanced, inter alia exploring the way in which a universal doctrine, apparently applying equally to all, can be seen to disadvantage the other or 'inferior' culture. But in suggesting that 'the transformation of the Indian is to be achieved by the waging of war' or that 'once fault is established, the war waged against the Indians is perpetual', he sets aside Vitoria's essential qualifications of any recourse to war.[143]

Some of Vitoria's Dominican colleagues and successors took issue with Vitoria's broad construction of the right to natural partnership and communication. Melchor Cano argued that some of the supposed rights were contrary to European practice, and dismissed the right to travel as an entitlement to rule with the comment: 'We would not be prepared to describe Alexander the Great as a traveller.'[144] Defenders of the Empire do not appear to have seized on Vitoria's complex arguments. The most prominent of these in the ensuing decades, Juan Gines de Sepulveda, preferred to argue from his own framework, 'the language of humanist jurisprudence'.[145]

But the imperialist interpretation of Vitoria raises more complex issues, any full discussion of which would go well beyond the scope of the present inquiry. Vitoria was not free from imperialist attitudes: his view of the American Indians was deeply ambivalent. On the one hand, the Indians met his criteria for perfect communities: their societies were ordered, and they had their own laws and rulers. Thus Spain must observe the law of nations in its relations with them. But in practice he does not accord them equal rights. He sees no problem in what came to be understood as economic imperialism: the law of nations allows a heavy Spanish presence, the mooring of ships and seemingly unrestricted mining rights which, as Cano pointed out, would not be acknowledged in Europe.

Moreover, Vitoria's language is often disparaging: he regularly refers to the Indians as barbarians and, even while arguing that they may have reasonable fears of the Spaniards, describes them as 'by nature cowardly, foolish and ignorant'.[146] He shows no respect for their culture, and not surprisingly, their religion is worthless. It is the duty of Christian missionaries to give them the opportunity to save their souls. And while he is

[143] Anghie, *Imperialism, Sovereignty and the Making of International Law*, pp. 23, 27.

[144] A. Pagden, 'Dispossessing the Barbarian: The Language of Spanish Thomism and the Debate over the Property Rights of the American Indians', in A. Pagden (ed.), *The Languages of Political Theory in Early Modern Europe* (Cambridge: Cambridge University Press, 1987), p. 89.

[145] Ibid., p. 93.

[146] Vitoria, 'On the American Indians', p. 282.

not prepared to endorse the view that Spain is entitled to take over their administration, because the barbarians are so lacking in mental capacity as to be unsuited to 'administering a commonwealth both legitimate and ordered in human and civil terms', nor is he prepared to reject it.[147] That is to say, he allows that this may well be the case.

The tensions in Vitoria's thought could be said to arise from his attempt to construct a single normative system for the relations among the established European states and their relations with peoples whom they are in the process of bringing under imperial rule – peoples at a different cultural and technical level who could not maintain a relationship with them on equal terms. In later centuries, as the empires became established, it was evident that if there was an international society of formally equal states, this was limited to the European system, while quite different, hierarchical norms regulated the relations between empire and colonies.[148] In the first decades of the Spanish empire it was quite unclear what norms might apply, as well as how the empire itself might be justified. Vitoria's bold attempt to resolve both questions through constructing a single, universal moral/legal order was to prove untenable, but in the attempt he exposed many of the major issues that had to be addressed by later theorists.

[147] Ibid., p. 290.

[148] See E. Keene, *Beyond the Anarchical Society: Grotius, Colonialism and Order in World Politics* (Cambridge: Cambridge University Press, 2002), especially chapters 3 and 4.

4 Alberico Gentili

The Italian jurist Alberico Gentili (1552–1608) is the third thinker to be included in this inquiry. Otto von Gierke as well as Martin Wight and Hedley Bull cite him in their respective lists of thinkers but, as in the case of Vitoria, disagree about the place to be accorded to him: Gierke claims him as a universalist, Wight is ambiguous, and Bull considers him a man of the *via media*.

Gierke offers his reason in the form of a footnote, half in German and half in Latin, which reads:

> Thus Albericus Gentilis, *de jure belli* ['On the Law of War'] (1588), pages 11–13, explains the binding force of the *jus gentium* by saying that, indeed, all the nations never came together, but that which over time has seemed acceptable to all, is to be regarded as having been decreed by the whole world; and he adds: as the rule of a state and the making of its laws are in the hands of a majority of its citizens, just so is the rule of the world in the hands of the aggregation[1] of the greater part of the world.[2]

Turning to Gentili's text for a better understanding of the above passage, one finds that the first half is part of an argument of how the law of nations was established. The second half – following the three words 'and he adds' – is embedded between two statements: one, if all known nations have used a certain code of laws, it may be inferred that all nations have used it, for the reason that from 'the known' one learns 'the unknown'; and, two, an unwritten law or custom of a state binds all its members, even if not everyone has agreed to it.[3] The additional information does not strengthen Gierke's case.

[1] The Latin word is *congregatio*, a difficult word in the present context. Usually it is translated as 'assembling together', 'union', 'society'.

[2] O. von Gierke, *Das Deutsche Genossenschaftsrecht*, vol. 4 (Graz: Akademische Druck und Verlagsanstalt, 1954), p. 362. The year 1588 in the quoted passage suggests that Gierke used the three commentaries rather than the three books of Gentili's *De Jure Belli*.

[3] A. Gentili, *De Jure Belli Libri Tres* [Three Books on the Law of War], vol. 2, transl. J. C. Rolfe, intro. C. Phillipson, *The Classics of International Law* (Oxford and London: Clarendon Press and Humphrey Milford, 1933, reprinted New York and London: Oceana Publications and Wildy & Sons, 1964), pp. 8, 9. For the Latin text,

Wight refers the reader to chapter 6 of book 1 of *De Jure Belli*, entitled 'That War May Be Waged Justly on Both Sides', in support of his argument that Gentili contributed to the theory of international legitimacy through his ideas about the just war[4] – which may be interpreted to mean that he accepts Gentili as a thinker of the *via media* but does not explain why he does so, except perhaps indirectly. Bull offers no reference. Wight includes him with the rationalists in a discussion of natural law and the *ius gentium*, but with the universalists when discussing the '*civitas maxima*, a great society or super-state'.[5] Bull sees Gentili, along with Vitoria, Suarez and Grotius, as sharing certain basic views on natural law and the just war, but having difficulty in freeing themselves from medieval notions of universalism.[6] The reasons, then, which led Gierke, Wight and Bull to adopt their respective positions remain rather unclear.

More recently, Richard Tuck has presented a strikingly different interpretation which places Gentili in a humanist or oratorical tradition stemming from the Roman empire which justifies war in a broad range of circumstances, in opposition to the restrictive doctrine of the scholastic school. He refers to Gentili's ideas about war as 'often extraordinarily brutal', and emphasizes in particular his endorsement of pre-emptive or preventive war and his support for the 'war party' led by Francis Bacon, advocating preventive war against Spain.[7] Although he does not use the category 'realist', he does see Machiavelli and raison d'état theorists as falling within the humanist tradition; in terms of Wight's categories, Gentili would be a realist.[8]

An assessment of these interpretations must await the detailed account of Gentili's views, but at this point it should be noted that Gentili's relation to humanism is by no means straightforward. Thomas Erskine Holland, who 'rediscovered' him in the nineteenth century, refers to him as 'a civilian of the old school',[9] alluding to his training in a tradition of legal scholarship inspired by the fourteenth-century jurist, Bartolus of

see A. Gentili, *De Jure Belli Libri Tres*, vol. 1, *A Photographic Reproduction of the Edition of 1612, The Classics of International Law* (Oxford and London: Clarendon Press and Humphrey Milford, 1933).

4 M. Wight, *Systems of States*, ed. and intro. H. Bull (Leicester: Leicester University Press for the London School of Economics and Political Science, 1977), p. 164.

5 M. Wight, *International Theory: The Three Traditions*, ed. G. Wight and B. Porter (Leicester: Leicester University Press for the Royal Institute of International Affairs, London, 1991), pp. 41, 72.

6 H. Bull, *The Anarchical Society: A Study of Order in World Politics* (London: Macmillan, 1977), pp. 28–32.

7 R. Tuck, *The Rights of War and Peace: Political Thought and the International Order from Grotius to Kant* (Oxford: Oxford University Press, 1999), pp. 16–50.

8 Ibid., p. 11.

9 T. E. Holland, *Studies in International Law* (Oxford: Clarendon Press, 1898), p. 16.

Sassaferrato. Gentili himself, in an early work which remains untranslated, disparaged the approach of prominent humanist jurists Alciati and Cujas for their pretensions to universal culture to the neglect of sound jurisprudence.[10] Nonetheless, in the humanist manner he was widely read in the classical literature, and he draws on all sources, including the contemporary humanists as well as the Bartolists and, more especially, the classical Roman authors, treating them all as authorities to be read critically. His advice to his students was 'to visit these moderns, but to dwell with the ancients'.[11] Randall Lesaffer, in discussing several ways in which Gentili's thought was influenced by humanism, suggests that he was seeking a *via media* between Bartolism and the newer approaches.[12]

On first meeting Gentili, one fact crystallizes quickly: the two earlier thinkers, Erasmus and Vitoria, are not unknown to him. He refers to them on numerous occasions,[13] sometimes using them simply as sources, at other times expressing opinions. And it is not difficult to detect that they produce different reactions. Erasmus causes displeasure. When inquiring into the question of the justice of war, for example, Gentili says:

> In fact, some cite Erasmus in our favour, others on the opposite side. Perhaps a third view will be nearer the truth, that the flighty dilettante did not know what he thought.[14]

Vitoria, on the other hand, is awarded the distinction of being 'learned'. 'But the learned Victoria [sic]', Gentili writes later, 'declares that [the] principle of not making war from religious motives is approved by all without exception'.[15]

Another point which becomes clear quickly is that Gentili is neither as resistant to exploration as Vitoria is nor does he possess the same ability

10 Ibid.

11 Ibid., p. 17.

12 R. Lesaffer, 'Alberico Gentili's *ius post bellum* and Early Modern Peace Treaties', in B. Kingsbury and B. Straumann (eds), *The Roman Foundations of the Law of Nations: Alberico Gentili and the Justice of Empire* (Oxford: Oxford University Press, 2010), pp. 217–20.

13 Regarding references to Erasmus, see, for example, A. Gentili, *De Legationibus Libri Tres* [Three Books on Embassies], vol. 2, transl. G. J. Laing, intro. E. Nys, The Classics of International Law (New York: Oxford University Press, 1924, reprinted New York and London: Oceana Publications and Wildy & Sons, 1964), p. 161; and Gentili, *De Jure Belli*, vol. 2, pp. 28, 29, 38, 135, 157, 261. Regarding references to Vitoria see, for example, Gentili, *De Jure Belli*, vol. 2, pp. 31, 39, 55, 89, 122, 126, 332.

14 Gentili, *De Jure Belli*, vol. 2, p. 29. This is perhaps Gentili's 'revenge' for the rather unflattering view which Erasmus expresses when he suggests that there should be as few laws as possible, and that these be as just and as clear as possible, for then 'there will be no need for that most grasping type of man who calls himself "jurisconsult" and "advocate"'. See D. Erasmus, *The Education of a Christian Prince*, transl. and intro. L. K. Born (New York: Columbia University Press, 1936), p. 234.

15 Gentili, *De Jure Belli*, vol. 2, p. 39.

to attract thinkers and writers as Erasmus does. He has neither Vitoria's mysteriousness nor Erasmus's lustre. The main facts of Gentili's life are known and agreed upon, and his writings, while at times obscure, have survived intact; yet few scholars have studied them closely. For example, the only substantial investigation of his life and works published in English in the twentieth century is Gesina van der Molen's *Alberico Gentili and the Development of International Law*, which appeared in 1937.[16] More recently, Gentili has achieved a new prominence in Tuck's reinterpretation of early modern political thought, and as the focal point in Benedict Kingsbury's and Benjamin Straumann's volume on the influence of Roman thought on the emerging study of international law.[17]

Gentili was born in 1552 at San Ginesio in Northern Italy in a well-established family, his father a physician with wide intellectual interests.[18] At the age of twenty-one he obtained his doctorate in civil law from the University of Perugia, and for the following three years was *praetor* (judge) at Ascoli. In 1575 he returned to San Ginesio to take up the position of municipal lawyer. He did not seek reappointment to this office in 1577, but devoted himself to private study. His father and he himself had become identified with the Reformation, and the threat of persecution from the Inquisition forced him to leave Italy in 1579.

In 1580 Gentili arrived in England and began to teach civil law at Oxford the following year. In 1587 he was appointed Regius Professor of Civil Law at that university, and retained this position until his death, although after 1590 he increasingly left the teaching to two deputies, Francis James and John Budden, moved to London, established a forensic

[16] G. H. J. van der Molen, *Alberico Gentili and the Development of International Law: His Life, Work and Times*, 2nd rev. edn (Leyden: A. W. Sijthoff, 1968). Gentili's translators also note this lack of interest. See J. C. Rolfe, in Gentili, *De Jure Belli*, vol. 2, p. 52a; and F. F. Abbott, in A. Gentili, *Hispanicae Advocationis Libri Duo* [Two Books of Spanish Advocacy], vol. 2, transl. F. F. Abbott, The Classics of International Law (New York: Oxford University Press, 1921, reprinted New York and London: Oceana Publications and Wildy & Sons, 1964), p. 9. A major Italian study appeared later in the century: D. Panizza, *Alberico Gentili, giurista ideologo nell'Inghilterra elisabettiana* [Alberico Gentilim Jurist Ideologue in Elizabethan England] (Padua: La Garangola, 1981).

[17] Tuck, *The Rights of War and Peace*, pp. 16–50; B. Kingsbury and B. Straumann (eds), *The Roman Foundations of the Law of Nations: Alberico Gentili and the Justice of Empire* (Oxford: Oxford University Press, 2010).

[18] Regarding details of Gentili's life and writings see, in addition to Molen, Holland, *Studies in International Law*, pp. 1–39; and E. Nys, 'Introduction', in A. Gentili, *De Legationibus Libri Tres*, vol. 2, pp. 11a–37a; C. Phillipson, 'Albericus Gentilis', in Sir J. Macdonell and E. Manson (eds), *Great Jurists of the World* (London: John Murray, 1913). A comparison of Gentili with Grotius has been offered by P. Haggenmacher, 'Grotius and Gentili: A Reassessment of Thomas E. Holland's Inaugural Lecture', in H. Bull, B. Kingsbury and A. Roberts (eds), *Hugo Grotius and International Relations* (Oxford: Clarendon Press, 1990).

practice there, and visited Oxford only on special occasions. In 1600 he became a member of Gray's Inn – the same Inn to which Francis Bacon belonged – and in 1605 was appointed to the office of Advocate to the Spanish Embassy, a position which required him to represent Spanish interests in the London Court of Admiralty. He held it until his death in London in 1608. The historian of Oxford Anthony Wood is recorded to have described him as 'the most noted and famous civilian and the grand ornament of the university of his time'.[19]

If Gentili's professional life knew diversity, so did the products of his mind. In the words of Holland, Gentili's numerous writings, all of which were included in the *Index of Prohibited Books* in 1603,

> touched upon an extraordinary variety of topics, dealing not only with questions of civil and international law, but also with witchcraft, casuistry, canon law, biblical exegesis, classical philology, the Vulgate, English politics, and the prerogative of the crown.[20]

Not all of them have been published, and those which have – they amount to approximately thirty books or treatises – are all in their original language, Latin, with the exception of three works which constitute Gentili's 'principal contributions to the science [of the law of nations]'.[21] These three works appeared in English in *The Classics of International Law* under their Latin titles – *De Legationibus Libri Tres*, *De Jure Belli Libri Tres* and *Hispanicae Advocationis Libri Duo* – and the present inquiry is based upon them. A fourth work recently translated (*De Armis Romanis*), also edited by Kingsbury and Straumann, is only indirectly relevant to the present topic.[22]

Gentili and the Events of His Time

Gentili's years in England (1580–1608) were a time rich in events for his adopted country;[23] the question here is whether his observations, like

[19] L. Markowicz (transl. with intro.), 'Latin Correspondence by Alberico Gentili and John Rainolds on Academic Drama', in J. Hogg (ed.), *Elizabethan and Renaissance Studies*, no. 68 (Salzburg: Institut fuer Englische Sprache und Literatur, 1977), p. 6.

[20] T. E. Holland, 'Gentili, Alberico (1552–1608)', in L. Stephen and S. Lee (eds), *The Dictionary of National Biography*, vol. 7 (London: Oxford University Press/Humphrey Milford, 1937–1938), p. 1004.

[21] Ibid., p. 1005. See also Molen, *Alberico Gentili and the Development of International Law*, pp. 330–31, on the other publications.

[22] B. Kingsbury and B. Straumann (eds), D. Lupher (transl.), *The Wars of the Romans: A Critical Edition and Translation of De Armis Romanis* (Oxford: Oxford University Press, 2011).

[23] See, for example, G. R. Elton, *England under the Tudors* (London: Methuen, 1956); and J. H. Elliott, *Europe Divided: 1559–1598* (Glasgow: Fontana/Collins, 1977).

those of Erasmus and Vitoria before him, may be described as realistic. For analytical purposes, the emphasis is again on conflict.

The four main areas of conflict which engaged English attention were: conspiracy at home; rebellion in the Netherlands; war at sea with Spain; and rebellion in Ireland. All of these find their way into Gentili's writings, not only acting as the initial spark, but also serving as examples or cases in his argumentation.

The Initial Spark

De Legationibus Libri Tres grew out of a diplomatic incident which had all the qualities of a Shakespearean drama centring on a plot to assassinate the Queen. In 1583 Don Bernardino de Mendoza, the Spanish ambassador to the English Court, was discovered to be implicated in the conspiracy. Gentili and Jean Hotman[24] were invited by the English government to advise on what ought to be done. In accordance with their advice, Mendoza was expelled in early 1584.[25] Later in the same year, Gentili made the rights and duties of ambassadors the subject of a disputation which he presented at the annual *comitia* (graduation ceremony) at Oxford and subsequently published. Further elaboration led to the work as it is known today: *De Legationibus Libri Tres*, which appeared in 1585.

For the *comitia* of 1588 Gentili chose as his topic the law of war. England had been at war with Spain since 1585, supported the rebellion in the Netherlands and was ready to fight the approaching armada. Nothing is known about the reception of his discourse, but it appeared shortly afterwards in the form of a series of three commentaries (1588–89). *De Jure Belli Libri Tres*, the work which is known today, was published nine years later in 1598.

Hispanicae Advocationis Libri Duo appeared posthumously in 1613, published by Gentili's brother Scipio, who gave it a subtitle, the English rendering of which is: *In which treatise different famous maritime questions according to the Law of Nations and the practice of today are explained and settled as clearly as possible*. It includes not only Gentili's cases as Spanish advocate, but also records of cases in which he represented English interests, and there are opinions concerned with private law rather than with maritime and prize law.[26]

[24] Jean Hotman, French jurist, teacher in civil law at Oxford, and secretary to the Earl of Leicester. See also Nys, 'Introduction', in Gentili, *De Legationibus*, vol. 2, p. 37a.

[25] Molen, *Alberico Gentili and the Development of International Law*, p. 49.

[26] A. Gentili, *Hispanicae Advocationis Libri Duo*, vol. 1, *A Photographic Reproduction of the Edition of 1661*, intro. F. F. Abbott, *The Classics of International Law* (New York: Oxford University Press, 1921).

Examples and Cases

One meets with references to events of his time in all three works, but with varying frequency. *De Legationibus* contains few references to the contemporary scene. Gentili has a reason for this: examples relating to Antiquity are preferable to those of recent origin, because they give embassies 'that degree of prestige which we assert they have, and which age so easily adds to all things'.[27] An important exception is the Mendoza case, where he argues: 'There was justice ... in England's recent treatment of the Spanish ambassador, who was dismissed for conspiring against the life of the sovereign and the safety of the kingdom.'[28]

In *De Jure Belli*, Gentili demonstrates his familiarity with the events of his time on numerous occasions. For example:

- He refers to the refusal by the King of Spain to submit to arbitration his claim to the crown of Portugal and remarks: '[H]e who tries to avoid a legal process distrusts the justice of his cause.'[29]
- He mentions the complaint by the Hanseatic cities about the pillage of their ships by the English fleet and comments: 'One must be regarded as an enemy who does what is pleasing to the enemy.' The comment is based on his knowledge that the Hanseatic ships supplied the Spaniards, the enemy of the English, with 'provisions and munitions of war'.[30]
- He takes up 'what is just now a burning question, namely, whether the English did right in aiding the Belgians against the Spaniards' and, in the course of his argument, observes:

  > [T]he Belgians, if vanquished in the war, would wholly change their condition, as we see in the conquered part of their country, which has now utterly fallen from its former state of liberty, and is grievously oppressed with garrisons and ruled by the mere nod of a sovereign.[31]

Hispanicae Advocationis Libri Duo derives exclusively from incidents which occurred in Gentili's own time, but for the most part his notes take the incidents as known, and set out only the legal arguments and pleas to be made, but refrain from political observations.[32]

[27] Gentili, *De Legationibus*, vol. 2, pp. 57–58.
[28] Ibid., pp. 112–13.
[29] Gentili, *De Jure Belli*, vol. 2, p. 20.
[30] Ibid., p. 267.
[31] Ibid., pp. 76–77.
[32] On this point, see also F. F. Abbott, 'Introduction', in Gentili, *Hispanicae Advocationis*, vol. 1, p. 10a.

It is clear that Gentili is a well-informed observer of events, and the evidence suggests that his judgements are sober; there is no indication that he tends to entertain unrealistic expectations.

Gentili and the Three Traditions of Thought

Gentili, the probable realist at the level of observation, is familiar with Machiavelli's writings, quotes from them on a number of occasions[33] and admits his admiration for the Florentine's 'remarkable insight'. Machiavelli and his 'precious' *Observations on Livy*, he writes, should be looked at as a model and imitated; yet 'the most distinguished of his class' is slandered, because his purpose is misunderstood. The truth is that,

> He was a eulogist of democracy, and its most spirited champion. Born, educated, and attaining to honors under a democratic form of government, he was the supreme foe of tyranny ... It was not his purpose to instruct the tyrant, but by revealing his secret counsels to strip him bare, and expose him to the suffering nations ... The purpose of this shrewdest of men was to instruct the nations under pretext of instructing the prince.[34]

Yet his admiration for Machiavelli's insight does not lead Gentili to take up the position which Wight and Bull identify as realist. He sometimes refers to adherents of this position as 'the unscrupulous'. For example, when making his case for the existence of the law of nature and of nations, he says: '[T]he unscrupulous will deny its existence.'[35] At other times he denotes their approach as 'Greek cunning and Punic craft'. The 'treacherous envoy' belongs to this category, and so does he who deceives the enemy.[36] As this chapter will show, Gentili puts his insights into reality to a use which differs from Machiavelli's, whether understood according to Gentili or differently.

Gentili's opposition to universalism or, as he himself formulates it, 'universal control and power to fall into the hands of one people' or 'one man',[37] is implicit in his whole work and will become apparent as this chapter proceeds. It is made explicit on a number of occasions, two of which are especially noteworthy.

[33] For example, Gentili, *De Legationibus*, vol. 2, pp. 153, 156; and Gentili, *De Jure Belli*, vol. 2, pp. 114, 199, 401.
[34] Gentili, *De Legationibus*, vol. 2, p. 156.
[35] Gentili, *De Jure Belli*, vol. 2, p. 5.
[36] See, for example, Gentili, *De Legationibus*, vol. 2, p. 67; Gentili, *De Jure Belli*, vol. 2, p. 349.
[37] Gentili, *De Jure Belli*, vol. 2, pp. 65, 66.

In his chapter 'Of the Overthrow of Kingdoms' he argues that the Roman emperor is not only not 'lord of the whole world'; he also has 'no right of action' against those territories which formerly belonged to the empire, to wit, territories which are now being held by the Turks and other barbarians; the French, the English and the Spaniards; Venice, Florence and other cities of Tuscany; and the pope of Rome.[38]

The other occasion is provided by his discussion of the question whether it is legitimate to make war when the only reason we have is fear that we ourselves may be attacked. In the course of his lengthy answer Gentili draws attention to a 'powerful argument' which, in his view, has proved acceptable to all ages, namely the idea that one ought to oppose those who 'are content with no bounds, and end by attacking the fortunes of all'. Is it not just, he inquires, that we oppose those who, like the Turks and the Spaniards, are 'planning and plotting universal dominion'? Is not this our aim, he reiterates a little later, 'that one man may not have supreme power and that all Europe may not submit to the domination of a single man'?[39] A just response to such a threat consists in preventive action, and he appeals to history. It was Lorenzo de Medici's unremitting concern, Gentili reminds his readers, that 'the balance of power[40] should be maintained among the princes of Italy. This he believed would give peace to Italy, as indeed it did so long as he lived.'[41]

The peace which results from an equal distribution of power, and the war which is fought in order to oppose the reach for universal political rule, are expressions of the same concern: the preservation of that which is 'right and just'. As he puts it at the end of his argument against universalism: 'No one's sovereignty must ever on any account be allowed to grow so great, that it is not permitted to call in question even his manifest injustice'.[42]

Gentili's explicit rejection of universalism as expressed above constitutes a first and serious challenge to Gierke's view of Gentili as a universalist.

[38] Ibid., pp. 112–13. See also the preceding chapter 'On not Reviving Old Causes for War', pp. 105–11. Even in relation to the German states, the Roman emperor is not 'a ruler of unlimited power', p. 50.

[39] Gentili entitles this chapter 'Of Defence on Grouds of Expediency', in Gentili, *De Jure Belli*, vol. 2, pp. 61–66; but here as elsewhere – see, for example, pp. 71, 211, 349, 350, 351 – he does not separate expediency from the idea of justice.

[40] The Latin text reads: '[R]es Italorum paribus libratae ponderibus forent', Gentili, *De Jure Belli*, vol. 1, p. 104, which a verbal translation might render as: '[T]he states of the Italians should be well-poised by equal weights'.

[41] Gentili, *De Jure Belli*, vol. 2, p. 65.

[42] Ibid.

The Perfect Ambassador

Gentili's imagination is not caught by either Erasmus's perfect temporal Christian prince or by Vitoria's perfect temporal community. His mind is inspired by the idea of the perfect ambassador, and he presents a portrait of it in *De Legationibus*.[43] As it represents an important aspect of his more general idea of the world as a 'lofty structure', perhaps even its distinguishing mark, its inclusion in this chapter under a separate heading is indicated.

Gentili attaches a twofold purpose to his creation. First, it is to instruct ambassadors how they 'ought to be' and how they 'ought to behave'.[44] Such knowledge is important in view of the function which they fulfil: '[A]n ambassador is one ... sent ... by the state, ... in the name of the state, ... as the representative of the state'; 'the ambassador is a statesman and is invested with the personality of his prince'; 'a bearer of messages, ... a judge of affairs'; '[ambassadors] represent one sovereign, and approach the other with the intention of negotiating with him on a basis of equality'.[45]

The second purpose is to correct an image of the ambassador with which he does not agree: the ambassador as the spy. Gentili mentions this view on a number of occasions,[46] but does not say how prevalent it was at his time or for how long it had existed. One of his sources is the French statesman and historian Philippe de Comines,[47] who is said to have met Machiavelli in 1494 but does not attribute to him such a 'degrading view'. A relevant passage in Comines's *Memoirs* relating to the year 1471 reads:

> Were it my Case, for one Ambassador they sent me, I would be sure to send them two; nay, though they were weary, and desir'd to have no more, I would not fail to send when I had Opportunity and Convenience; for there is no Spy so good, and so safe, nor can have such Liberty to pry and inform himself.[48]

The assigned task is indeed not small, and one way to acquaint oneself with the object – the portrait of the perfect ambassador – is to watch Gentili create it. Two categories of 'essential qualities' are involved.

[43] See also K. R. Simmonds, 'Gentili on the Qualities of the Ideal Ambassador', *Indian Year Book of International Affairs*, vol. 13, II, 1964.

[44] Gentili, *De Legationibus*, vol. 2, p. 135.

[45] Ibid., pp. 7, 139, 158, 169.

[46] Ibid., pp. 53, 170. For a comparison of Gentili's views with other writings on diplomacy at the time, see G. Mattingly, *Renaissance Diplomacy* (Harmondsworth: Penguin, 1965), pp. 201–12, 222–28.

[47] Gentili, *De Legationibus*, vol. 2, p. 178; Gentili, *De Jure Belli*, vol. 2, p. 237.

[48] P. de Comines, *Memoirs*, transl. and annotated Mr Uvedale, 2nd edn, vol. 1 (London: Bettesworth & Pemberton, 1723), p. 270.

'Graces and Refinements'

Perhaps because he is interested in stage-plays and acting,[49] Gentili begins his portrait by delineating the 'external circumstances'. The stage has to be set properly or, as he puts it, '[The Ambassador's] equipment and suite should be marked by a splendor commensurate with the dignity of him who has sent him.'[50]

Next comes the actor. The perfect ambassador is endowed with 'blessings of nature' and 'blessings of fortune'. The former include 'a comely appearance', beauty based on dignity and vigour linked to courtesy. A 'good personal appearance', Gentili remarks, is especially important with barbarians. 'Blessings of fortune' comprise a distinguished origin and position, for 'a man of ignoble station' can hardly assume the personality of a prince.[51]

With the next stroke of his brush, Gentili adds talents which are partly inborn and partly acquired and developed: ready wit and eloquence – two characteristics which help to win friends, 'the greatest art of ambassadors'.

Purely acquired qualities come next. There is a knowledge of languages. The perfect ambassador knows his own language, a universal language – Gentili suggests Latin for his day and age in preference to Greek – and the language of the state or sovereign to whom he is sent. The reason is this: '[T]he wise ambassador will never have [an interpreter].'[52]

There is a knowledge of history – past and contemporary. The study of the past generates learning, helps to arrive at a norm for one's own conduct and enables one to understand the present and to foresee the future. And there is a knowledge of philosophy, that branch of it which is concerned with morals and politics:

> This is in a sense the soul of history, for it includes and explains the causes of all words, deeds and issues, and so does not suffer historical knowledge to be a bare and empty thing, but brings it within the field of well-defined and useful practical experience.[53]

The group 'graces and refinements' is now complete except for a few finishing touches. The perfect ambassador walks in the 'sunlight' rather

[49] On this aspect of Gentili's life and work, see Markowicz, 'Latin Correspondence', p. 62; J. Rainolds, *The Overthrow of Stage-Plays by the Way of Controversy between D. Gager and D. Rainolds*, 1599 (New York and London: Johnson Reprint, 1972); J. W. Binns, 'Alberico Gentili in Defense of Poetry and Acting', *Studies in the Renaissance*, vol. 19, 1972.

[50] Gentili, *De Legationibus*, vol. 2, p. 198.

[51] Ibid., pp. 141, 143. Gentili applies the term 'barbarians' to 'uncivilized' peoples.

[52] Ibid., pp. 148, 151.

[53] Ibid., p. 156.

than buries himself in books; that is, his knowledge of languages, history and philosophy is not acquired at the cost of practical experience. He is familiar with 'practical politics and the administration of high offices',[54] and he is experienced in foreign travel. The perfect ambassador is more than thirty years of age.

'Virtues'

Gentili endows the perfect ambassador with four virtues – fidelity, fortitude, temperance and prudence – and attributes their parentage to nature and diligence. Fidelity is important because '[h]e who shows good faith ... has a claim on good faith'; courage enables one to perform one's duty 'in spite of violence of any kind'; temperance places 'a seemly limit on things', and prudence permits 'a shrewd analysis of the truth'.[55]

When prudence, which, according to Gentili, 'directs and regulates all the virtues', is linked to fidelity, the perfect ambassador knows how to behave in a situation where there is a conflict between duties to his state or prince and duties to his religion, his integrity, and the situation; when prudence accompanies courage, he discerns when to be persevering and when to defer to circumstances; and when prudence joins temperance, he understands in which circumstances a word or deed is appropriate.[56]

Prudence has its own regulatory device. In order to avoid deception, the perfect ambassador studies the person who says or does something (the adviser) and that which is being said or done (the situation). If both agree in what they convey, there is no problem. If they disagree, the perfect ambassador chooses the situation rather than the adviser as the basis for his decision: 'A conclusion ... based on the situation is more reliable.'

All the virtues which Gentili considers essential in the perfect ambassador are now present, and he completes the portrait by adding the following detail: those who accompany the perfect ambassador are 'of such character that everyone of them could perform the duties of the embassy'.[57] The finished product is dedicated to Philip Sidney, 'a living image and example of the perfect ambassador'.[58] It fits neither the realist way of thinking about the world nor that of the universalists.

[54] Ibid., p. 161.
[55] Ibid., pp. 162, 164, 166, 169.
[56] Ibid., pp. 172, 173–74, 182–85, 189–91.
[57] Ibid., pp. 194, 197.
[58] Ibid., p. 201.

The State, a Public Part of the World

In contrast to his usual practice, Gentili does not offer a definition of the state.[59] This may be an indication of his concern to differentiate himself from the political philosophers, who since the time of Plato and Aristotle have devoted themselves to theorizing about the state and what happens within it. As he puts it in his introductory chapter to *De Jure Belli*,

> For the moralist, whether he treats of the private customs of individuals or aims at the highest good in some other way always confines himself within the city-state,[60] and rather limits himself to the foundations of the virtues than rears lofty structures.[61]

And when a political thinker has looked beyond his own state, so Gentili finds, it was for the purpose of establishing its own needs. An example comes readily to his mind:

> And although [our own Justinian] discussed the law of nature and of nations … as well as the cause of wars, prisoners, slaves, and some other topics relating to the subject: he nevertheless considered them all from the standpoint of his own state and explained them with reference to its requirements.[62]

Gentili refers to the state as a community 'joined together by common laws'.[63] But for the most part he takes the state as something given, and observations about it are little more than side-products of his larger concern – those 'lofty structures' neglected by the political philosophers. They throw light on three aspects of the state as part of his larger enterprise: its formal position and the roles of rulers and subjects.

The Formal Position of the State

The state with which Gentili is concerned may be Christian or non-Christian, Catholic or Protestant, as long as it is represented by a *princeps* or is constituted by a *princeps populus* – a prince or people who are sovereign: that is to say, they have no 'earthly judge' and acknowledge no 'judge or superior'. He uses the terms a 'free prince' or 'Sovereign',

[59] See, for example, his attempts at defining 'ambassador', in Gentili, *De Legationibus*, vol. 2, pp. 5–8; and 'law of nations' (pp. 8–11), 'war' (pp. 12–14) or 'peace' (p. 290) in Gentili, *De Jure Belli*, vol. 2.

[60] The Latin word is *civitas*, and a more appropriate translation in the present context would be 'state'.

[61] Gentili, *De Jure Belli*, vol. 2, p. 3.

[62] Ibid., p. 4.

[63] Ibid., p. 72.

or a 'free people' or occasionally 'sovereign people'.[64] And, like Vitoria, he includes in this category those princes or peoples who have religious, feudal or treaty ties to pope, emperor or some other ruler, provided that jurisdiction in and dominion over their realms or territories are theirs.[65]

To the *princeps* – prince or people – Gentili accords the title of 'public citizen', whose realm is a 'public part of the world'.[66] To the *princeps* he attaches the right and duty to act externally, that is, to maintain the law of nations. This includes actions such as going to war; making peace; sending and receiving ambassadors; entering into public agreements; helping another prince;[67] and redressing a wrong committed by another prince or, as he expresses it, acting as 'the magistrate of the law of nations'.[68]

The Use and Abuse of Power by Those Who Rule

Gentili notes that states can have different 'forms' – they may appear as kingdoms, republics or empires – and a particular state can change from one form to another, but he abstains from discussing the differences between them or indicating his preferred 'form'. Equally, he speaks of 'absolute or modified sovereignty' and of what he calls the 'magistrate' or prince of a 'free state' without telling his readers what he understands by these terms or hinting at any preference on his part.[69]

This disinterest may have its origin in the position he has taken up: he is not a political philosopher. It also may stem from his conception of power. Gentili identifies 'power' as 'that which we can do legitimately and without injustice'. 'Fullness of power' he explains as 'that which is good and praiseworthy', adding that, however 'absolute' power may be, 'nothing unseemly is admitted'.[70]

[64] Ibid., p. 15; Gentili, *De Legationibus Libri Tres*, vol. 1, *A Photographic Reproduction of the Edition of 1594*, intro. E. Nys, *The Classics of International Law*, New York: Oxford University Press, 1924, p. 9. Gentili's translator Laing translates *liber* as 'independent'. See Gentili, *De Legationibus*, vol. 2, p. 11.

[65] Gentili, *De Legationibus*, vol. 2, p. 11; Gentili, *De Jure Belli*, vol. 2, pp. 20–21. Those who do not enjoy the status of *princeps* internally are identified by Gentili as dependent states, subject states, subject peoples or petty sovereigns. 'The term territory', as Gentili explains in *De Jure Belli*, vol. 2, p. 384, 'is used both of land and water', that is, '[t]he adjacent part of the sea belongs to one's dominion'. However, the prince's dominion over this part of his territory is limited, as, according to Gentili, the sea is open to all as far as its use is concerned (pp. 90–92).

[66] See, for example, Gentili, *De Jure Belli*, vol. 2, pp. 15, 68, 102.

[67] Ibid., pp. 15–21, 67–73, 360–66; Gentili, *De Legationibus*, vol. 2, pp. 59–95, 96–126.

[68] See, for example, Gentili, *De Legationibus*, vol. 2, p. 108; Gentili, *De Jure Belli*, vol. 2, p. 92.

[69] Gentili, *De Jure Belli*, vol. 2, pp. 15, 20, 111, 117–19.

[70] Ibid., p. 227.

Given this view of power, it may not matter who wields it – an absolute ruler of a kingdom or a magistrate of a free republic. It may not even matter whether the ruler is legitimate or illegitimate. As he puts it,

> Each of them is master, and law perhaps is the basis of each one's sovereignty. A king rules over his subjects because they want him to do so, a tyrant in spite of them. Yet a tyrant is none the less a prince.[71]

For Gentili the important point seems to be to *what end* power is exercised. '[Power] is not for purposes of tyranny, but of administration.' He offers no detailed explanation as to where the one begins and the other ends, but points to the existence of a general criterion – the common good. As he formulates it variously, '[a] good ruler ... will always bear in mind that kingdoms were not made for kings, but kings for their kingdoms', or, 'governments are constituted, not for the advantage of any individual, but for that of the community'.[72]

There is no definition of the common good or advantage, but it may be close to what he calls 'reason of state', namely peace, security and justice, as the following propositions suggest: a prince desires to be 'the father of his people ... fountain head of peace and love',[73] and 'a principality' is meant to be 'a protection for mankind'.[74]

Thus, when thinking about the use or abuse of power, Gentili considers the final cause of power (the end) rather than its formal cause (the extent) – to use sixteenth-century language – although he does not leave the topic without admitting that '[p]ower is always under suspicion' and positing the following rule, borrowed mainly from Baldus de Ubaldis, the Italian legal scholar of the fourteenth century:

> A prince who makes a contract with his subjects is bound to them by natural law, by the law of nations, and by the civil law ... [T]he prince is indeed superior to every positive law, but ... he is subjected to reason, because he is a reasonable being; therefore his acts cannot prevail against reason and therefore he is bound by a compact.[75]

The Subject or Citizen: 'Participant in the Burdens and Honours of the State'

Although Gentili devotes considerable space to this topic, the discussion is not systematic; rather, his comments are scattered over many pages.

[71] Gentili, *De Legationibus*, vol. 2, p. 76.
[72] Gentili, *De Jure Belli*, vol. 2, pp. 76, 349, 372.
[73] See, for example, ibid., pp. 47, 100–02, 289–90, 353–55, 413.
[74] Ibid., pp. 349–50. The Latin word is *principatus*, the meaning of which is identified by the context as 'state'.
[75] Ibid., p. 378.

The compact between ruler and subject is mutually binding. The subject is entitled to just rule and protection by the ruler; in return, he is obliged 'to render loyal obedience'. Gentili does not explain the concept of loyal obedience; it seems to include the idea that the subject 'owes it to his prince and country to fight for them'; and it appears to extend to the principle that the subject, as a private citizen, has no right to revolt against an oppressive ruler. 'Rebels are enemies', for they 'secede from those under whose authority they are.'[76] However, he makes an exception for the subject who holds a public office. He may 'defend himself against a sovereign even by means of war'. The context is religious conflict, but the same holds in 'other cases of the same kind'. But the private citizen 'has no recourse but to follow the order of Christ and flee'.[77]

It becomes clear that this is not his last word: Gentili has a different answer to the problem. He refers to such a prince as a tyrant and permits his punishment by another prince; that is, he places the force to secure internal justice and security outside the state. As he puts it in the context of his chapter 'On Defending the Subjects of Another Against Their Sovereign',

> And unless we wish to make sovereigns exempt from the law and bound by no statutes and no precedents, there must also of necessity be some one to remind them of their duty and hold them in restraint.[78]

And the context makes it clear that that 'some one' is a 'sovereign'.

The links which the above discussion establishes between the inside of the state and its outside may be summarized as follows: he who has jurisdiction and dominion internally, the *princeps*, is public citizen externally; administration rather than tyranny is appropriate for the state which is a public part of the world; if tyranny exists inside, the outside is entitled to intervene.

The World, a Lofty Structure

Gentili's 'lofty structure' may be seen as a rather modern composition presenting an indefinite number of vertical divisions, four horizontal partitions and three distinct yet related materials which give cohesion to the whole. Gentili left his creation nameless; some commentators assert or imply that he attached the words *societas gentium* to it.[79]

[76] Ibid., pp. 50–52, 114, 371; Gentili, *De Legationibus*, vol. 2, p. 85.
[77] Gentili, *De Jure Belli*, vol. 2, pp. 52, 77.
[78] Ibid., pp. 69, 74–78.
[79] For example, Phillipson, 'Albericus Gentilis', p. 116; also his 'Introduction', in Gentili, *De Jure Belli*, vol. 2, p. 20a; K. R. Simmonds, 'Alberico Gentili at the Admiralty Bar,

The Frame

Identical at each of the four horizontal levels, the vertical divisions are constituted by the states or public parts of the world. They are basic to Gentili's construct: they have existed since the early age of mankind, and their continued existence appears to be taken for granted. Individual states may be born or die, but states in a sense are immortal.[80]

The four horizontal partitions reflect different features of their component parts, the states, resulting in different patterns or groupings of the basic units at each level. The first level presents the idea of formal equality. States may differ in many ways – Gentili especially mentions size, power, rank and religion – but from a legal point of view they are identical, having the same rights and the same obligations. As he puts it, there is no 'supervision of one sovereign by another', but 'one sovereign is said to be on an equality with another'.[81]

At the second level the idea of foreignness appears. It makes for a pattern which distinguishes between 'one's own state' and all the other states. Gentili's interest in 'examin[ing] this very matter of a foreign nation' is expressed in a lengthy discussion which may be abbreviated in the following way:

> [T]he law says ... that independent allies are foreign to us ... [T]he ... old grammarians teach that a foreigner is one whom we speak of as belonging to a foreign nation, to an alien land, as coming from another people ... Virgil [says] ... that every land which is free and not beneath our sceptre is foreign ... Those who are not subjects are foreigners ... A foreigner is a resident alien, not a citizen.[82]

The distinction between 'the self' and 'the others' cannot be blurred, neither by an individual moving from one country to another nor by two states concluding an alliance.

The third level shows the idea of foreignness from a different angle. Foreign states in relation to one's own state may be enemies, friends or neither of the two. Gentili defines the enemy as one 'who [has] officially

1605–1608', *Archiv des Voelkerrechts*, vol. 7, 1958–59, pp. 7, 8; and Molen, *Alberico Gentili and the Development of International Law*, p. 115.

[80] Gentili, *De Legationibus*, vol. 2, p. 51; Gentili, *De Jure Belli*, vol. 2, p. 414. There is no evidence in Gentili's work to support P. Guggenheim's assertion that 'Alberico Gentil [sic] sees the obligatory basis of the law of nations in the fact that, although the peoples have never been united, the evolution goes in the direction of a "supernational community" [communauté superétatique]'. P. Guggenheim, 'Contribution à l'Histoire des Sources du Droit des Gens' [Contribution to the History of the Sources of the Law of Nations], *Recueil des Cours*, vol. 94, II, 1958, p. 23.

[81] See, for example, Gentili, *De Jure Belli*, vol. 2, pp. 38–41, 74, 75, 323; Gentili, *De Legationibus*, vol. 2, pp. 11–12.

[82] Gentili, *Hispanicae Advocationis*, vol. 2, pp. 105–06.

declared war upon us, or upon whom we have officially declared war' and adds: '[An enemy] is the equal of his opponent.'[83] 'If friendship is contracted', he writes at the beginning of his chapter 'Of Friendship and Alliance', 'by this term something of no slight importance is designated.' And he explains what he means by this statement: states which agree to be friends do not thereby agree 'to become one body' and 'to regard all [their] possessions ... as common property' – but they agree to aid one another in case of necessity, whether they make this commitment explicit, as in an alliance providing for mutual aid in the event of one of them being 'wronged', or whether they leave it unspecified, for '[i]f this is not so, what is gained by that agreement and that title of friendship?'[84]

For those states which are neither enemies nor friends in relation to one's own state, Gentili does not have a name. They may act like enemies, friends or neutrals, although he does not use the latter term. It is at this level and in this context that his lofty structure displays an irregularity, for he argues that 'it is lawful neither to lend aid to infidels nor to accept aid from them'. There may be war with infidels and there may be peace, but no treaty of friendship or alliance. Gentili does not explain this restriction, which Vitoria does not impose, but he may have in mind his contention that 'nations are more closely united by a common religion than by the tie of any other law or by the terms of a treaty'.[85]

At the fourth level, states group themselves according to their religious beliefs, and Gentili finds that there is no state which has no religion. 'Name me one such nation, if you can.' The resultant pattern is characterized by diversity – all religions are present, having followings of various sizes – but this does not establish a relationship of dependence between groupings and their constituent parts. As he puts it, '[r]eligion is a relationship with God. Its laws are divine, that is between God and man; they are not human, namely, between man and man.'[86] Religion may form a link amongst states, but it does not affect their status of being sovereign.

With the fourth level, Gentili's structure has reached its upper extension. It stands for the idea of a plurality of states.

The Cohesive Materials

The first to be noted is the idea of human society. Gentili also calls it the 'association of the human race' or 'that great community' and he draws

[83] Gentili, *De Jure Belli*, vol. 2, pp. 12, 15.
[84] Ibid., pp. 387–88.
[85] Ibid., pp. 72, 402. For a discussion of this issue, see N. Malcolm, 'Alberico Gentili and the Ottomans', in Kingsbury and Straumann (eds), *The Roman Foundations of the Law of Nations*, pp. 139–45.
[86] Gentili, *De Jure Belli*, vol. 2, p. 41.

attention to the fact that all along the ages there have been men who believed that 'the whole world was, as it were, one commonwealth ... all men were one people and fellow citizens, being, so to speak, like a single herd grazing in a common pasture'.[87] Did not Aristotle call the world 'a greater city'? Philo, the Jewish-Hellenistic philosopher, held the view that '[the world] is a great state, having the form of one commonwealth'. Did not Tertullian, the theologian, likewise see the world as 'the one commonwealth of all, and the common city of all'? Gentili goes on to affirm that there is 'a bond of fellowship among men', and that 'the world forms one body'.

> [N]ature has made us all kindred, since we have the same origin and the same abode. She has implanted in us love for one another and made us inclined to union ... the nations of the earth are united through this human society.[88]

It is statements such as these that have led some commentators to see Gentili as a universalist. But it becomes clear that, as in the case of Vitoria, they are not to be taken literally. There is a certain natural and moral unity of mankind, but no political unity. Their world commonwealth is not a political institution, still less a political actor. Actions on behalf of the world community can be taken only by a public citizen, a sovereign.[89]

Most societies have their outsiders, and human society is no exception. Excluded from it, according to Gentili, are two categories of men: pirates and rebels. 'Pirates', he writes, 'are the common enemies of all mankind.' 'To pirates and wild beasts no territory offers safety.'

> How can men who have withdrawn from all intercourse with society and who ... have broken the compact of the human race, retain any privileges of law, which itself is nothing else than a compact of society?[90]

As for rebels, a subject on which he remains uncommunicative,[91] they are 'enemies to the extent of losing their citizenship', and they are not given 'the benefit of a new law, to wit, the law of nations'.[92]

The second material to bind together Gentili's structure is the law of nature and of nations. In the first chapter of *De Jure Belli*, he offers his

[87] Ibid., pp. 3, 67, 291.
[88] Ibid., pp. 67, 68.
[89] Ibid., pp. 15–21, 68.
[90] Ibid., p. 22; Gentili, *Hispanicae Advocationis*, vol. 2, p. 18; Gentili, *De Legationibus*, vol. 2, p. 79.
[91] As he explains in *De Jure Belli*, vol. 2, p. 321: 'Such rebels cannot be discussed in a few words; but I am not treating that subject, which belongs to civil law.'
[92] Ibid., pp. 23–24.

definition of the law of nations which, he claims, 'the authors and founders of our laws were unanimous in giving'.

> [T]he law of nations is that which is in use among all the nations of men, which native reason has established among all human beings, and which is equally observed by all mankind. Such a law is natural law. The agreement of all nations about a matter must be regarded as a law of nature.[93]

He does not define the law of nature, but it may be inferred that it is what native reason has established among all human beings. He goes on to ask 'what this natural reason is, or how is it made manifest', but his answer does not bring greater clarity. It is 'evident of itself' and cannot be further explained.[94] He also refers to 'a more elegant definition of the law of nations' 'that there are everywhere certain unwritten laws, not enacted by men, but given to them by God'. He refers to such laws as inborn, not learned but instinctive, but also as 'wrested, drawn and forced out of nature herself'.[95]

The last expression may derive from Gentili's struggling with the question, which also troubled Vitoria: why, if the law of nature is so evident, is there so much disagreement over what is lawful and right? One answer is to point to human imperfection: not only dullness, unscrupulousness and perversity, but even the wisest of the sages are 'but men, born to error and to disagree', even though 'it is the habit of philosophers and other wise men to speak according to the promptings of nature'.[96]

A second answer is suggested in a less well-known work, a collection of readings and letters, untranslated. Here he draws a distinction between 'the first' and 'the secondary or derived' law of nature and of nations. The first is concerned with 'the worship of God; the honouring of father and mother; the differentiation of peoples; the separation of dominions', and the second with 'wars, treaties, obligations, and other things of this kind', and it owes its status of being secondary or derived to the fact that 'from that separation of dominions have followed wars, treaties, etc.'[97] The first may well be generally agreed, the second more subject to dispute, but Gentili does not further explain the import of the distinction. It may be analogous to Vitoria's distinction between laws perceived directly or by a

[93] Ibid., p. 8.
[94] Ibid., p. 10.
[95] Ibid., pp. 9–10.
[96] Ibid., pp. 5–8, 11.
[97] Translated from *Lectiones et Epistolae …* [Readings and Letters …], Latin text in Molen, *Alberico Gentili and the Development of International Law*, pp. 114, 115. See also Gentili, *De Jure Belli*, vol. 2, p. 331.

simple inference and those arrived at by a longer chain of reasoning, and thus more prone to dispute.

Gentili's definition of the law of nations has been criticized for its lack of clarity.[98] His two formulations bring together a number of different elements; his exposition is rather discursive – not a rigorous definition, but a general conception. As such, however, it is coherent and provides a foundation for his analysis. He very rarely departs from it, on one occasion proposing a distinction between the law of nature and the law of nations, but he never returns to it.[99]

He fills out his general description of the law by giving an account of its origin and how it came to be developed. God gave the law to men when they needed it: '[T]he law of nations is a portion of the divine law, which God left with us after our sin'.[100] Men knew when they transgressed it. Not only the words of good and wise men, but 'the actions of great and good men' were in accordance with the promptings of nature.

Good and wise men were not the property of any particular people, but the inclination to do what ought to be done according to natural reason existed in all peoples. The observance of this law everywhere was not the result of a single decision, 'not ... that all nations actually came together', but it was the manifestation of natural reason over time and space. The law of nations established itself like a custom and, as such, it is binding upon all, even if not everyone has agreed to it.[101]

The third material to give cohesion to Gentili's creation is the principle of good faith, which stands in opposition to 'treachery', 'trickery', and 'deception'. It permeates all dealings between princes, states and their

98 Gentili's 'lack of clarity' in his 'general definition of the law of nations' is underlined by a scholar such as C. von Kaltenborn, *Die Vorlaeufer des Hugo Grotius auf dem Gebiete des Jus naturae et gentium sowie der Politik im Reformationszeitalter* [The Predecessors of Hugo Grotius in the Study of the Law of Nature and of Nations as well as Politics in the Age of the Reformation] (Leipzig: Gustav Mayer, 1848, reprinted Frankfurt am Main: Sauer & Anvermann, 1965), p. 231; nevertheless Kaltenborn is prepared to credit Gentili with the distinction of being 'the first more important author of the modern law of nations' (p. 228). For a more positive assessment of Gentili's definition, see J. Waldron, '*Ius Gentium*: A Defence of Gentili's Equation of the Law of Nations and the Law of Nature,' in Kingsbury and Straumann (eds), *The Roman Foundations of the Law of Nations*. It is puzzling that Waldron initially sees Gentili's natural law/law of nations as positive law, but he goes on to qualify this, referring to its 'Janus-faced status ... descriptive and normative', making for 'a rich and textured source of both moral and legal insight' (p. 291).

99 '[N]ot only is the civil law an agreement and a bond of union among citizens, but the same is true of the law of nations as regards nations, and the law of nature as regards mankind'. Gentili, *De Jure Belli*, vol. 2, p. 124.

100 Gentili, *De Jure Belli*, vol. 2, pp. 7–8.

101 Ibid., p. 8. This is a point emphasized by C. L. Lange, 'Histoire de la Doctrine Pacifique et de son Influence sur le Développement du Droit International' [History of the Doctrine of Peace and Its Influence on the Development of International Law], *Recueil des Cours*, vol. 13, III, 1926, p. 225.

representatives, in times of peace and in war. Good faith constitutes 'the essence of the law of nations'.[102] It may equally be seen as a prerequisite for the observance of the law of nations: a norm so basic that to breach it undermines the whole structure of norms of the law of nations, and for this reason it is singled out as the third strand of the cohesive materials.

The presence of these three cohesive materials means that the normal or natural state or condition of Gentili's lofty structure is peace which, as he agrees with St Augustine, is 'ordered harmony': '[O]rder is the proper distribution of things, which ... is the nature of justice.'[103]

With this observation, Gentili's 'world', so far as it concerns its form or appearance, is complete. The activities to which it gives rise – Gentili singles out commerce, diplomacy and war – are discussed in the next three sections of this chapter.

Commerce as a Link

Regarding the origin of commerce, Gentili is not very communicative. All that he is prepared to say is that it was before the institution of embassies which was 'after the separation of the nations, the foundation of kingdoms, the partition of dominions';[104] and he does not hint at which came first – commerce or war. His indefiniteness in relation to time is offset by his certainty regarding purpose – a certainty which he shares with other thinkers. Their argument may be presented in the following way.

God made the earth one, for men to see. Gentili's source is William Camden's *Britannia*:

> [T]here is no land so remote, no island so secluded, that the sight does not reach it from some other land ... [T]his was so planned by God, in order that men might have this unity before their eyes and mutual access on every hand.[105]

He then qualifies this a little: 'This applies well to nearly all parts of the earth.' But although God made the earth one, he did not distribute its products equally: 'Here the crops of grain are richest, there grapes grow best.' A reason for this natural inequality is offered by Seneca, the Roman statesman and philosopher: 'Commodities are distributed over different regions, in order that it may be necessary for mortals to have commerce with one another.' This suggests that, while one purpose of commerce is

[102] See, for example, Gentili, *De Jure Belli*, vol. 2, pp. 145, 191, 361; Gentili, *De Legationibus*, vol. 2, pp. 87, 162. On the principle of good faith in Gentili's writings, see L. Ehrlich, 'L'Interprétation des Traités' [Interpretation of Treaties], *Recueil des Cours*, vol. 24, IV, 1928, pp. 12–15.

[103] Gentili, *De Jure Belli*, vol. 2, p. 290.

[104] Gentili, *De Legationibus*, vol. 2, p. 51.

[105] Gentili, *De Jure Belli*, vol. 2, p. 89.

to bring about a more even distribution of the riches of the earth, and it has another, higher purpose which Gregoras, the Byzantine historian, states more fully:

> But if nature had given everything equally to all men, the reasons for loving one another would readily be destroyed; for it is through this inequality that we ask and give in turn without ceasing. This is the law of friendship and its strongest bond.[106]

Thus the end and aim of commerce lies not only in making the world more 'complete', but also in linking it more closely. '[C]ommerce', Gentili writes, 'is in accordance with the law of nations' which was devised 'to bring men together'.[107]

For commerce to attain its purpose it is necessary that nobody exclude himself from participation in the interchange of things. Gentili quotes Gregoras again:

> If anyone is so greedy that he does not wish the good things of life to be distributed, he will have to take heed that he does not ... establish a law upon the earth which sanctions every kind of wickedness and does away wholly with all intercourse and commerce.[108]

It is equally necessary that nobody be excluded from taking part. Gentili mentions the case of the ancient Megarians who were 'forbidden all intercourse and commerce and kept from the harbours of the Athenians'. Their complaint, in his view, was just. The Athenians acted 'contrary to the law of nations'. He also refers to the non-Christians of his own day and states his position unequivocally: 'Commerce with infidels is not forbidden.'[109]

The right and duty of all peoples to participate in the interchange which 'makes the completeness of the universe' becomes, at a different level of the argument, the 'right of way' or the duty not to close the lines of communication. Gentili insists: 'All routes are free by nature' and by nature the use of harbours and the sea is open to all. His source is Hermes Trismegistus, the ancient Egyptian god of wisdom: '[I]n harbours, navigation, communication, and accommodation is the strongest bond of human interdependence.'[110]

There is one constraint which he places on commerce: it must not do harm to the state, for 'the principle on which states are governed' is to

[106] Ibid., p. 88.
[107] Gentili, *De Legationibus*, vol. 2, p. 119.
[108] Gentili, *De Jure Belli*, vol. 2, p. 88.
[109] Ibid., also p. 401. Megara was an important city-state from the eighth century BC, with Sicilian and Black Sea colonies.
[110] Ibid., pp. 86–91.

avoid suffering harm. Reason of state may take precedence over reason of commerce in cases such as these: 'The law of trade is just; but that of maintaining one's safety is more so. The former is a law of nations, the latter of nature.'[111]

In times of peace, a state may prohibit the importation of certain goods if they present a risk to the physical, mental or moral health of its members; it may forbid the exportation of a commodity if it needs it itself; for reasons of security it may refuse access to certain parts of its territory. In times of war, a state which is engaged in a just war may prevent commerce from aiding its enemies.[112]

Apart from these and similar instances – limited in time and/or extent – the interference with commerce constitutes a denial of a 'privilege of nature', a violation of the law of nature and of nations, and furnishes a just cause for war.[113] Gentili leaves his readers in no doubt that commerce is an essential activity within his lofty structure – the world.

Diplomacy as a Link

The term 'diplomacy' had not yet been coined when Gentili wrote about that branch of politics which subsequently came to be defined as:

> The management of international relations by negotiation; the method by which these relations are adjusted and managed by ambassadors and envoys; the business or art of the diplomatist; skill or address in the conduct of international intercourse and negotiations.[114]

Gentili uses the term *legatio*, which the Latin dictionary and his translators render as 'embassy', and he does not always assign the same meaning to it. When, for example, he speaks of sending or receiving an embassy, undertaking or being on an embassy, the word 'mission' comes readily to one's mind; when he writes '[t]he term embassy, though strictly connoting a public function, is used both of public and private negotiations', he denotes the substance of the enterprise; and when he says 'embassies assembled from all parts', one thinks first and foremost of the people engaged in the enterprise.[115] So, the point which Harold Nicolson makes

[111] Ibid., p. 101. This is one of the rare instances where Gentili distinguishes between the two laws, but not in the way suggested in note 99 to this chapter.

[112] Ibid., pp. 87–90, 101–03, 267.

[113] Ibid., pp. 86, 90.

[114] C. T. Onions (ed.), *The Shorter Oxford English Dictionary on Historical Principles*, 3rd edn, vol. 1 (Oxford: Clarendon Press, 1967), p. 514. According to the same source, the term 'diplomacy' was coined in 1796.

[115] Gentili, *De Legationibus*, vol. 2, pp. 14, 18.

about the term 'diplomacy' can also be made about its predecessor, the term 'embassy', to wit: it denotes 'several quite different things'.[116]

In terms of the purpose of the institution, Gentili distinguishes five 'types' of embassy, only two of which remain significant.

Purposes

'The embassy for the transaction of business' arose, he has no doubt, after the formation of states and the establishment of commerce. He is even prepared to be slightly more precise about the age of this embassy: '[W]e certainly shall not ... abandon the view of those who set it down to the credit of Belus', the founder of Babylon, in 4000 BC.

But if Belus was the 'visible reason', necessity was its underlying cause:

> But since it was inevitable that obligations and negotiations should arise between organizations having such reciprocity of rights as exists between nations, commonwealths and kings, and since those organizations are either unwilling or, as often happens, unable to meet (certainly states can not meet), it was absolutely necessary ... that others should be appointed, who by representing the organizations would be able to transact the necessary business. These representatives, moreover, had to be persons ... not subject to him to whom they are sent. Otherwise the distinction of sovereignties would not be kept intact.[117]

The business with which this embassy is charged consists of 'peaceful negotiations' and 'negotiations pertaining to war'.[118]

The most recent of all embassies is the 'time or resident embassy':

> By a time embassy or time ambassadors, I mean those who are sent on no specific or definite business but for a period of time sometimes prescribed, sometimes not, with the understanding that while they are on the embassy they shall be responsible for the negotiation and performance of everything which during the whole period may happen to be in the interest of the person sending them.[119]

It is Gentili's opinion that the resident embassy goes back to Roman times. Rome accommodated 'embassies of the provincials and the allied nations' for a period of time, and the custom became more widespread under the popes, 'for on their manifesting a tendency to have their own ambassadors everywhere, other princes imitated the practice'.

[116] H. Nicolson, *Diplomacy*, 3rd edn (London and New York: Oxford University Press, 1965), p. 13.
[117] Gentili, *De Legationibus*, vol. 2, pp. 51, 52.
[118] Ibid., p. 14.
[119] Ibid., p. 14.

The time or resident embassy owes its existence, not to necessity, but to a 'good reason':

[O]ccasions for negotiation arise so frequently between princes that it would be more inconvenient to keep sending ambassadors than to maintain them always at one another's court.[120]

The categories no longer relevant include the embassy of courtesy, to offer congratulations or condolences; the free embassy, for one engaged in private business but given the status of ambassador; and the sacred embassy, the messenger sent by a God or to a God on some sacred mission.[121]

Law

The age of the various kinds of embassies, and the reasons for them, point to the existence of a law relating to embassies:[122]

[I]f all antiquity, if Greece and Rome in so many ways ... attest that embassies enjoyed the highest honor among them, are we not justified in claiming a like distinction for them among ourselves and among all nations, now and forever?[123]

Of the rights which he ascribes to this law, three are especially instructive. First, the right to send embassies is enjoyed by all public citizens, that is, independent princes or states, and 'ought not to be disturbed on account of religious differences'. Dependent princes or states have certain limited rights. Rebels, pirates and brigands never have this right, but it may be conceded in a situation like civil war, when 'each faction lays claim ... to the whole organization of the state'.[124]

Second, to the right to send embassies corresponds the duty to receive them. The exceptions which Gentili grants to this 'eternal law' are of two kinds. A state may refuse to admit embassies if they mean interference with the 'transaction of business', slighting of the 'dignity of the state', or 'danger of any kind'. These are what he calls 'adequate reasons'. Their justification:

[U]nless one had the privilege of forbidding the coming of embassies, considerable confusion would be introduced by this alone into the law of nations,

[120] Gentili, *De Legationibus*, vol. 2, pp. 52–53, 99.
[121] Ibid., pp. 9–10, 18–19, 20–21.
[122] Gentili's translator Laing translates *jus legationum* for most of the time as 'right of embassies', occasionally as 'law of embassies'.
[123] Gentili, *De Legationibus*, vol. 2, pp. 52–53.
[124] Ibid., pp. 76, 79, 82, 85–90. Gentili never explains whether he sees a link between 'the rebel' and 'civil war'.

which insists and orders that control over one's own affairs shall be final and inviolable.[125]

'Intrinsic reasons' constitute the other kind of exception. A state may refuse to admit those embassies which are not necessary for the 'intercourse of nations', that is, the free embassy, the embassy of courtesy, and the resident embassy.[126]

And finally, ambassadors are inviolable. This, according to Gentili, is the most majestic and prestigious principle of all. It holds irrespective of whether ambassadors find themselves 'under the laws of allies' or 'amid the weapons of the enemy'. Its disregard invites disaster. He cites from the records of history to make the point:

> [T]he sacrilegious treatment of ambassadors was either punished with the utmost severity, or was given such unfavourable publicity that the loss of prestige which resulted may be regarded as more serious than all the rest of the damage.

This reaction, he submits, is proof of the strict enforcement of the principle's observance. And inviolable are not only the ambassadors, but all those who accompany them, and the ambassadors' effects.[127]

Gentili raises a number of specific issues in order to show how far the principle of inviolability extends. For example, it is his view that:

- It holds even if an ambassador is suspected of having been sent for the purpose of spying. The country to which he goes may refuse to admit him or, if it has admitted him, may expel him, but it may not do harm to him. Suspicion is not sufficient.[128]
- It holds even if an ambassador is found to be planning to commit an offence. The case which he discusses in detail is the ambassador who conspires against the life of the prince to whom he has been dispatched. '[D]ismissal is the proper treatment', he rules, for 'the mere consideration of plans' is not sufficient to justify doing violence to the ambassador.[129]
- It ceases to hold if an ambassador is found to have committed an offence. Gentili distinguishes between an offence which constitutes a violation of the 'legal obligations in the country of his embassy' and an offence against the law of nations. While in both cases the law according to which the ambassador is to be judged is the law of nations,[130]

125 Ibid., pp. 69, 70.
126 Ibid., pp. 94–95. Gentili mentions that Henry VII, for example, did not allow resident ambassadors into his realm for fear that they were spies. Gentili, *De Legationibus*, vol. 2, p. 170.
127 Ibid., pp. 59, 96, 101, 103–04.
128 Ibid., pp. 65–68.
129 Ibid., pp. 113–14.
130 Ibid., pp. 97, 106, 108, 111, 113, 123.

in the former case – he mentions business and lawsuits – the measure of the punishment is provided by the principle 'like for like', and the judge of the ambassador, the magistrate of the law of nations, is the prince of the country of his embassy.[131] In the case of an offence against the law of nations – he refers to the ambassador who injures the prince of the country of his embassy by word or deed – the ambassador must be surrendered or punished 'with great severity by [his] own nation'. 'I hold', he writes, 'that an ambassador … should be put to death or be surrendered, if he has inflicted even the slightest injury upon the sovereign.'[132]

- Lastly, it is his view that a prince who does violence to an ambassador should not hope for the safety of his own ambassador.[133]

As the above examples indicate, the principle of inviolability extends far, but not so far as to protect those who themselves violate it.

Gentili's treatise *De Legationibus* provides a comprehensive account of the institution of diplomacy at the time, and also makes clear that he regards diplomacy as one of the central aspects of the relations among states, very much as Wight and Bull see it as an essential institution of international society.

The Question of War

War, which Gentili defines as 'a just and public contest of arms',[134] has a remote origin. '[W]ho doubts', he says in *De Legationibus*, 'that wars occurred soon after the separation of the nations'? In *De Jure Belli* he identifies its origin as necessity:

> [W]ar has its origin in necessity; and this necessity arises because there cannot be judicial processes between supreme sovereigns or free peoples unless they themselves consent, since they acknowledge no judge or superior.[135]

The necessity must be 'real' and 'actual', which means that unless an attempt is made first to resolve the conflict by the use of argument – Gentili points to the many cases of arbitration that every age is known to have adopted in preference to war – war cannot be said to be necessary.[136]

131 Ibid., pp. 107, 108–10, 125.
132 Ibid., pp. 98, 113, 122.
133 Ibid., pp. 72–74.
134 Gentili, *De Jure Belli*, vol. 2, p. 12. Gentili cannot mean this literally, and purely descriptively: he goes on to insist that war must be just, and to distinguish war from brigandage (pp. 13–14). He sees war as a legitimate conflict between states, regulated by generally accepted rules.
135 Gentili, *De Legationibus*, vol. 2, p. 52; Gentili, *De Jure Belli*, vol. 2, p. 15.
136 Gentili, *De Jure Belli*, vol. 2, pp. 15–16.

The fact that the necessity of war is admitted into his lofty structure does not mean that every war is so admitted. War as the arbiter of last resort must be just, that is, 'lawful' and 'perfect in all its parts', or, as he also says, 'we hold the firm belief that questions of war ought to be settled in accordance with the law of nations, which is the law of nature'.[137] And necessity is only one of the elements which go into demarcating a just from an unjust war.

In presenting his idea of the war which is 'perfect in all its parts', Gentili distinguishes four causes which, borrowing from Aristotle, he calls the efficient cause, the material cause, the formal cause, and the final cause.[138]

Efficient Cause

The efficient cause is the *princeps*. For a war to have a claim to justice, it must be undertaken by a sovereign: a public citizen, a 'free prince' or 'free people'. '[P]rivate individuals, subject peoples, and petty sovereigns' have no right to resort to war as 'they can obtain their legal rights before their superiors' tribunal'.[139]

Material Cause

As for the material cause of war, Gentili distinguishes between divine, natural and human causes.

Divine Causes Divine causes are treated with scepticism. Men claim, he says, that they fight a war on the command of their god, but 'we must go to the root of things and consider whether their religious feeling in these instances is correct'. 'Religious feeling' is not a just cause for war: '[N]o man's rights are violated by a difference in religion, nor is it lawful to make war because of religion.' And he adds: '[I]f men in another state live in a manner different from that which we follow in our own state, they surely do us no wrong.'[140]

Natural Causes Regarding natural causes of war – his main concern under this heading – his basic position is that 'no war is natural', for 'by nature' men are all akin: 'If man's desires are boundless and there is not sufficient glory and power to satisfy them, that is not a law

137 Ibid., pp. 5, 13.
138 Ibid., p. 35.
139 Ibid., pp. 15, 20.
140 Ibid., pp. 37, 41.

of nature, but a defect.'[141] While rejecting the idea that any war can be natural, Gentili admits, as just, wars undertaken 'under Nature's guidance'. This category includes defensive war and offensive war.

Defensive war

- 'Necessary defence', which he defines as 'the repelling of force by force', is the most generally accepted of all rights.[142]
- 'Defence on grounds of expediency', which he identifies as a war made 'through fear that we may ourselves be attacked'. The cause of fear must be justified, that is, suspicion is not enough – a condition which, he admits, is not always easily determinable, but he offers a guideline – powerful and ambitious princes should be opposed: 'Do not all men with complete justice oppose on one side the Turks and on the other the Spaniards who are planning and plotting universal dominion?'[143]
- 'Defence for the sake of honour' which, in his language, is a war undertaken for 'the sake of others'.

'The other' may be a prince, and help may justly be offered on the principle that 'nature has established among men kinship'. The tie of natural kinship is at times reinforced by an alliance, a treaty, a common religion, a common border or the fear that if the 'other's' enemy is a great power, it may become even greater if it succeeds in conquering the 'other'.[144]

'The other' may be a people which suffers from its unjust and cruel prince. Help may justly be rendered on the same principle as above: '[T]he subjects of others do not seem to me to be outside of that kinship of nature.' Sometimes, necessity and expediency add support to honour as the reason for helping 'to ward off injury'. As he observes in the case of English help to the Dutch against their Spanish rulers, 'if that bulwark of Europe ... should be broken down by the Spaniards, nothing would be left as a bar against their violence.'[145]

Offensive war

- Offensive war for reasons of 'necessity'. It is Gentili's view that necessity may force a people and its prince to make war if, for example, they cannot otherwise maintain their existence, or an emergency compels

[141] Ibid., p. 54, 56.
[142] Ibid., pp. 58, 59.
[143] Ibid., pp. 61–64. See also the discussion of universalism earlier in the chapter.
[144] Ibid., pp. 67, 71–73.
[145] Ibid., pp. 74–78.

them to leave their country and find a place somewhere else.[146] Such a war is just.

- Offensive war for reasons of 'expediency'. Here he has in mind the right of a state to undertake a war in response to a wrong received. It is 'perfectly clear', he writes, that a state may avenge a wrong suffered at the hand of another state if the latter fails to right the wrong itself, for example, by returning wrongfully seized property.[147]
- Offensive war for 'natural reasons', by which he means the right to go to war if a 'privilege of nature' is refused, for example, the right of way, access to harbours or the right to engage in commerce and trade.[148]
- Offensive war for 'honourable reasons', that is, 'in behalf of others'. If a people sins against the laws of nature – one of Gentili's examples refers to the Indians being punished by war by the Spaniards for killing innocent human beings for the purpose of eating them – it is just to make war on it.[149] Gentili, then, concedes a just material cause of war not only to the sovereign who fights a war of defence; he also grants it to the prince or people who undertakes an offensive war, provided the latter is fought in defence of a right which accords with natural or human law.

A major consequence of his approach is that he is prepared to consider that a just material cause may be present on both sides. In support of his view he advances three reasons:

- Princes not being 'cognizant of that purest and truest form of justice' – divine justice – can aim at no more than justice as man understands it, and if they think they act in pursuit of this justice, they cannot be called unjust.
- The prince being obliged to help 'allies, friends, kindred [and] neighbours', thereby 'justly rouses against himself the arms of the adversary whom he is attacking'.
- Justice, like other virtues, is not 'limited to a point'. One side may have a just cause, for example, defending its right to engage in commerce, and the other may have a still more just cause, such as securing the country's safety.[150]

This appears to suggest that in most cases the decision to wage war is justified; indeed, he goes so far as to claim that '[i]n general, it may be

[146] Ibid., pp. 79–82.
[147] Ibid., pp. 83–85.
[148] Ibid., pp. 86–92.
[149] Ibid., pp. 122–27.
[150] Ibid., pp. 31–33. The example is taken from p. 101.

true in nearly every kind of dispute, that neither of the two disputants is unjust'.[151]

Human Causes Human reasons form Gentili's third and last category of material causes of war. It is his contention that the violation of a 'man-made' law may constitute a just cause of war. Amongst other examples he mentions the breaking of a treaty and, more prominently, rape, a crime which he considers to have been responsible, for example, for the 'undying enmity between the Greeks and Barbarians'.[152]

Formal Cause

Both the requirement that a war be just in all its parts and the possibility that a just material cause may be present on both sides make it essential that the formal cause of war – the conduct of war – be just. As Gentili variously puts it, '[o]f all our laws … that one seems to me the clearest which grants the rights of war to both contestants'; or, with Cicero: 'In war an enemy retains his religion and his rights.'[153]

The whole of the second book of *De Jure Belli* is devoted to the question of justice in war. A few examples must suffice to document the general theme:

- The prince who has decided to make war must inform the prince against whom the war is to be made of his intention: 'This is the voice of God. This is natural law, that before you take hostile steps, you first utterly renounce the friendship or common tie which you have with the men in question.'[154]
- Poisoning is a weapon not to be used against the enemy. His nineteenth, and last, reason in a long argument is that 'war ought to be limited to things which it is within human power to resist'.[155]
- '[T]he rights of humanity and the laws of war' require that those who have surrendered be spared.[156]
- Farmers and religious men are safe, for 'there can be no war with unarmed men'; traders, travellers and other people who happen to sojourn with the enemy are safe, for they are not the enemy. Only if

[151] Ibid., p. 31.
[152] Ibid., pp. 93, 95.
[153] Gentili, *De Jure Belli*, vol. 2, pp. 33, 131.
[154] Ibid., p. 132.
[155] Ibid., p. 158.
[156] Ibid., p. 216.

they help the enemy do these people become the enemy and are treated as such.[157]

- It is the law of nations and of humanity 'to bury the dead or to turn them over to their countrymen when they ask for them'.[158]

Final Cause

The fourth ingredient of Gentili's idea of the just war is the just conclusion of war – the final cause or end of war: peace. As noted earlier, peace is defined by Gentili in a general way as 'ordered harmony', 'the proper distribution of things'; when he applies it to the conclusion of war, it becomes 'the orderly settlement of war'. He adds: '[O]ur definition ... has the provision about justice, which is what we seek in this cessation of war, along with order and the assignment of his own to each man.'[159]

Gentili distinguishes between a situation where, at the end of war, there is a victor and a vanquished, in which case the establishment of peace is the responsibility of the victor alone; and a situation where arms are laid down by agreement and war is settled by both sides.

In the first situation, the victor assumes the role of judge and should, if the peace which he makes is to be lasting, take into account not only his own rights, but also those of the vanquished. The punishment which he decides and which is intended to achieve 'solace for injury and security for the future' should depend, not on what he is 'able' to do, but on 'the character of the persons concerned, the nature of the offence, the time, the age, the sex'. Too much severity may not be in the interests of peace:

> For one who has been injured beyond his deserts will not be tranquil, but will continually desire revenge; and one who is forced to accept pitiless conditions will carry the burden only so long as he is under the necessity of obedience.[160]

Too little severity may, at times, not be conducive to a lasting peace either. A vanquished enemy who has done evil in the past and would do evil in the future because of his 'inclination' must not be given the opportunity to do so. Gentili quotes Lentulus, a Roman commander: 'Since we cannot put an end to your perfidy, we will above all break your power.'[161]

The third book of *De Jure Belli* reveals the many questions which may come up for consideration and judgment by the victor when he makes

157 Ibid., pp. 262–63, 266–67.
158 Ibid., pp. 122–27.
159 Ibid., p. 290.
160 Ibid., pp. 291, 293, 296, 353, 354.
161 Ibid., p. 357.

peace: the payment of expenses and losses of war; the imposition of tribute; the acquisition of territory; the removal of treasures and ornaments; the sacking of cities; the punishment of the enemy's leaders and soldiers; the internal organization of the state; and particular aspects of it such as religion, language and customs. When making peace, Gentili writes: '[T]he victor may, without violating the laws of nature, do anything which tends to make his victory firm and ensure a peace which is just to himself and to the vanquished.'[162]

The idea of justice is of equal importance in the other situation: the settlement of war by mutual agreement. Whatever the decisions which enter the agreement – Gentili discusses questions relating to the laws of each party; territories; towns and buildings; prisoners; arms and armies; friendship and alliance – they need to be based on the principle of 'right and justice' in order to achieve a peace which is 'perpetual and assured'.[163]

Assessment

Although Vitoria and Gentili stand in different intellectual traditions, their thinking on the just war appears to be remarkably similar. They address the same range of questions and there are few differences in their answers: Vitoria does not endorse preventive war; Gentili does not include preventing the preaching of the Christian religion.[164] But Gentili does not emphasize preventive war to the extent that Tuck's interpretation would lead one to expect.

Perhaps the most significant difference is on the question whether war can be just on both sides. Vitoria's prince, knowing that only one side can have a truly just cause, must ponder the matter deeply and consult the views of wise men; he takes account of the possible costs and goes to war only with extreme reluctance. Gentili does not challenge the prince to question the justice of his cause, at least not very deeply. He must first seek to resolve disputes peacefully, but if this fails, he knows that there is normally a just cause for fighting. There is a major difference in the two thinkers' attitude to war: the Erasmian strand in Vitoria is absent in Gentili; his tone is matter-of-fact; he appears to see war as quite normal.

162 Ibid., p. 359.
163 Ibid., p. 361.
164 However, Neil Malcolm points out that although Vitoria does not refer explicitly to pre-emptive war, he permits war to 'ward off' an injury. 'His thinking may well have included the notion of "averting" in the sense of preventing.' Malcolm, 'Alberico Gentili and the Ottomans', p. 136.

Moderation

The idea of moderation is easily traceable in Gentili's work. Sometimes it remains implicit, but is stated with unusual rhetorical force in the following quotation from St Bernard:

> The unique power and inmost marrow of all the virtues is moderation. Hold to the mean, if you do not wish to lose moderation; a middle course is the seat of moderation and moderation is virtue.[165]

However, it becomes clear that this is not quite his own position. In his discussion of the qualities of the ideal ambassador, as we have seen, temperance needs to be combined with prudence, which 'directs and regulates all the virtues'. In particular temperance, or moderation, is not to be equated with restraint. 'To spare is not always a sign of compassion, but sometimes is a fault or due to cowardice.'[166] What is indispensable is discretion (i.e. prudence): 'Discretion … is the mistress of zeal and mercy. When they are blind in the eye of discretion, men are wont to seize upon one or the other of these and to occupy the extremes.'[167] This appears to express the essentials of his line of thought. Understood in this sense, moderation consists in observing 'the proper limit'.[168]

The proper limit, as one discovers when one examines the particular instances to which he applies the general idea, may be drawn at more than one level. In fact, it is possible to distinguish three situations. In the first place, to be moderate means to refrain from, or to limit, the use of force. For example, in Book One of *De Jure Belli*, Gentili argues for arbitration in place of war, and submits examples drawn from all periods of history in order that:

> [T]hose who avoid this kind of contest by arbitration and resort at once to … force, may understand that they are setting their faces against justice, humanity, and good precedent.[169]

In Book Two of the same work, as noted above, he insists that a justly conducted war demands that the innocent – children, women, farmers, religious people, traders and travellers – be spared. But he stops short of endorsing Polybius's view that 'it is mad and utterly raving' if the enemy's temples, colonnades and statues are destroyed, for these things 'yield no profit in themselves and [their] destruction does no damage to the

165 Gentili, *De Jure Belli*, vol. 2, p. 294.
166 Ibid.
167 Gentili, *De Legationibus*, vol. 2, p. 166; Gentili, *De Jure Belli*, vol. 2, p. 228.
168 Gentili, *De Jure Belli*, vol. 2, p. 295.
169 Ibid., pp. 15–16.

enemy'.[170] If the enemy has destroyed one's own temples and the like, it is legitimate to retaliate in kind, or he will not be deterred from such actions in the future.[171] Nonetheless, the general tenor of his discussion is to condemn needless destruction.

Second, to be moderate means not to go beyond what is lawful and just. For example, the punishment of an ambassador who is discovered to conspire against the life of the prince to whom he has been sent must be expulsion and not death. As noted above, this is the position which Gentili takes up in *De Legationibus*, and he offers the following reason for it:

> We commit a grave offense against the law of nations, if in our efforts to repel violence we go beyond the proper limit. To put to death such an ambassador would be to show cruelty far transcending the requirements of the case.[172]

In *De Jure Belli* he argues that to kill the captured leaders of the enemy, unless there is a just reason, amounts to 'severity' which 'ought not to be shown'. If there is such a reason, death may be 'approved', but torture must not be applied: 'Who will defend the Spaniards when they inflicted a wretched death upon some great kings of the New World?'[173]

Finally, to be moderate means not to go as far as what would be lawful and just. For example, Gentili concludes his chapter 'Of Cruelty toward Prisoners' in Book Two of *De Jure Belli* by saying:

> But surely it is fitting to restrain the violence of war as much as possible ... [E]ven if it is allowed you to do harm, the permission must yet be used with moderation. Also if it has been allowed you as an arbiter to impair our rights, you must do so with moderation and to a slight degree.[174]

In his chapter 'Of the Vengeance of the Victor' in Book Three of *De Jure Belli* he argues that there is a limit to punishment and the question ought to be, not what the vanquished deserve, but what befits the victor. Quoting the Greek historian Polybius, he writes: '[T]hose who are endowed with minds, when they decide to punish the enemy, do not first consider what he may suffer in accordance with his deserts, but rather what they themselves may do with propriety.' For example, it is not against the law to pillage churches and take sacred objects, but, as he notes: 'I should prefer to show respect to moderation and honour, and to refrain from doing what is permitted by the laws.'[175]

170 Ibid., pp. 255, 261–63, 270.
171 Ibid., pp. 271–72.
172 Gentili, *De Legationibus*, vol. 2, p. 112.
173 Gentili, *De Jure Belli*, vol. 2, pp. 322, 324–25.
174 Ibid., p. 239.
175 Ibid., pp. 292, 313.

Gentili thus measures the idea of moderation in terms of what is lawful and just, and this in turn depends on the particular instance under consideration. It normally makes for restraint, but not in all circumstances.

Conclusion

Gentili offers the first systematic presentation of major features of the idea of international society as envisaged by Gierke, Wight and Bull. Erasmus had expressed an outlook on international relations which accords with this conception, and Vitoria had offered a powerful sketch of its central claims, but the idea is not expressed explicitly: it has to be discerned by the reader, brought to the surface as it were. In Gentili, the sketch is elaborated into a tolerably systematic account of three of the five institutions which Bull sees as essential to international society: diplomacy, international law, and war.[176] And he alone of the four thinkers studied here brings in the balance of power, Bull's fourth institution. In the case of international law, although he does not theorize about its role in international relations, his discussion amounts to a depiction of how it functions in practice, through providing the rules which regulate international conduct. His discussion of the balance of power, although brief, draws attention to its role in maintaining the states system through opposing attempts to establish a universal political order. As to Bull's fifth institution, the special role of the great powers, the states system had not yet developed to the point where this could be realized, or even envisaged.

Gentili cannot match Erasmus's eloquence or Vitoria's philosophical grounding of the law of nations, but the practical jurist can claim a place in the history of international thought as the first to offer an explicit account of the idea of international society – what might be termed its phenomenology. He makes no claim to present its philosophical foundations, and thus may have little to offer the political philosopher,[177] but to the international relations specialist he is surely a major figure. But perhaps one qualification needs to be made at this point. If the overall design of his main works is clear and systematic, the same cannot be said of his detailed exposition, especially in the longer chapters of *De Jure Belli*, where the accumulation of classical and biblical examples tends to obscure his line of argument. This may be one cost of his lack of philosophical rigour, and another would be the varying formulations of his

[176] Bull, *The Anarchical Society*, pp. 101–229.

[177] This refers to the views of David Boucher, discussed in the Introduction. See D. Boucher, *Political Theories of International Relations: From Thucydides to the Present* (Oxford: Oxford University Press, 1998), pp. 8, 16, 19.

concepts and his minor inconsistencies, all of which may provide one explanation for the long neglect of his work.

What of the alternative interpretations? We have seen that the universalist reading of Gentili is unconvincing: his references to the world as a great city, a state or a commonwealth, are metaphors that acquire no political substance, and whatever his attitude to the Roman empire may have been, he strongly opposes any empire with universalist ambitions in his own time.[178] There is no contemporary reaffirmation of the universalist interpretation.

Of much greater interest is Tuck's interpretation, which has sparked a lively debate. His postulate of a Roman humanist or oratorical tradition revived by sixteenth- and seventeenth-century scholars has prompted a new interest in the influence of Roman thought in that period, exemplified in the Kingsbury and Straumann volume which, like Tuck, takes Gentili's work as a focal point.[179] Several chapters discuss Tuck's characterization of this tradition and Gentili's place within it, and in particular his thinking on pre-emptive war, with widely differing assessments.[180]

Notwithstanding the attractions of Tuck's bold reinterpretation, this study has found his account of Gentili unpersuasive. In the light of Gentili's volume on the just conduct of war and his pervasive theme of moderation, it is difficult to understand his view that Gentili's ideas on war were 'often extraordinarily brutal'. He places Gentili's view of pre-emptive/preventive war in the context of wide-ranging Roman debates on the topic, but not of Gentili's overall thinking on the justification of war, where it does not have the prominence which Tuck would lead one to expect. Moreover, as Bull makes clear, Gentili's defence of preventive war on balance-of-power grounds is compatible with a theory of international society no less than with realism.[181] It all depends on the context – and this Tuck leaves out of his account. Tuck does not use the category 'Realist', but the reader coming from international relations theory will surely understand him in this sense, especially since he associates the humanist tradition with Machiavelli and raison d'état thinking.

[178] In *De Armis Romanis*, Gentili presents a dialogue between a speaker who defends the justice of the Roman empire and one who denies it. Contributors to the Kingsbury and Straumann collection are divided on the question of whether Gentili's own views were those of the affirmative speaker.

[179] Tuck, *The Rights of War and Peace*; Kingsbury and Straumann (eds), *The Roman Foundations of the Law of Nations*.

[180] For a wide-ranging discussion of Gentili's views on pre-emptive war, see P. Pürimäe, 'Alberico Gentili's Doctrine of Defensive War and Its Impact on Seventeenth Century Normative Views', in Kingsbury and Straumann (eds), *The Roman Foundations of the Law of Nations*. See also chapters by Panizza and Malcolm.

[181] Bull, *The Anarchical Society*, pp. 101–26.

It is beyond the scope of this study to assess the adequacy of Tuck's account of this tradition, and of its radical opposition to scholasticism; but the closeness of Gentili's views on the just war to those of Vitoria at least raises a question about this latter point.

However, while Gentili is not a 'hard' realist, one who denies the relevance of moral considerations in international politics, could he be seen as a realist in terms of other criteria? His seeming acceptance of the normality of war smacks of realist thinking. But it goes too far to suggest that Gentili's project 'was essentially to give a legal interpretation to Machiavelli's doctrine of the ruler's unlimited moral right to take all necessary means for the protection of the state'.[182] Gentili's own comment on Machiavelli would suggest otherwise, and it seems out of character for his thinking to accord this kind of unconditional priority to a single goal of this kind. His focus is not on the ruler or the state but on the 'lofty structure'. He is first and foremost a jurist, his thinking grounded in the Bartolist tradition of legal thought. His thinking as a whole accords with the international society paradigm; if there is a realist flavour to some of his utterances, this is a secondary strand in his thought.

[182] Pürimäe, 'Alberico Gentili's Doctrine of Defensive War', p. 195.

5 Hugo Grotius

Hugo Grotius (1583–1645) elicits a unanimous response on the part of Otto von Gierke, Martin Wight and Hedley Bull: they not only accord him a place on their respective lists of thinkers but also assign him to the same tradition of thought – the tradition which Gierke refers to as 'the dominant theory, decisive for the future of the law of nations', Wight at times as the Grotian tradition, and Bull as 'the Grotian or internationalist tradition'. However, the reasons which they adduce in support of their decision and the methods for establishing them vary.

Gierke emphasizes the presence of the idea of human society in Grotius's thought. But he limits himself to a footnote to his proposition, cited in Chapter 1, that in this tradition the binding force of the *jus gentium* was based on a *societas gentium*, in which the idea of state sovereignty coexisted with the unity of mankind. He gives six references to *De Jure Belli ac Pacis* which offer various propositions concerning human society, some of them rather cryptic but including the statement, also noted by Wight, that 'Kings, in addition to the particular care of their own state, are burdened with a general responsibility for human society'.[1]

Wight's reasons for appropriating Grotius for this tradition are presented most fully in 'Western Values in International Relations'. First, observing that the tradition of thought which is representative of Western values has 'the quality of a *via media*', Wight cites Grotius's dictum: 'A remedy must be found for those that believe that in war nothing is lawful, and for those for whom all things are lawful in war.'[2]

[1] O. von Gierke, *Das Deutsche Genossenschaftsrecht*, vol. 4 (Graz: Akademische Druck und Verlagsanstalt, 1954), pp. 361–62. The six references are: IIc8, §26; IIc 15, §5; IIc 15, §12; IIc 20; IIc 21, §3; IIc 3, §6.

[2] M. Wight, 'Western Values in International Relations', in H. Butterfield and M. Wight (eds), *Diplomatic Investigations: Essays in the Theory of International Politics* (London: George Allen & Unwin, 1969), p. 91. Wight does not identify the edition of *De Jure Belli ac Pacis* to which he refers. His translation differs in detail from that in The Classics of International Law. See H. Grotius, *De Jure Belli ac Pacis Libri Tres* [Three Books On the Law of War and Peace], vol. 2, transl. Latin edition of 1646 by F. W. Kelsey, with the collaboration of others, *The Classics of International Law* (Oxford: Clarendon Press,

When outlining this tradition's conception of the nature of international society, characterizing it as 'complex', 'lacking in intellectual conciseness' and employing a language 'full of qualifications', Wight says:

> In Grotius's description of international society there is a fruitful imprecision. *Communis societas generis humani, communis illa ex humano genere constans societas, humana societas, magna illa communitas, magna illa universitas, magna illa gentium societas, mutua gentium inter se societas, illa mundi civitas, societas orbis* – such is his range of language.[3]

Turning to the question of order in international society, in support of his point that '[t]he notion that there could be a lawless or delinquent state has been integral to this conception of international society', Wight reports the incident which led to Grotius's composition of *De Jure Praedae* and quotes its opening paragraph.[4] This understanding of international society, Wight argues, insists that the delinquent state deserves punishment.[5] Next, on the question of intervention, he notes that '[b]etween the opposing positions of non-intervention and intervention, there is a central doctrine of what might be called the moral interdependence of peoples'. He quotes the same passage as Gierke, referred to above, and notes further that '[Grotius] refused to allow oppressed subjects to take up arms in their own behalf, but permitted a foreign Power to intervene for them'.[6]

In concluding his argument Wight addresses the question of international morality, but refers to Grotius only in general terms: '[T]he Greeks never developed the theory of a society of states mutually bound by legal rights and obligations. There was no Greek Grotius'.[7]

Wight's course of lectures, published as *International Theory*, is organized in terms of themes, not individual thinkers, and thus contains no extended discussion of Grotius, but a later publication, based on a special lecture series in 1959–60, offers a wide-ranging discussion of his

1913–1927, reprinted New York and London: Oceana Publications and Wildy & Sons, 1964), p. 20.

[3] Wight, 'Western Values', p. 102. Translated: the universal society of the human race, that universal society comprising the human race, human society, that great society, that great whole, that great society of nations, the mutual society of nations, that world state, world society.

[4] H. Grotius, *De Jure Praedae Commentarius* [Commentary on the Law of Prize and Booty], vol. 1, transl. Original Manuscript of 1604 by G. L. Williams, collab. W. H. Zeydel, *The Classics of International Law* (Oxford and London: Clarendon Press and Geoffrey Cumberlege 1950, reprinted New York and London: Oceana Publications and Wildy & Sons, 1964), p. 1, quoted by Wight, 'Western Values', pp. 104–05.

[5] Wight, 'Western Values', p. 105.

[6] Ibid., pp. 116, 119. It may be noted that these points are already present in Vitoria and Gentili, and in the just war tradition more generally.

[7] Ibid., pp. 126–27.

moral and political thought and his links with later thinkers.[8] His general theme is the richness and complexity of Grotius's thinking; he does not, however, enlarge on his earlier account of his view of international society.

The perusal of Bull's writings for reasons which may have induced him to link Grotius to the tradition which 'views international politics as taking place within an international society'[9] leads one to conclude that the establishment of such reasons is not one of Bull's concerns; rather, he takes Grotius's membership of this tradition as something given, and applies it to questions that are his concern.

For example, in *The Anarchical Society*, he offers a detailed account of the tradition of thought in question. He speaks of it as 'the Grotian tradition' and calls its adherents 'the Grotians', but he does not speak of Grotius nor does he refer to his writings. There is a footnote in which he gives the two meanings in which he uses the word 'Grotian': the idea that there is a society of states and 'the solidarist form' of this society – but he does not tell the reader where to find these two ideas in the writings of Grotius.[10] Perhaps his references to some of Grotius's ideas on war, such as his condemnation of wars without any cause as 'wars of savages' or the approval of only those wars which 'remedy an injury received', can be taken as reasons why Grotius is seen to fit the *via media*.[11]

'The Grotian Conception of International Society' looks at the disagreement between two members of the *via media*, Grotius – the 'solidarist' – and Lassa Oppenheim – the 'pluralist' – in relation to three questions – the place of war in international society, the sources of the law which binds its member states, and the place of the individual in 'the society of states' – and evaluates the appropriateness of their ideas to the functioning of international society in the twentieth century.[12] In spite of its promising title, this investigation reveals little about Bull's reasons for appropriating Grotius for the *via media*. It states: 'Both assert the existence of an international society and of laws which are binding on its member states in their relations with one another', that both reject '[t]he pacifist and militarist positions … [as] inimical to the idea of international society' and approve of certain wars as being legitimate.[13]

[8] M. Wight, *Four Seminal Thinkers in International Theory: Machiavelli, Grotius, Kant, and Mazzini*, ed. G. Wight and B. Porter (Oxford: Oxford University Press, 2005), pp. 29–61.

[9] H. Bull, *The Anarchical Society: A Study of Order in World Politics* (London: Macmillan, 1977), p. 24.

[10] Ibid., pp. 26–27, 322.

[11] Ibid., pp. 45, 109.

[12] H. Bull, 'The Grotian Conception of International Society', in Butterfield and Wight (eds), *Diplomatic Investigations*.

[13] Ibid., p. 53.

Somewhat more helpful is 'The Importance of Grotius in the Study of International Relations'. Grotius's work is 'cardinal', Bull writes, because it formulates one of the 'classic paradigms' in terms of which international relations have been thought about in modern times, and this is the idea of international society. He goes on to identify five characteristics: it accords a central place to natural law; its extent is worldwide; it accommodates not only states but also individuals and non-state groups; it is marked by 'solidarism'; and it accords little or no place to formal international institutions.[14] As one pursues his references, one meets with many of Grotius's ideas, but his conception of international society remains elusive.

Thus, while the information supplied by Gierke, Wight and Bull provides much food for thought, it does not answer the question: what is Grotius's idea of international society? He thence becomes the fourth thinker to be included in this study.

The other three thinkers – Erasmus, Vitoria and Gentili – are no strangers to Grotius. He knows Erasmus well, but this is not obvious from his books. *De Jure Belli ac Pacis* does not go beyond referring to him as 'my fellow-country man' and grouping him with those who show 'the utmost devotion to peace'; that is, those who 'have come to the point of forbidding all use of arms to the Christian'.[15] It is Grotius's correspondence which reveals his closeness to Erasmus. Here, Grotius portrays him as the example, the 'greatest man', the man who has done so much toward showing the way to a 'legitimate reformation' and whom 'we Hollanders' cannot thank sufficiently, the man who is on his side in his struggle for religious peace.[16]

Vitoria does not figure in Grotius's correspondence, but he is given a great deal of attention in *De Jure Praedae*: references to the Spaniard's works are numerous and Grotius offers them in support of his own arguments. He credits him with 'irrefutable logic' and 'thoroughly sound'

[14] H. Bull, 'The Importance of Grotius in the Study of International Relations', in H. Bull, B. Kingsbury and A. Roberts (eds), *Hugo Grotius and International Relations* (Oxford: Clarendon Press, 1990), pp. 71, 78–91.

[15] Grotius, *De Jure Belli ac Pacis*, vol. 2, p. 20. Is this perhaps the origin of the image of Erasmus as the pacifist *par excellence*?

[16] See, for example, his letters to Salmasius of 23 June 1630 and to Episcopius of 15 December 1630, in *Briefwisseling van Hugo Grotius* [Correspondence of Hugo Grotius], vol. 4, ed. B. L. Meulenbroek ('S-Gravenhage: Martinus Nijhoff, 1964), pp. 234, 297; to Wtenbogaert of 26 January 1632, in *Briefwisseling van Hugo Grotius*, vol. 5, ed. Meulenbroek ('S-Gravenhage: Martinus Nijhoff, 1966), p. 15; and to Willem de Groot of 14 April 1640, in *Briefwisseling van Hugo Grotius*, vol. 11, eds Meulenbroek and P. P. Witkam ('S-Gravenhage: Martinus Nijhoff, 1981), p. 203.

conclusions.[17] In *De Jure Belli ac Pacis* he speaks of Vitoria's 'sound judgement' only once.[18] He refers to his writings, and not always favourably:

> I have seen ... special books on the law of war, some by theologians, as Franciscus de Victoria ... others by doctors of law ... All of these ... have said next to nothing upon a most fertile subject.[19]

Gentili also is well known to Grotius – a point established by both his correspondence and his books. In a letter of 1615, for example, Grotius refers to Gentili as an 'eminent' jurisconsult – eminent because of his writings on the law of nations and on public law; and in letters of 1622/23 from Paris to his brother Willem in Holland, Grotius urgently requests, among other works, Gentili's *De Jure Belli* and *Hispanicae Advocationis* as he needs them for a 'commentary'.[20] In *De Jure Praedae* and *De Jure Belli ac Pacis*, the references to Gentili are numerous. In the former work, the emphasis is on agreement, and Gentili finds himself amongst the 'jurisconsults of the greatest renown'.[21] In the latter work, disagreement is evident, Grotius rejecting some of Gentili's views as 'untenable', 'unacceptable' and erroneous. The 'Prolegomena' contains the following acknowledgement: 'Knowing that others can derive profit from Gentili's painstaking, as I acknowledge that I have, I leave it to his readers to pass judgement on the shortcomings of his work.'[22]

Grotius, then, is familiar with all three thinkers, and in relation to two of them, Vitoria and Gentili, he reveals a change in attitude, the reasons for which are not readily available, but which tend to overstate his own originality.

Who is Hugo Grotius or – his Dutch name – Huig(h) de Groot? The existing literature is likely to identify him as extraordinarily gifted – a prodigy, 'one of the greatest men of Europe', or 'the miracle of Holland'

[17] Grotius, *De Jure Praedae*, vol. 1, pp. 221, 284. He also drew heavily on Vitoria in his early *Commentarius in Theses XI*. See P. Borschberg, *Hugo Grotius 'Commentarius in Theses XI'* (Berne: Peter Lang, 1994), pp. 48–53.

[18] Grotius, *De Jure Belli ac Pacis*, vol. 2, p. 745.

[19] Ibid., p. 22. For formulations of disagreement see, for example, ibid., pp. 98, 178, 506, 592.

[20] Extracts from these letters are given by C. van Vollenhoven, 'On the Genesis of *De Jure Belli ac Pacis* (Grotius, 1625)', *Verspreide Geschriften* [Various Writings], vol. 1 (Haarlem and 'S-Gravenhage: Tjeenk Willink & Zoon and Martinus Nijhoff, 1934), pp. 361–63.

[21] Grotius, *De Jure Praedae*, vol. 1, p. 218.

[22] Grotius, *De Jure Belli ac Pacis*, vol. 2, p. 22. See also pp. 184–85, 639. For a more extensive discussion of Grotius's reaction to Gentili, see P. Haggenmacher, 'Grotius and Gentili: A Reassessment of Thomas E. Holland's Inaugural Lecture', in Bull, Kingsbury and Roberts (eds), *Hugo Grotius and International Relations*.

as is still being echoed to this day.[23] Yet few scholars seem to have felt inclined to record and examine this greatness closely. The standard work, W. S. M. Knight's *The Life and Works of Hugo Grotius*, goes back to 1925, has no claim to completeness,[24] and does not always escape the weakness, which Knight attributes to others, of failing to apply a critical mind to the facts at hand. Not only is there no 'fully documented' modern biography of Grotius; there also is no modern critical edition of his works. Comprehensive studies of his thought are all but absent.[25] Specialized studies, of which the twentieth century produced a good number, especially in relation to his legal writings, often do not distinguish themselves by a searching approach.[26] Criticisms formulated in earlier centuries have been given little attention by twentieth-century scholarship.[27]

[23] See, for example, C. S. Edwards, *Hugo Grotius: The Miracle of Holland: A Study in Political and Legal Thought*, intro. R. A. Falk (Chicago: Nelson-Hall, 1981); and the 'Preface' to *Netherlands International Law Review*, vol. 30, no. 1, 1983. A dissenting voice is mentioned by H. F. Wright who, in his study of 'The Controversy of Hugo Grotius with Johan de Laet on the Origin of the American Aborigines', includes a letter which de Laet, 'a geographer, historian, philologian and naturalist of no little skill', writes to the young Grotius wishing him 'a better mind and greater modesty'. See H. F. Wright, 'Some Less Known Works of Hugo Grotius', *Bibliotheca Visseriana*, vol. 7 (Lugdunum Batavorum: E. J. Brill, 1928), pp. 211–28. For a further dissenting voice from the past, see Sir Robert Filmer's 'Observations Upon H. Grotius De Jure Belli ac Pacis', in J. P. Sommerville (ed.), *Sir Robert Filmer: Patriarcha and Other Writings* (Cambridge: Cambridge University Press, 1991).

[24] For example, he does not mention the Anglo-Dutch negotiations of 1615, although he discusses those of 1613 at great length; nor does he refer to or make use of the regular reports on political events which Grotius sent to his brother-in-law, N. van Reigersberch, in Holland, after 1621. See W. S. M. Knight, *The Life and Works of Hugo Grotius*, The Grotius Society Publications No. 4 (London: Sweet and Maxwell, 1925).

[25] For a beginning, see A. Eyffinger, 'In Quest of Synthesis: An Attempted Synopsis of Grotius' Works According to their Genesis and Objective', *Grotiana*, New Series, vol. 4, 1983.

[26] Examples that come to mind include: H. Vreeland, Jr., *Hugo Grotius the Father of the Modern Science of International Law* (New York: Oxford University Press, 1917); C. van Vollenhoven, 'Grotius and Geneva', *Bibliotheca Visseriana*, vol. 6 (Lugdunum Batavorum: E. J. Brill, 1926), pp. 5–81; C. van Vollenhoven, *The Framework of Grotius' Book De Jure Belli ac Pacis (1625)* (Amsterdam: Noord-Hollandsche Uitgeversmaatschappij, 1931). For a more searching approach, see P. Haggenmacher's study *Grotius et la Doctrine de la Guerre Juste* [Grotius and the Doctrine of the Just War] (Paris: Presses Universitaires de France, 1983).

[27] See, for example, H. Lauterpacht's reaction to criticisms voiced by Pufendorf, Barbeyrac and Stewart, 'The Grotian Tradition in International Law', in E. Lauterpacht (ed.), *International Law: Being the Collected Papers of Hersch Lauterpacht*, vol. 2, Part I (Cambridge: Cambridge University Press, 1975), pp. 308, 330. Political theorists seem to be more mindful of past criticisms. See, for example, A. C. 't Hart, 'Hugo de Groot and Giambattista Vico', *Netherlands International Law Review*, vol. 30, no. 1, 1983, pp. 12, 23; D. F. Scheltens, 'Grotius' Doctrine of the Social Contract', *Netherlands International Law Review*, vol. 30, no. 1, 1983, pp. 43–44; and R. Tuck, 'Peter Haggenmacher, Grotius et la Doctrine de la Guerre Juste', *Grotiana*, New Series, vol. 7, 1986, pp. 87–88.

It is the uneven nature of the existing literature, together with contradictory statements embedded therein, the occasional dismantling of an 'established truth', and laconic statements, such as '[i]n fact De Groot the man of history and Grotius the genius of legend are almost two different people'[28] which suggest that Grotius has yet to be discovered. An important step in this direction is the publication in 1990 of *Hugo Grotius and International Relations*.[29]

Life and Works

The following details about his life and writings are offered as a way of introducing him.[30] Grotius was born in 1583 at Delft, Holland, into a family of influence and ambition, which placed a high value on humanist learning. At first educated privately, he attended the University of Leyden from 1594 to 1597 – young but not exceptionally so for the initial degree in classical languages and literature. The sources disagree on whether any study of law, normally undertaken later, was included. In 1598 he accompanied a diplomatic mission led by Admiral Count Justin of Nassau, a member of the house of Orange, and the *Landsadvocaat* (also referred to as Advocate-General or Chief Counsellor or, after 1618, Grand Pensionary) Johan van Oldenbarneveldt to Henry IV, King of France. He remained in France for several months, probably in Orleans, where he received a doctorate in law from the University of Orleans.[31]

Toward the end of 1599, Grotius was admitted to the bar at the *Hof van Holland* (Court of Holland) and the *Hooge Raad* (Supreme Court of Holland, Zeeland and West Friesland) at The Hague. In 1601 the States of Holland and West Friesland appointed him official historian and in 1607 Grotius became *Advocaat-Fiscaal* (Advocate-General of the Fisc)

[28] D. P. O'Connell, *Richelieu* (London: Weidenfeld & Nicolson, 1968), p. 303.

[29] Bull, Kingsbury and Roberts (eds), *Hugo Grotius and International Relations*. Not to be neglected either is J. den Tex, *Oldenbarneveldt*, 2 vols, transl. from Dutch by R. B. Powell (Cambridge: Cambridge University Press, 1973). More recently Renée Jeffery has offered a reinterpretation of Grotius in the context of a study of the evolution of the 'Grotian tradition'. See R. Jeffery, *Hugo Grotius in International Thought* (New York: Palgrave Macmillan, 2006).

[30] For accounts of Grotius's life see, for example, E. Dumbauld, *The Life and Legal Writings of Hugo Grotius* (Norman, OK: University of Oklahoma Press, 1969); C. G. Roelofsen, 'Grotius and the International Politics of the Seventeenth Century', in Bull, Kingsbury and Roberts, *Hugo Grotius and International Relations*; Borschberg, *Hugo Grotius 'Commentarius in Theses XI'*, pp. 19–30; and Jeffery, *Hugo Grotius in International Thought*, pp. 1–14. The most comprehensive account is Knight's biography.

[31] As Knight indicates, there were 'doctors by favour' and 'effective doctors', and Grotius must have been one of the former, unless 'the university had ceased to observe its old conditions'. Knight, *The Life and Works of Hugo Grotius*, p. 38.

of Holland, Zeeland and West Friesland. A year later he married Maria van Reigersberch, the daughter of an influential family in Zeeland.

The year 1613 saw his appointment to a major public office, *Pensionary* of Rotterdam,[32] which gave him a seat in the States of Holland and West Friesland and, later, a seat in the States-General of the United Provinces. The year 1613 also witnessed his participation, as its spokesman, in a diplomatic mission to England to review the long-standing maritime rivalry between the English and the Dutch. In 1615, a second Anglo-Dutch conference took place, this time at The Hague, Grotius again being the spokesman for the Dutch.

In 1616 he became a member of the *College van Gecommitteerde Raaden*, a committee responsible for the administration of Holland and West Friesland, under the leadership of Oldenbarneveldt. The risks of high office at a time of deep religious conflict became evident in 1618 when the *Stadhouder* Maurits, Prince of Orange, had Oldenbarneveldt, Grotius and some others arrested and charged with treason. Oldenbarneveldt was executed in 1619, Grotius was sentenced to lifelong imprisonment and forfeiture of all his property, and the *Stadhouder*[33] took over the reins of government.

Grotius was allowed access to books and had them delivered by the trunkload, eventually escaping in a trunk and fleeing to Paris, where he spent the next ten years, writing *De Jure Belli ac Pacis* (1624–25) and other works. Late in 1631 he returned to Holland for a few months and, as he was refused permission to return to public life, left again to spend about three years, of which there is no record, at or near Hamburg. From 1635 to 1645 he was again in Paris, this time as Sweden's ambassador to the Court of France.

The year 1645 saw the termination of his ambassadorship, his voyage via Holland to Sweden, and his death at Rostock in Pomerania – three years before the Peace of Westphalia and five years before the house of Orange was to hand back political power to Holland's oligarchs.

His first publications were literary, including poetry and translations, among them a work in mathematics. Histories soon followed, notably on the history of his native province, Holland, *A Treatise on the Antiquity of the Commonwealth of the Battavers, Which Is Now the Hollanders*.[34] He wrote extensively on the religious and theological controversies of the day,

[32] The *Pensionary* was 'the recognized representative and negotiator of the city'. Knight, *The Life and Works of Hugo Grotius*, p. 136.

[33] Sometimes termed Lieutenant-Governor: the representative of the sovereign, initially the King of Spain, later the States-General of the United Provinces.

[34] H. Grotius, *A Treatise on the Antiquity of the Commonwealth of the Battavers, Which Is Now the Hollanders*, transl. T. Woods (London: John Walker, 1649).

pleading for religious toleration and seeking to bridge the gulf between Catholicism and Protestantism. The most widely read of his works was *True Religion* [*De Veritate Religionis Christianae*] (1627).[35]

His juridical works were not limited to those on the law of nations. The *Jurisprudence of Holland* (1631), frequently reissued, was long a standard work.[36] *De Jure Praedae* (manuscript, 1605) was commissioned by the United Dutch East India Company as a defence of the seizure by one of its captains of a Portugese ship carrying rich merchandise. It was not published, being too long and complex to serve the original purpose, and Grotius himself may have found the timing inopportune. Also probably written at this time, the *Commentarius in Theses XI*, a succinct defence of the justice of the Dutch war against Spain, offers an example of his skills as advocate.[37] The *magnum opus* on which his reputation rests, *De Jure Belli ac Pacis*, written in Paris in 1624–25, was surprisingly popular, given its prolixity and, to most of today's readers, the obscurity of its arguments.

In contrast to Vitoria's Thomism or Gentili's Bartolism, it is not possible to assign Grotius to any specific intellectual tradition. From early childhood he was exposed to humanist culture through his family's contacts with writers and scholars, and this was deepened through his university study of classical languages and literature, which opened the way to a rudimentary acquaintance with a range of disciplines. He developed an early interest in mathematics, and presumably in law, but there is no record of any formal legal studies. His few months in Orleans would have acquainted him with French legal thinking, but no more than that.

Thus Haggenmacher's claim that Grotius may be seen as an exponent of the systematic strand in French legal humanism is open to question.[38] It is true that the argument of *De Jure Praedae* was tightly structured in terms of a set of rules and laws set out in the first chapters, but nothing of this remains in *De Jure Belli ac Pacis*. Haggenmacher's thesis that Book II presents a systematic statement of the full gamut of rights is unconvincing. Readers who have struggled with lengthy chapters, puzzling how these may relate to the ostensible theme, the justifiable causes of war, may be more likely to echo Voltaire's wry comment: 'He is very learned … but what has circumcision to do with the laws of war and peace?'[39] There

[35] H. Grotius, *True Religion* (Amsterdam: Theatrum Orbis Terrarum, 1971).
[36] H. Grotius, *The Jurisprudence of Holland*, transl. with brief notes and a commentary R. W. Lee, vol. 1 (Oxford: Clarendon Press, 1926).
[37] Borschberg, *Hugo Grotius 'Commentarius in Theses XI'*.
[38] Haggenmacher, 'Grotius and Gentili', pp. 159–60.
[39] Cited in E. Keene, *Beyond the Anarchical Society: Grotius, Colonialism and Order in World Politics* (Cambridge: Cambridge University Press, 2002), p. 41.

is even the suggestion that some of the chapters may come from another manuscript scarcely linked to the topic.[40]

Indeed Grotius's own description of his approach is to the point: like the early Christians, he was committed to no particular philosophy: 'None encompassed all truth, and none which had not perceived some aspect of truth.' Thus he would 'gather up into a whole the truth which was scattered among the different philosophers'.[41]

Grotius and the Events of His Time

Grotius lived in a turbulent age, his public career shaped by the political and religious struggles in the Netherlands, and the second half of his life witnessing the Thirty Years' War, in the diplomacy of which he was a participant. A number of levels of conflict may be distinguished. There was conflict within Holland amongst its oligarchs over political, economic, military and religious issues; conflict between Holland and the other six 'provinces' of the northern Netherlands, linked together in what is variously called the United Provinces, the Rebel Provinces or the Dutch Republic, over essentially the same questions, but argued in terms of the principle of provincial sovereignty; conflict between the United Provinces and the Spanish South Netherlands, hence Spain, over the question of freedom from Spain – a struggle which engages its protagonists not only on Dutch soil but also in other parts of Europe and outside Europe; conflict between the United Provinces and other European powers, within Europe and beyond, in Africa, Asia and America, over questions of commerce and/or colonies; and there was conflict between the successive Grand Pensionaries and Princes of Orange over all of these points.[42]

[40] A. Nussbaum, *A Concise History of the Law of Nations*, rev. edn (New York: Macmillan, 1954), p. 103.

[41] Grotius, 'Prolegomena', *De Jure Belli ac Pacis*, vol. 2, p. 24.

[42] Regarding the Netherlands see, for example, P. Geyl, *The Revolt of the Netherlands: 1555–1609*, 2nd edn (London and New York: Ernest Benn and Barnes & Noble, 1980); P. Geyl, *The Netherlands in the Seventeenth Century: I. 1609–1648* (London: Ernest Benn, 1961); J. Huizinga, *Dutch Civilization in the Seventeenth Century and Other Essays*, sel. P. Geyl and F. W. N. Hugenholtz, transl. A. J. Pomerans (London: Collins, 1968); den Tex, *Oldenbarneveldt*; and J. L. Price, *Culture and Society in the Dutch Republic During the Seventeenth Century* (New York: Charles Scribner's Sons, 1974). Regarding the wider context see, for example, T. Aston (ed.), *Crisis in Europe: 1560–1660: Essays from Past and Present* (London: Routledge & Kegan Paul, 1965); H. G. Koenigsberger, *The Habsburgs and Europe: 1516–1660* (Ithaca and London: Cornell University Press, 1971); M. Roberts (ed.), *Sweden's Age of Greatness: 1632–1718* (London: Macmillan, 1973); C. Wilson, *The Transformation of Europe: 1558–1648* (London: Weidenfeld & Nicolson, 1976); and G. Parker, *Europe in Crisis: 1598–1648* (Glasgow: Fontana, 1979).

His books reveal very little of his views of these conflicts. *De Jure Belli ac Pacis* was prompted by his revulsion against the unrestrained violence 'throughout the Christian world',[43] but it makes no reference to contemporary events; its examples, and the controversies with which it engages, are drawn from the ancient world. The *Jurisprudence of Holland* deals with principles, not current issues. *De Jure Praedae* appears to be an exception. Although it consists mainly of legal arguments for the justice of the Dutch action, it includes a long historical chapter on the incident, but this makes no claim to provide an objective record. Grotius writes as an uncompromising advocate. The nineteenth-century historian, Robert Fruin, observes:

> [The Historica] are ... a protracted indictment of the Portuguese, a defence of the East India Company. Whatever does not serve this purpose is left unrecorded by the barrister. Whatever would bear witness against his clients is concealed by him ... De Groot ... cannot be acquitted of willful partiality in writing this narrative.[44]

De Jure Praedae was not published until 1868, but its twelfth chapter was released anonymously under the title *Mare Liberum* in 1609.[45] Addressed to the rulers and free peoples of Christendom, it presents its case for the right of navigation and the freedom of commerce. Events are not discussed in the course of the argument, only principles. The

[43] Grotius, *De Jure Belli ac Pacis*, vol. 2, p. 20. As other possible initial sparks, the secondary literature suggests (and on the whole rejects) *Le Nouveau Cynée* by Émeric Crucé, or personal ambition on the part of Grotius. See van Vollenhoven, 'On the Genesis', pp. 352–61. Knight, however, does not hesitate to see *De Jure Belli ac Pacis* as a bid for a place of influence in public affairs, and Roelofsen as 'at least partly that'. See Knight, *The Life and Works of Hugo Grotius*, pp. 191–92, and Roelofsen, 'Grotius and the International Politics of the Seventeenth Century', pp. 122–23. Tuck's discussion of revisions in the second edition of *De Jure Belli ac Pacis* lends some support to this view. See R. Tuck, *The Rights of War and Peace: Political Thought and the International Order from Grotius to Kant* (Oxford: Oxford University Press, 1999), pp. 97–102.

[44] R. Fruin, 'An Unpublished Work of Hugo Grotius', transl. from an essay in Dutch (1868), *Bibliotheca Visseriana*, vol. 5 (Lugdunum Batavorum: E. J. Brill, 1925), p. 48. A similar, although less harshly formulated, reproach for unreliability is levelled by another historian against Grotius on the latter's reporting of his interviews with James I in 1613. See den Tex, *Oldenbarneveldt*, vol. 2, p. 563.

[45] H. Grotius, *Mare Liberum, Sive de Iure Quod Batavis Competit Ad Indicana Commercia Dissertatio* [Dissertation on the Freedom of the Seas or the Right which Belongs to the Dutch to Take Part in the East Indian Trade], transl. with a revision of the Latin text of 1633 R. van Deman Magoffin, ed. with intro. note J. Brown Scott, *The Classics of International Law* (New York and London: Oxford University Press and Humphrey Milford, 1916). Sometimes the original date of publication is given as 1608. For an informative account of 'The Genesis of Grotius' Mare Liberum', see F. de Pauw, *Grotius and the Law of the Sea*, transl. P. J. Arthern, Éditions de l'Institut de Sociologie (Brussels: Université de Bruxelles, 1965), pp. 14–22.

same is true of 'The Colonial Conferences between England and the Netherlands in 1613 and 1615'. Grotius, who is credited with the formulation and presentation of the argument on the Dutch side, submits principles rather than events.[46]

A Treatise on the Antiquity of the Commonwealth of the Battavers, Which Is Now the Hollanders, published in 1610, is a response to the conflict which separated Holland and its *Landsadvocaat* from the other six provinces of the United Provinces and the Prince of Orange over the question of who is or ought to be in control of affairs, and, in turn, was intended to influence the course of events.[47] Later in life Grotius conceded that 'it contained assertions which … proceeded rather from his love of freedom and his native country than from earnest research'.[48] The later history, *Annales et Histoires des Troubles du Pays-Bas*[49] (not published until 1657), the story of the war with Spain up to and including the year of the truce in 1609, is descriptive rather than interpretative, and in that quality, it is not a faithful reflection of reality. 'The extremes on either side' in the course of this war, as Knight observes, 'receive little consideration, being, as often as not, entirely ignored'.[50]

For a number of reasons, then, Grotius's historical and legal writings are an unfruitful source in relation to the question of realism on the part of their author *vis-à-vis* the events of his time.

The same cannot be said of his correspondence. The many weighty volumes published by Martinus Nijhoff show Grotius as he participates in a far-flung communications network, informing and being informed, on the events of the times – great and small, good and bad, nearby and distant, expressing his views and seeking those of others, intent on seeing things as they are.

In order to give an impression of the nature of his observations, a few excerpts from letters written from France are presented here:

23 November 1626: Here we have ten days to the beginning of the Assembly of Notables … Cardinal Rochefocaud will preside, which is not to the liking of many as he is very much in the service of the Pope … We understand here that the Persian and the Turc are about to conclude peace, which will make it possible

[46] G. N. Clark and W. J. M. van Eysinga, 'The Colonial Conferences between England and the Netherlands in 1613 and 1615', Part I, *Bibliotheca Visseriana*, vol. 15 (Lugdunum Batavorum: E. J. Brill, 1940), pp. 1–270, and Part II, *Bibliotheca Visseriana*, vol. 17 (Lugdunum Batavorum: E. J. Brill, 1951), pp. 1–155.

[47] Grotius, *A Treatise on the Antiquity*.

[48] Fruin, 'An Unpublished Work of Hugo Grotius', p. 47.

[49] H. Grotius, *Annales et Histoires des Troubles du Pays-Bas* [The Annals and History of the Troubles of the Low-Countries] (Amsterdam: Iean Blaev, 1662).

[50] Knight, *The Life and Works of Hugo Grotius*, p. 276.

for the Turc to display his strength against Hungary which, in turn, will enable France to advance against the German emperor.[51]

4 February 1628: I have seen the proposal by the Spaniards and Imperials, Poland and Danzig included, to Luebeck ... It aims at greatly reducing the traffic into our country and reinforcing the other side at sea ... Cardinal Bernulle has written to Richelieu's people including a proposal for an agreement between Spain and the United Provinces mediated by France ... I am afraid that the accord will come to nothing ... From England no help is to be expected.[52]

16 October 1636: The good news regarding Poland pleases me all the more as the truce with Sweden is so long that few peace agreements between powerful neighbours have lasted as long. At sea, in Burgundy, and Picardy things are 'in balance' ... The English and the Dutch are in conflict over the question of a tax on the herring, and the free entry of the English into Flanders ... Meanwhile both desire to enrich themselves with the help of the wealth of the Orient.[53]

20 October 1640: We hear that the King of Spain tries to establish peace with the Sultan, and that he is likely to succeed; the former now has many things on his hands, and the latter wants to take revenge on the Polish cossacks and, as I believe, on Moscow, and with Persia the situation is uncertain ... The agreement between Sweden and the United Provinces is said to be of no great importance. Sweden, I don't think, has much to fear from Denmark.[54]

It is not only the twentieth-century reader of Grotius's correspondence who is prepared to acknowledge him as a well-informed and discerning observer. Grotius's contemporaries are quite ready to do the same. As the Spanish King Philip IV writes to Francisco de Moncada, Marquis de Aytona, Governor of the Spanish South Netherlands, to whom he communicates 'conditions to attract Hugo Grotius ... to the services of His Majesty', in 1634: 'Of all those who live today Hugo Grotius has the most perfect insight into the situation of the Rebels.'[55]

Grotius and the Three Traditions of Thought

This section inquires whether Grotius, like Erasmus, Vitoria and Gentili, sees himself as taking up a position between the realists on the one hand and the universalists on the other.

As we have seen, Grotius likes to think of himself as representing no particular pattern of thought, but, like the early Christians, he seeks 'to

[51] Grotius to Nicolaes van Reigersberch, in *Briefwisseling van Hugo Grotius*, vol. 3, eds P. C. Molhuysen and B. L. Meulenbroek ('S-Gravenhage: Martinus Nijhoff, 1961), pp. 83–85.

[52] Ibid., pp. 231–33.

[53] Grotius to Israel Jasky, in *Briefwisseling van Hugo Grotius*, vol. 7, ed. B. L. Meulenbroek ('S-Gravenhage: Martinus Nijhoff, 1969), pp. 441–42.

[54] Grotius to Nicolaes van Reigersberch, in *Briefwisseling*, vol. 11, pp. 574–75.

[55] Grotius to Nicolaes van Reigersberch, in *Briefwisseling*, vol. 3, pp. 465–66.

assemble the truth that was scattered' among the different various philosophies. Thus, in *De Jure Belli ac Pacis* he lists as an unjust cause of war 'the title to universal empire', whether advanced by the Roman emperor or the pope. The emperor's claim, he argues, is 'absurd, as if he had the right of ruling over even the most distant and hitherto unknown peoples'. It is not only contrary to reason, but, no matter what Dante thinks, it is also disadvantageous to mankind, for like 'a ship', it 'may attain to such a size that it cannot be steered'. Even if the advantages outweighed the disadvantages, 'the right to rule by no means follows', for such a right has its origin in consent or punishment, and neither of these applies. The Roman emperor is no longer entitled even to all that the Roman people once possessed, for changes have occurred due to war, treaties, abandonment and internal developments. And as far as the papal claim is concerned, the Church has no rights over peoples 'outside the bounds of Christendom', and within these bounds, it is not entitled 'to rule over men in the manner of this world'.[56]

De Jure Praedae exhibits the same negative attitude towards universalism. Chapter Twelve, the later *Mare Liberum*, contains the statement that 'no person is the master of all mankind', hence nobody is entitled to grant the exclusive use of the sea to 'any particular man or nation'. The same chapter borrows Vitoria's ideas against the pope's temporal rule of the world in order to divest the Portuguese of any rights over the East Indian peoples as a result of the papal donation. '[T]here is no person who has the power to bestow by grant that which is not his own.'[57] Grotius thus is constant in his rejection of universalism: reason, practicability and law all speak against it.

Less readily assessable is his attitude towards the realist tradition. At one level, and this is easily discernible, Grotius gives the impression of being distant or negative in regard to it. He never mentions Machiavelli's name, nor is there any sign that he is familiar with his writings.[58] Thomas Hobbes, a near contemporary, is mentioned in Grotius's correspondence. In 1643 he writes to his brother Willem that he has seen *De Cive*, that he approves of its views concerning kings, but that he disagrees with the foundations upon which its propositions rest, in particular, the idea that war between all men is natural.[59]

[56] Grotius, *De Jure Belli ac Pacis*, vol. 2, pp. 551–54.

[57] Grotius, *De Jure Praedae*, vol. 1, pp. 222–24, 247–48, 257–58.

[58] In contrast to Charles Marini, one of his correspondents. See, for example, *Briefwisseling*, vol. 11, pp. 170, 329.

[59] Reproduced in part by C. van Vollenhoven, 'The Growth of Grotius' *De Iure Belli ac Pacis* as It Appears from Contemporary Correspondence', *Bibliotheca Visseriana*, vol. 8 (Lugdunum Batavorum: E. J. Brill, 1929), p. 167.

Scholarship has not yet established the existence of a link from Machiavelli to earlier 'Machiavellians', but Grotius singles out one – Carneades, the Greek philosopher and founder of the New Academy who lived from 215 to 129 BC – in order to attack in him all those 'who view this branch of law [the whole law of war and peace] with contempt as having no reality outside of an empty name'; who declare that 'nothing is unjust which is expedient'; and who say that 'might makes right'. Carneades is wrong to divide 'all law into the law of nature and the law of particular countries', for there is also the law of nations.[60]

The 'Academics', Grotius argues in *De Jure Praedae*, are wrong to negate justice properly so called. It is not true, he holds, that the justice which is based on nature has regard only for the self, and that civil justice is no more than a matter of opinion, for they overlook that 'justice which is characteristic of humankind' – outward-looking justice expressing regard for the other.[61]

At this level, then, Grotius's disapproval of the realist tradition of thought is obvious. At another level his attitude towards this set of ideas becomes visible only after a careful examination of his writings. It is an enterprise which takes one well beyond the 'Prolegomena' of *De Jure Praedae* and that of *De Jure Belli ac Pacis*.

The Fatherland

The idea which inspires Grotius is not Erasmus's perfect temporal Christian prince, nor is it Vitoria's perfect temporal community or Gentili's perfect ambassador. Grotius is moved by the idea of the fatherland.

Many of the titles of his writings contain a reference to his native country, for example, *A Treatise on the Antiquity of the Commonwealth of the Battavers, which is now the Hollanders, Ordinum Hollandiae ac Westfrisiae pietas ... vindicata*[62] and *The Jurisprudence of Holland*; and his country, or an aspect of it, provides their subject matter. In other cases, the title does not mention his native country, nor does the subject matter deal with it, but Grotius uses the introduction to establish a link between the one and the other. For example, *True Religion* is intended 'to benefit all my Countrey-men, but specially Sea-faring-men ... in farre-distant-forren Countries'[63] when meeting with the enemies of Christianity. There are

[60] Grotius, *De Jure Belli ac Pacis*, vol. 2, pp. 9–15.
[61] Grotius, *De Jure Praedae*, vol. 1, pp. 12–13.
[62] Translated: The public worship of the States of Holland and West Friesland ... defended.
[63] Grotius, *True Religion*, p. 4.

also cases where the title does not refer to his country, although the work itself is concerned with it. An example is *De Jure Praedae.*

Grotius never makes a secret of the close link between his writings and his country. In 1618, following his arrest at The Hague, he puts it this way: 'My inclination to serve the Country is shown in my Writings … and also in my deeds.'[64] In 1632, after approximately ten years in France, he writes:

> During all the time that I have been in France, I have not only seized upon all occasions but also searched for them … to serve my fatherland … Several writings which I have published … are my witnesses before all the world of my constant affection for this land.[65]

And after his death, on the occasion of the publication of *Annales et Histoires des Troubles du Pays-Bas* by his children, the latter write in their dedication to the States of Holland and West Friesland: '[Y]ou will see that, until the last moment of his life, this author has preserved a perpetual love for his fatherland.'[66]

The country which is close to Grotius's heart and mind is not the whole of the Netherlands, nor its northern part, the United Provinces, but one of the provinces, the most powerful – Holland. 'Grotius … preferred to think of himself as a Hollander … and to treat the other provinces as mere allies … of Holland.' These words come from the Dutch historian Johan Huizinga, and his colleague Peter Geyl puts it this way: 'This Hollander … identified without a qualm the *Respublica Battava* with the fatherland.'[67]

Grotius's many efforts to serve his fatherland include an image which he creates of it. It displays the following features.

Great Age

Holland is a very old 'true commonwealth'. In *De Jure Praedae* he gives as its age 'seven centuries'; in *A Treatise on the Antiquity* he traces its birth back to 'before the time of Julius Caesar, yea, peradventure some hundred years before'.[68]

[64] Vreeland, *Hugo Grotius the Father*, p. 104.
[65] *Briefwisseling*, vol. 5, no. 1727, of 14 January 1632.
[66] Grotius, *Annales et Histoires des Troubles du Pays-Bas*, p. 4.
[67] Huizinga, *Dutch Civilization in the Seventeenth Century*, p. 74n; Geyl, *The Revolt of the Netherlands*, p. 292.
[68] Grotius, *De Jure Praedae*, vol. 1, p. 169; Grotius, *A Treatise on the Antiquity*, p. 11.

Love of Independence

Holland has always been an independent commonwealth. It was 'established by a people of a free original beginning in a free Land', and it retained its independence, even during 'the flourishing time' of the Romans. Holland 'never was subject neither to the Lawes nor Customes of the Emperor, nor of the Empire'. When there were attempts at subjugation – and there were two, towards the end of the Roman empire and during the reign of Philip II – the Battavers, now the Hollanders, took up arms and defended their liberty, such that 'the principall Soveraignty over the Hollanders hath been among themselves, and never depended upon any forraigne Authority'.[69]

A Moderate Government

Holland has always had the same form of government – a government of the nobles, 'the principall best men' distinguished by their birth or wealth or understanding, 'the Fathers of the Fatherland'. Such a government shares the advantages of 'Regall Authority' – majesty and dignity – and of 'the Authority of the Common People' – equal liberty – and avoids the disadvantages of both of them – the rule of one man, which is subject 'to many errours', and the rule of 'the Common People who are ignorant'. Such a government is not only good in itself. As the experience of many centuries shows, it 'well agrees' with the Hollanders' 'nature and manner of life'.[70] Hence, it ought to be preserved.

A Virtuous People

The people of Holland distinguish themselves by their 'undaunted courage and fidelity', their 'extraordinary fortitude' and 'inviolable good faith', their 'candour and foresight', their 'justice', their gentleness and compassion, their 'modesty and goodwill', their 'aptnesse for all sorts of warre', their skill as navigators. Even God approves of them: '[I]t has been His pleasure to reveal the glory of our race to the farthest regions of the world created by Him.'[71]

69 Grotius, *A Treatise on the Antiquity*, pp. 12, 84, 85.
70 Ibid., pp. 6–8, 141, 148; Grotius, *De Jure Praedae*, vol. 1, p. 341.
71 Grotius, *De Jure Praedae*, vol. 1, pp. 171, 178, 180, 210, 365; Grotius, *A Treatise on the Antiquity*, pp. 43, 46; Grotius, *True Religion*, p. 4.

Valued as an Ally

Holland, because of its government and because of its people, has always been a sought-after ally – both in war, as a 'confederate' of many a people, and in peace, as a partner in marriage alliances.[72] A country displaying such traits is surely worthy of support.[73]

The State and the Ruler

Grotius's discussion of the state is somewhat more elaborate than that of Vitoria or Gentili, but he takes up essentially the same issues. It is not a unified presentation, but various aspects of the state are discussed in different contexts. They may be presented as: the definition of the state; its origin and purpose; civil or sovereign power; and ruler and subject.

Definition

Grotius offers various definitions of the state. Sometimes the idea of community is emphasized: 'The state is a complete association of free men, joined together for the enjoyment of rights and their common interest.'[74] At other times the accent is on self-sufficiency, as in the following example, which he credits to the accounts of Thucydides, Cajetan, and Vitoria:

> [A] state must be conceived of as something ... self-sufficient, which in itself constitutes a whole entity; something ... possessed of its own laws, courts, revenue, and magistrates; something endowed with its own council and its own authority.[75]

And there is one instance, singled out by Gierke, where the concept of sovereign power appears in a definition of the state. It is a definition, the ingredients of which Grotius attributes to Plutarch, Paul, Seneca, Aristotle and Alfenus, which does not distinguish between state and people:

72 Grotius, *A Treatise on the Antiquity*, pp. 104–07.

73 There is one piece of writing, only recently published under the title 'De Republica Emendanda', which – if Grotius is the author, as its editors are inclined to think – would mean that in 1598/1600 Grotius was prepared to argue against particularism, provincial sovereignty, and the independence of Holland, and for unification, a central government, and 'a true republic'. See H. Grotius, 'De Republica Emendanda: A Juvenile Tract by Hugo Grotius on the Emendation of the Dutch Polity', eds A. Eyffinger, P. A. H. de Boer, J. T. de Smidt and L. E. van Holk, *Grotiana*, New Series, vol. 5, 1984.

74 Grotius, *De Jure Belli ac Pacis*, vol. 2, p. 44.

75 Grotius, *De Jure Praedae*, vol. 1, p. 63.

> [A] people … [has] a single essential character, a single spirit … [T]hat spirit or essential character in a people is the full and perfect union of civic life, the first product of which is sovereign power; that is the bond which binds the state together, that is the breath of life which so many thousands breathe.[76]

Grotius himself nowhere indicates a preference for any one of the definitions, nor does he discuss or compare them. And he does not offer a definition of the state which places the civil or sovereign power apart from the community or people, such as Louis XIV's 'l'état c'est moi', although, as shown below, the idea is present in his works. In fact, Grotius is not so much interested in the state as in civil or sovereign power.[77]

Origin and Purpose

Grotius does not ascribe the origin of the state to natural law, but to various practical reasons such as 'the weakness of isolated households against attack'. In *De Jure Praedae* he invokes the lawlessness of the pre-state condition. '[M]any persons', he writes, 'either failed to meet their obligations or even assailed the fortunes and the very lives of others', getting away, for the most part, without punishment. To which he adds a practical consideration: the increasing number of human beings. The latter reason figures exclusively in *The Jurisprudence of Holland*.[78] In *De Jure Belli ac Pacis* he terms such reasons 'expediency' and is concerned to identify a role for natural law: the law of the state thus founded derives ultimately from natural law: those who have established the state are obliged to abide by the pact they have agreed to. In a rather convoluted image he suggests that 'nature may be considered, so to say, the great-grandmother of municipal law'.[79]

Grotius portrays the purpose of the state by ideas such as 'self-protection through mutual aid' and the 'equal acquisition of the necessities of life', 'peace and order',[80] 'mutual advantage', thereby tying it to the reasons which made for its establishment. There is one occasion, however, where he identifies a purpose which links the state to an entity larger than itself – human society. The state was founded, he submits in

[76] Gierke, *Das Deutsche Genossenschaftsrecht*, vol. 4, p. 286; Grotius, *De Jure Belli ac Pacis*, vol. 2, pp. 310–11.

[77] The 'absence of philosophical reflection' in Grotius regarding the state is the subject matter of a critical literature on the part of political theorists. See, for example, Scheltens, 'Grotius' Doctrine of the Social Contract', pp. 43–60.

[78] Grotius, *De Jure Praedae*, vol. 1, pp. 19, 20, 92; Grotius, *The Jurisprudence of Holland*, vol. 1, p. 7; Grotius, *De Jure Belli ac Pacis*, vol. 2, pp. 14–16, 149.

[79] Grotius, *De Jure Belli ac Pacis*, vol. 2, p. 15.

[80] Grotius, *De Jure Praedae*, vol. 1, p. 20; Grotius, *De Jure Belli ac Pacis*, vol. 2, pp. 53, 139, 141; Grotius, *The Jurisprudence of Holland*, vol. 1, p. 17.

De Jure Praedae, not for the purpose of destroying 'the society which links all men as a whole', but rather in order 'to fortify that universal society by a more dependable means of protection'.[81] As the discussion proceeds, it becomes clear that a primary purpose of the state, once established, is to preserve the order thus constituted.

Civil or Sovereign Power

These are closely related, although the precise relationship is not made clear. Grotius defines civil power as '[t]he moral faculty of governing a state', although his writings, especially *De Jure Praedae*, impart to it a second meaning – civil power is the power which inheres in the state and makes it 'self-sufficient' or 'perfect'.[82] He offers various formulations of the legislative, executive and judicial powers of the state, but does not elaborate on them,[83] being more interested in the concepts of sovereignty and sovereign power. He offers this definition:

> That power is called sovereign whose actions are not subject to the legal control of another, so that they cannot be rendered void by the operation of another human will.[84]

In the external context, sovereignty means the absence of subjection to another state or ruler, or, to put it positively, the possession of independence. 'Truly, there is no greater sovereign power set over the power of the state and superior to it, since the state is a self-sufficient aggregation.'[85] Being independent or being subject to none means having the right to make war, to conclude peace, to enter into treaties and to act as 'the guardian and vindicator of the divine law, the natural law and the law of nations'.[86]

In the internal context he does not discuss in what sovereign power consists, although he attributes to it, in statements scattered through his writings, some of the same rights as to civil power, but rather looks at questions such as: in whom does sovereign power reside? What may terminate it? What constitutes an abuse of sovereign power and does it confer the right of rebellion?

[81] Grotius, *De Jure Praedae*, vol. 1, p. 19.
[82] Grotius, *De Jure Belli ac Pacis*, vol. 2, p. 101; Grotius, *De Jure Praedae*, vol. 1, pp. 25–26, 283–84.
[83] Grotius, *De Jure Belli ac Pacis*, vol. 2, pp. 101–02. As Dunning observes, 'with the art of government – the questions of organization and of administrative policy – [Grotius] had nothing to do'. See W. A. Dunning, *A History of Political Theories: From Luther to Montesquieu* (New York and London: Macmillan, 1949), p. 179.
[84] Grotius, *De Jure Belli ac Pacis*, vol. 2, p. 102.
[85] Grotius, *De Jure Praedae*, vol. 1, p. 28.
[86] Grotius, *De Jure Belli ac Pacis*, vol. 2, pp. 100–03, 130–37, 504–05, 804–05.

Sovereign power may reside in the community – a case considered exclusively in *De Jure Praedae*[87] – but, as Grotius argues in *De Jure Belli ac Pacis*, it is wrong to assume that it always does. Depending on its needs or inclinations, a community may transfer its sovereign power in its entirety to one or to several persons. A ruler may also receive sovereign power not from 'the will of the people', but from God or through a victorious war. It also may be the case that a community retains part of its sovereign power, transferring the other part to one person or to several persons.[88] Whatever a community's form of government – and he mentions some further possible forms – it should not, he holds, 'be measured by the superior excellence of this or that form ... in regard to which different men hold different views, but by its free choice'.[89]

How is sovereignty extinguished? A particular state may perish, either in its 'body' or in its 'form or spirit'; and when this happens, sovereign power perishes with it. As destructive causes of the body Grotius mentions the sea; earthquakes; voluntary destruction; pestilence; rebellion (that is, when 'the citizens withdraw from the association of their own accord'); and war which disperses a people such that 'it cannot unite again'. The form or spirit of a state is destroyed when, as a result of war, 'its entire or full enjoyment of common rights has been taken away'.[90]

Factors which, however, do not extinguish the body or spirit of a state are: migration; sharing a ruler with another state; uniting in a 'confederation' with one or more states (that is – and he borrows the idea from Strabo – 'forming a system'); concluding an unequal alliance; paying tribute; and feudal tenure.[91]

Ruler and Subject

The subject is 'under the rule of another', that is, of another human will – the sovereign power. Being 'truly subject' and as such 'part of the state' or 'part of the ruler' entails the duty to obey.[92] This duty appears equally strong in *De Jure Praedae* where Grotius says: 'The gods have assigned to the prince the supreme power of judgement; to the subjects, the glory of

[87] See, for example, Grotius, *De Jure Praedae*, vol. 1, pp. 283–89, 25–26, 63, 299–301. The term Grotius uses here is sometimes 'sovereign power' and at other times 'civil power' or simply 'power'.
[88] Grotius, *De Jure Belli ac Pacis*, vol. 2, pp. 103–09, 123–30.
[89] Ibid., p. 104.
[90] Ibid., pp. 312–14.
[91] Ibid., pp. 103, 130–37, 314–15.
[92] Grotius, *De Jure Praedae*, vol. 1, pp. 61–62, 144; Grotius, *De Jure Belli ac Pacis*, vol. 2, pp. 165, 578, 587–95.

obedience has been left'; and in *De Jure Belli ac Pacis* where he reminds the reader of Seneca's dictum: 'The rule of a king, just and unjust, you must endure.' His reason: '[B]eyond doubt the most important element in public affairs is the constituted order of bearing rule and rendering obedience.'[93]

In the event of abuses of power, such as engaging in an unjust war, showing disrespect for divine law, natural law or the law of nations, disregarding the laws of the country or violating a pledge, the subject might refuse to obey an order or may withdraw from the ruler, i.e. go into exile but, with the few exceptions noted below, may not use force against the sovereign power.[94]

If the subject is treated unjustly, even if the treatment is such that 'no one is warranted in inflicting', subjects have no right to take up arms. 'Others' may do it on their behalf.[95] That is, he permits intervention from the outside or what he calls 'the exercise of the right vested in human society' as a response to injustice on the part of the sovereign power.

This 'law of non-resistance', as Grotius presents it, derives its strength not only from the purpose which underlies the state – the maintenance of tranquillity, peace and order; it also is upheld by the Hebraic law, the Gospel and the practice of the early Christians. The formation of civil society and the creation of the state supersede the natural right to ward off injury.

Grotius deals briefly with the exceptional cases where the ruler may be resisted by force:

- the ruler who rules by mandate only (the community having retained the sovereign power) oversteps the 'bounds defining his office';
- the ruler 'renounces' or 'abandons' the sovereign power;
- the ruler proceeds to transfer the people to some other ruler;
- the ruler intends to destroy the people;
- the ruler violates a clause the very observance of which was the condition on which the sovereign power was 'granted' to him;
- the ruler attempts to gain for himself a part of the sovereign power which does not belong to him; and
- the right to resist 'in a particular case' was agreed upon when the people transferred the sovereign power to the ruler.[96]

[93] Grotius, *De Jure Praedae*, vol. 1, p. 76 (quoting Tacitus); see also pp. 79, 125, 128; Grotius, *De Jure Belli ac Pacis*, vol. 2, pp. 140, 143.

[94] Grotius, *De Jure Bellis ac Pacis*, vol. 2, pp. 138–40, 253–54, 587–90; Grotius, *De Jure Praedae*, vol. 1, pp. 77–78.

[95] Grotius, *De Jure Bellis ac Pacis*, vol. 2, p. 584. It is a right which he does not present without attaching qualifications.

[96] Grotius, *De Jure Belli ac Pacis*, vol. 2, pp. 157–59. Grotius grants the right of resistance in three further cases, all of which relate to a 'usurper' of sovereign power (pp. 160–61).

Grotius does not subsume the above seven instances under a 'law of resistance', but they may be taken to express the view that a violation of 'the constituted order' on the part of the ruler entails the right of resistance on the part of the ruled.

Grotius's ideas about sovereignty portray those in whom it is vested – the state and/or the ruler(s) – as having no superior above them and as being supreme in relation to those whom they rule – the citizens or subjects. The origin of the state and its purpose make, on the part of those who rule, for a concern with order rather than justice in relation to those whom they rule.

Human Society: Another Kind of Commonwealth

The idea of human society appears in a number of Grotius's writings; Gierke makes it the sole reason for appropriating their author for the *via media*; and Wight gives it as one of his reasons. What is this idea and what is its place in Grotius's thinking?

An answer may be attempted by examining the origin of human society, the members of human society, the law of human society, and human society from the point of view of states and rulers. The third of these proves to be highly problematic.

Origin

Human society, according to Grotius, owes its existence to a 'natural disposition' on the part of man: 'But among the traits characteristic of man is an impelling desire for society, that is, for the social life – not of any and every sort, but peaceful.'[97] This does not mean that man is not 'regardful of self'. On the contrary, 'in human affairs the first principle of a man's duty relates to himself'.[98]

Human society has existed as long as mankind, i.e. long before states, and continues to exist together with them.[99]

[97] Grotius, *De Jure Praedae*, vol. 1, p. 92; Grotius, *De Jure Belli ac Pacis*, vol. 2, p. 11.

[98] Grotius, *De Jure Praedae*, vol. 1, p. 9; see also pp. 21, 29, 45, 103; and Grotius, *De Jure Belli ac Pacis*, vol. 2, pp. 142, 173, 186–90. This side of Grotius's view of man is often not discussed by the secondary literature. See, for example, Lauterpacht, 'The Grotian Tradition in International Law', pp. 333–36. It provides the foundation for Tuck's 'Hobbesian' interpretation of Grotius. See Tuck, *The Rights of War and Peace*, pp. 78–127.

[99] See, for example, Grotius, *De Jure Praedae*, vol. 1, pp. 11–19; and Grotius, *De Jure Belli ac Pacis*, vol. 2, pp. 186–88.

Membership

He does not offer a definition of human society, but refers, for example, to 'the mutual tie of kinship among men'.[100] He has many names for it: apart from human society, possibly the most frequently used term, he speaks of mankind, the brotherhood of man, the world state, commonwealth, that society which embraces all mankind and that great society 'the human race is like a great people, and hence some philosophers call this world a city'.[101] Human society includes all human beings, even pirates and tyrants, and knows of no outsiders.[102] As in the case of Vitoria and Gentili, it is clear that expressions such as 'world state' or 'commonwealth' are not to be taken literally.

Law

The law which is proper to human society, as indeed to all human conduct, is natural law. We may consider first Grotius's definition of this law, then his discussion of its subject matter.

In *De Jure Praedae*, the law of nature is inherent in all living creatures, it is 'the law instilled by God into the heart of created things, from the first moment of their creation, for their own conservation'.[103] There is a law specific to man, which he terms the primary law of nations, for man, in contrast with all other beings, is endowed by God 'with the sovereign attribute of reason' – and reveals itself in 'the mutual accord of nations'.[104]

In *De Jure Belli ac Pacis* he offers a radically changed definition, rejecting the former distinction as of 'hardly any value': 'For, strictly speaking, only a being that applies general principles is capable of law'.[105] He now offers his well-known definition:

> The law of nature is a dictate of right reason, which points out that an act, according as it is or is not in conformity with rational nature, has in it a quality of moral baseness or moral necessity; and that, in consequence, such an act is either forbidden or enjoined by the author of nature, God.[106]

[100] Grotius, *De Jure Belli ac Pacis*, vol. 2, p. 582.

[101] H. Grotius, 'Defensio', in Wright, 'Some Less Known Works of Hugo Grotius', p. 169. See also Grotius, *De Jure Praedae*, vol. 1, pp. 14, 19, 265; 13, 16, 50; 13; 93; 248, 261; Grotius, *De Jure Belli ac Pacis*, vol. 2, pp. 25, 197, 309, 504, 584; 17, 45, 799; 15; 510.

[102] See, for example, Grotius, *De Jure Praedae*, vol. 1, pp. 13, 315; Grotius, *De Jure Belli ac Pacis*, vol. 2, pp. 373–74, 793–94.

[103] Grotius, *De Jure Praedae*, vol. 1, p. 33; see also pp. 8–11.

[104] Ibid., pp. 8–9, 11–12. This is an example of the word *gens* or nation being used in the non-political sense, that is, as not referring to distinct political entities.

[105] Grotius, *De Jure Belli ac Pacis*, vol. 2, p. 41.

[106] Ibid., pp. 38–39; see also p. 468. For comments on Grotius's conception of the law of nature as a product of the divine will and of man's reason derived from God's reason

His definition in *The Jurisprudence of Holland* is along similar lines. The existence of this law, Grotius holds, can be proved by referring to reason itself – there are 'certain fundamental conceptions which no one can deny ... without doing violence to himself'. God himself cannot change it. 'Just as even God, then, cannot cause that two times two should not equal four, so He cannot cause that which is intrinsically evil be not evil.'[107] This he terms proof *a priori*. There can also be proof *a posteriori*, by reference to the statements of philosophers, historians, poets, orators, and other 'men of wisdom' such as those 'inspired by God', when these are in agreement.[108]

Natural law, then, is immutable. But he goes on to say, 'the thing, in regard to which the law of nature has ordained', can change. Thus, some things belong to the law of nature if 'no provision has otherwise been made; but provisions in relation to those things which the law of nature permits can be made, and have been made, by both the will of God and the will of man'.[109]

In *The Jurisprudence of Holland*, he formulates this proviso even more broadly:

> That which is forbidden by the law of nature may not be enjoined by positive law, nor that which is enjoined by the first forbidden by the second, circumstances remaining unchanged.

Indeed, '[t]hings may be so changed by another law, or by the voluntary act of man, that the obligation of the law of nature ceases to apply in the circumstances'.[110]

The idea of immutability, then, as a distinction between natural and volitional law – Gierke might consider it the most important distinction[111] – is not inseparable from the law of nature as Grotius presents it.

see, for example, D. P. O'Connell, 'Rationalism and Voluntarism in the Fathers of International Law', *Indian Year Book of International Affairs*, vol. 13, part II, 1964; and Haggenmacher, *Grotius et la Doctrine de la Guerre Juste*, pp. 466–70, 496–523.

107 Grotius, *De Jure Belli ac Pacis*, vol. 2, p. 40.

108 Ibid., p. 23. Grotius presents the two lines of reasoning – proof *a priori* and proof *a posteriori* (pp. 42–44). See also Grotius, *De Jure Praedae*, vol. 1, p. 59. For a discussion of his method see, for example, B. P. Vermeulen, 'Grotius' Methodology and System of International Law', *Netherlands International Law Review*, vol. 30, no. 1, 1983, pp. 376–78; and, more, briefly, G. Schwarzenberger, 'The Grotius Factor in International Law and Relations: A Functional Approach', in Bull, Kingsbury and Roberts (eds), *Hugo Grotius and International Relations*, pp. 305–06.

109 Grotius, *De Jure Belli ac Pacis*, vol. 2, pp. 40, 57, 178–79, 192, 205, 207, 250–51, 297.

110 Grotius, *The Jurisprudence of Holland*, vol. 1, p. 7.

111 Gierke, *Das Deutsche Genossenschaftsrecht*, vol. 4, p. 282.

All this suggests that there may be difficulties, or ambiguity, in applying the rules of natural law in practice, a doubt which is strengthened when we turn to the question of its subject matter. Grotius presents this at two different levels. The first is general and abstract. In *De Jure Praedae* he lists laws including:

It shall be permissible to defend [one's own] life and to shun that which threatens to prove injurious ... It shall be permissible to acquire for oneself, and to retain, those things which are useful for life ... Let no one inflict injury upon his fellow ... Let no one seize possession of that which has been taken into the possession of another ... Evil deeds must be corrected ... Good deeds must be recompensed ... Individual citizens should not only refrain from injuring other citizens, but should furthermore protect them, both as a whole and as individuals.[112]

If laws conflict with one another, they are assigned a priority; for example, the first two take precedence over those that follow.[113] These laws and a set of accompanying rules are followed systematically in the overall argument.

In *De Jure Belli ac Pacis* he identifies a collection of items assembled in a paragraph of the 'Prolegomena' as belonging to the law of nature 'properly so-called':

[T]he abstaining from that which is another's, the restoration to another of anything of his which we may have, together with any gain we may have received from it; the obligation to fulfill promises, the making good of a loss incurred through our fault, and the inflicting of penalties upon men according to their deserts.[114]

Items such as 'self-defence' and 'self-assistance' occur elsewhere in the work.[115] There is no attempt at a systematic listing, nor is the argument structured in terms of these rules. Especially in this latter work, the content of the law of nature remains unclear.

The second level is more concrete, but brings no greater clarity. Three kinds of situation may be distinguished. First, there are principles of law which, because of the general context and of statements elsewhere in the texts, the reader is inclined to see as manifestations of the law of nature but which Grotius fails to identify as such. For example:

- The right of innocent use. To this he attributes 'the right to the use of running water' or, as he also puts it: '[A] river ... is the property of the people through whose territory it flows, or of [its] ruler'; but 'any one

[112] Grotius, *De Jure Praedae*, vol. 1, pp. 10–15; see also p. 75.
[113] Ibid., pp. 21, 29, 45, 103.
[114] Grotius, *De Jure Belli ac Pacis*, vol. 2, pp. 12–13.
[115] Ibid., p. 52.

may drink … from it'. He also ascribes to it 'the right of passage over land and rivers'. These should be 'open to those who, for legitimate reasons, have need to cross over them'.[116]

- The right of temporary sojourn: 'To those who pass through country it ought to be permissible to sojourn for a time for any good reason'.
- The right of permanent residence: to foreigners 'expelled from their homes' a permanent residence 'ought not to be denied'.[117]

These principles are contained in the chapter 'Of Things which Belong to Men in Common', the initial proposition of which is that '[s]ome things belong to us by a right common to mankind'; they are clearly supportive of human society; but Grotius relates them only to 'the old community of property', not the law of nature.[118]

Second, there are other principles which Grotius does relate to the law of nature, but which he is prepared to sacrifice without ado to positive law. For example, by the law of nature, a man has the right to hunt wild animals, fish and birds. This is true, he says, 'so long as municipal law does not intervene'.[119] From 'the force of natural liberty' a man derives the right to buy things which he needs for life at a fair price, to refuse to sell what belongs to him, or to seek marriage abroad. These are permitted by the law of nature, unless 'annulled by any statute law'.[120] Nature confers upon all men the right to resist in order to avoid injury, but 'the state … in the interest of public peace and order, can limit that common right of resistance'.[121]

Third, there are principles which Grotius treats differently in different contexts. For example, in *De Jure Praedae*, the freedom of commerce is securely tied to the law of nature, and 'cannot be abrogated' – even though, elsewhere, 'under the primary law of nations … there were no commercial transactions'.[122] In 'The Colonial Conferences between England and the Netherlands in 1613 and 1615', he negates the principle of the freedom of commerce by confronting it with another principle of 'the law of nations' – the principle that agreements are to be kept.[123]

[116] Grotius, *De Jure Belli ac Pacis*, vol. 2, p. 196.
[117] Ibid., p. 201.
[118] Ibid., pp. 186, 195, 196. The law of nature did in fact change, as Grotius notes in a later passage, from 'its original state' to 'the state which followed the introduction of property ownership' (p. 295).
[119] Ibid., p. 192.
[120] Ibid., pp. 203–05.
[121] Ibid., p. 139. For further examples of the will of man interfering with the law of nature, see pp. 253, 296, 297, 298, 334, 335, 354–55.
[122] Grotius, *De Jure Praedae*, vol. 1, pp. 227, 257.
[123] Clark and van Eysinga, 'The Colonial Conferences', vol. 15, p. 188. See also section on Commerce later in this chapter.

Excluded from individual ownership is the sea, for it is 'common to all under natural law'. Not even parts of the sea are exempted from this rule, for 'if parts of the sea could become property, the entirety … could also'. In *De Jure Belli ac Pacis* 'the law of nature presents no obstacle' to acquiring 'a part of the sea'.[124]

As the preceding examples indicate, the emphasis is on those things which, in the end, the law of nature neither enjoins nor forbids. Human society takes on an uncertain and changing appearance.

States and Rulers

Nature, it is Grotius's view, rejects as a man-made fiction the distinction between 'people grouped as a whole and private individuals'. States and rulers, however, do not do likewise. From their point of view, there is a difference, and this difference is 'civil power'. Civil or sovereign power entitles states and rulers to act in accordance with their interests, and these interests may or may not be those of human society, which means two things. First, in the internal context, they may, 'in the interest of peace and order', enact laws which are not in harmony with the law of nature; and if they fail to observe contracts concluded with their subjects, the latter have no right to compel them.[125]

Second, in the external context, states and rulers may adopt laws which are contrary to the law of nature, such as the rules governing formal war;[126] they may act as the 'guardians and vindicators' of the law of nature and, for example, uphold the freedom of commerce or punish wrongdoing anywhere in the world, but they also may decide not to – their interests may be better served by disregarding these rights. As Grotius holds, one people is not bound to defend another people from wrong.[127]

The observance of the law of nature is 'binding upon all kings', according to a statement in *De Jure Belli ac Pacis*, but, as the texts at large reveal, much of what Grotius is concerned with relates to that which is not obligatory according to this law, which means, states and rulers have a choice.[128] As Grotius presents it, human society cannot be certain of support by states and rulers. C. C. Roelofsen observes that 'Grotius'

[124] Grotius, *De Jure Praedae*, vol. 1, p. 232; Grotius, *Mare Liberum*, p. 29; Grotius, 'Defensio', p. 194; Grotius, *De Jure Belli ac Pacis*, vol. 2, pp. 209, 211.
[125] Grotius, *De Jure Belli ac Pacis*, vol. 2, p. 384.
[126] Ibid., pp. 461, 651–52.
[127] See sections on 'Commerce' and 'The Question of War' later in this chapter.
[128] Grotius, *De Jure Belli ac Pacis*, vol. 2, p. 121.

natural law, though theoretically predominant, actually only has a slight influence. It is hard to find what, according to Grotius, is the substantive content of its rules.'[129] The present findings support Roelofsen's thesis.

To conclude, in *De Jure Praedae*, Grotius speaks of human society as 'commended to us so frequently and so enthusiastically by the ancient philosophers' and in *De Jure Belli ac Pacis* he notes that 'the force of the relationship which nature has wished to prevail among men' is being restored, but his own treatment of the matter does not amount to a statement on behalf of human society.[130]

A Plurality Rather Than a Society of States and Rulers?

There are sentences in Grotius's writings which attract the eye and mind of those interested in the idea of international society. For example, the 'Prolegomena' of *De Jure Belli ac Pacis* refers to 'certain laws ... between all states, or a great many states' having 'in view the advantage, not of particular states, but of the great society of states'; Book Two identifies 'international law' as affecting 'the mutual society of nations in relation to one another'; and the concluding chapter of Book Three draws attention to the importance of keeping good faith, 'for not only is every state sustained by good faith ... but also that greater society of states'.[131] *De Jure Praedae* is in no way outdistanced by *De Jure Belli ac Pacis*, for, in its 'Prolegomena', it presents the idea that:

> [O]wing to the existence of a common good of an international nature, the various peoples who had established states for themselves entered into agreements concerning that international good.[132]

However, the expectations which these utterances raise remain largely unfulfilled. Their wording, it is true, is more suggestive in the English language in *The Classics of International Law* than in the Latin original. But the Latin text is suggestive enough, even if one makes allowance for the often non-political meaning of the word *gens* or 'nation'.[133]

[129] C. G. Roelofsen, 'Some Remarks on the "Sources" of the Grotian System of International Law', *Netherlands International Law Review*, vol. 30, no. 1, 1983, p. 77.

[130] Grotius, *De Jure Praedae*, vol. 1, p. 13; Grotius, *De Jure Belli ac Pacis*, vol. 2, p. 715.

[131] Grotius, *De Jure Belli ac Pacis*, vol. 2, pp. 15, 295, 860. As noted earlier, 'international law' is better translated as 'law of nations'.

[132] Grotius, *De Jure Praedae*, vol. 1, p. 26.

[133] H. Grotius, *Hugonis Grotii De Jure Belli et Pacis Libri Tres* [Hugo Grotius, On the Law of War and Peace, Three Books], vol. 1, ed. W. Whewell (Cambridge: Cambridge University Press, 1853); H. Grotius, *De Jure Praedae Commentarius*, vol. 2, *The Collotype Reproduction of the Original Manuscript of 1604, The Classics of International Law* (Oxford and London: Clarendon Press and Geoffrey Cumberlege, 1950), p. 12. Haggenmacher mentions four passages in the 'Prolegomena' of *De Jure Belli ac Pacis* (§ 2, 17, 32, 39–41) which he thinks may have given rise to

Expectations remain unfulfilled because Grotius does not provide the ingredients necessary to put substance into the statements referred to above. Like *fata morgana*, they lure the searcher into traversing the many pages of his writings without leading to what they promise. The findings gathered together in the course of this exploration are presented in this and the following sections. They amount to a picture of international relations which is fragmented, indeed.

Let us see how it takes shape.

Plurality and Equality

First, and readily discernible, is the idea of a plurality of independent states and rulers. Grotius attests to their presence everywhere when he says:

> [I]n every part of the world we find a division into just such united groups, with the result that persons who hold themselves aloof from this established practice seem hardly worthy to be called human beings.[134]

Although he qualifies this – states are absent 'on the sea, in a wilderness, or on vacant islands', and where 'men live in family groups and not in states' or 'in any region where the people have no government' – he is firm in his insistence that states are immortal.[135] Their permanence is immediately attributable to man, for 'mans wisdome and policy have some stroke in point of government', but ultimately 'the preservation of Commonwealths' is imputable to 'an all-guiding providence'.[136] As noted earlier here, claims to universal rule by pope and/or emperor have no room in this scheme of things.

Also clearly visible is the idea that states and rulers are formally equal. It appears in *De Jure Praedae* when he says, '[o]ne state … is not in subjection but in contraposition … to another state', and in *De Jure Belli ac Pacis* when he speaks of 'the equal rights' of those who 'are subject to no one', or when he reminds his audience that among the Greeks, according to Thucydides, 'colonies in respect to legal independence were on the same plane as the mother cities'.[137] States and rulers may differ in power

'the extensive interpretations which the work has received and hence to the title itself of founder of international law commonly attributed to its author'. Haggenmacher, *Grotius et la Doctrine de la Guerre Juste*, pp. 618–19, 451–52.

134 Grotius, *De Jure Praedae*, vol. 1, p. 20.

135 Ibid., p. 88; Grotius, *De Jure Belli ac Pacis*, vol. 2, pp. 92, 310, 506.

136 Grotius, *True Religion*, pp. 35–37; see also Grotius, *De Jure Belli ac Pacis*, vol. 2, p. 310.

137 Grotius, *De Jure Praedae*, vol. 1, p. 27; Grotius, *De Jure Belli ac Pacis*, vol. 2, pp. 130–36, 504–05, also his comment on 'What Rank Is to Be Observed among Equals, even Kings', p. 252. Likewise, unequal treaties do not negate formal equality. See Keene, *Beyond the*

or prestige, civilization or religion, but these factors do not affect their formal standing.

The Law of Nations

The next component is highly problematic. It is the law which 'Carneades passed over altogether', the law which holds between states and rulers.[138] Its problematic nature is not immediately obvious but appears as one follows Grotius's answers to the two closely related questions: what is the law of nations? What is its subject matter?

As in the case of natural law, Grotius later simplified his initial definition and terminology. In *De Jure Praedae*, he termed it the 'secondary or volitional law of nations' (the primary law, as noted above, being essentially natural law); in *De Jure Belli ac Pacis* it is simply the law of nations, sometimes retaining 'volitional' to emphasize this aspect. In contrast to Gentili, he insists on a clear distinction between natural law, coming from God, and the law of nations, a product of agreement among states:

> [The volitional law of nations] is broader in scope than municipal law ... [it] has received its obligatory force from the will of all nations, or ... of many nations, for ... outside of the sphere of the law of nature ... there is hardly any law common to all nations.

'The law of nations', he adds, 'is the creation of time and custom.'[139] The proof of its existence 'is found in unbroken custom and the testimony of those who are skilled in it'.[140] He does not define 'custom' but accords it a high standing; he endorses Seneca's reference to 'laws which are unwritten but more sure than all written law'.[141]

It is noteworthy that he refers to 'a law common to all nations' rather than 'existing between' them, even though in the 'Prolegomena' he identified it as a law between states.[142] In the texts at large he has both meanings, more often the latter. In an obscure passage in the chapter 'On Acquisitions Commonly Said to be by the Law of Nations', referring to

Anarchical Society, pp. 48–52. In spite of the presence of this idea in Grotius's writings, Haggenmacher insists on its absence. See Haggenmacher, *Grotius et la Doctrine de la Guerre Juste*, p. 546; and P. Haggenmacher, 'On Assessing the Grotian Heritage', in T. M. C. Asser Instituut (ed.), *International Law and the Grotian Heritage: A Commemorative Colloquium Held at The Hague on 8 April 1983 on the Occasion of the Fourth Centenary of the Birth of Hugo Grotius* (The Hague: T. M. C. Asser Instituut, 1985).

[138] Grotius, *De Jure Belli ac Pacis*, vol. 2, p. 15.

[139] Ibid., p. 44.

[140] Ibid.

[141] Ibid., p. 450.

[142] Ibid., p. 15.

certain Greek laws which were followed by the Italians and their neighbours, he states:

> This law of nations is not international law, strictly speaking, for it does not affect the mutual society of nations in relation to one another; it affects only each particular people in a state of peace … a single people can change its determination without consulting others.

Over time, he goes on, there may be a different common custom, 'and therefore a different law of nations (improperly so called)'.[143] This appears to discredit the formal definition, but he does not elaborate nor return to the question.

In the 'Prolegomena' to *De Jure Praedae* he posits a twofold division. The first category has 'the force of an international pact', and includes the inviolability of ambassadors, the burial of the dead and judicial procedure.[144] The second category lacks 'the force of a pact': it is not law, but rather 'accepted custom' and contains 'provisions relative to servitude, to certain kinds of contract, and to order of succession'. These provisions, Grotius holds, may be abrogated by individual states, because they owe their existence to a chance accord.

> [They] have been adopted in identical form – either imitatively or as a coincidence – by all or … a majority of nations, in accordance with their separate and individual interests.[145]

De Jure Belli ac Pacis does not give this twofold division, perhaps because custom is now given a higher standing, but some of its elements reappear occasionally. At the end of the nineteenth chapter of Book Two, Grotius offers a list of items which he subsumes under the law of nations. Apart from 'the right of legation' and 'the right of sepulchre' they include: '[T]he right to things possessed for a long time [prescription], the right of succession … and the rights which are created by a contract no matter how unfair'. All these rights, he submits, impose an 'obligation by virtue of the volitional law of nations', which may be interpreted to mean that he accords them the same status, and the wording which he chooses suggests the status of 'pact' or 'law'.[146]

An assessment of Grotius's account of the law of nations must await the discussion of commerce, diplomacy and war in the following sections,

[143] Ibid., p. 295.

[144] Grotius, *De Jure Praedae*, vol. 1, pp. 26, 27, 250. Regarding judicial procedure, Grotius states the following rule: 'Neither the state nor any citizen thereof shall seek to enforce his [sic] own right against another state or its citizen save by judicial procedure' (p. 27).

[145] Grotius, *De Jure Praedae*, vol. 1, pp. 27, 162.

[146] Grotius, *De Jure Belli ac Pacis*, vol. 2, p. 461; also pp. 24, 28–29, 208, 260, 295, 309, 608.

but it may be instructive to examine his comments on the other topics just referred to. How do they relate to his definition? And are they placed in a larger context which could be seen as a notion of international society?

'Provisions relating to certain kinds of contract' are discussed in *De Jure Praedae*, surprisingly, in the category of custom, in *De Jure Belli ac Pacis* as law. Contracts in general are discussed in terms of natural law, treaties in terms of the law of nations. He presents a classification of treaties – as merely reaffirming natural law, or as adding something further, as equal or unequal – and inquires whether they may be concluded with 'strangers to the Christian religion'. He discusses treaties in the context of peace and war, the latter being rather more prominent. In a later chapter he turns to peace treaties, not to questions of general principle but the technical details of negotiating them.[147] All in all, his discussion remains concrete and practical: he does not refer back to his general account of the law of nations, nor give expression to any wider context that might indicate a concept of international society.

Atypically, the right of sepulchre, the obligation to permit the burial of the dead, provides an illustration of Grotius's main contentions on the law of nations. It is a long-established custom, demonstrated by many examples and the words of many authorities: '[W]ith great unanimity the ancients agreed that war is not lawfully undertaken if it is denied'.[148] Again, there is no hint of an idea of international society, even though the example could readily be seen in this light.

Other examples are less satisfying. He affirms the right of prescription no less categorically: 'By universal customary law ownership is by possession exceeding the memory of man ... in accordance with the volitional law of nations'. But very few examples or authors are offered in support.[149] The law of succession is described in great detail, but beyond agreement on a few very general principles such as the precedence of the eldest son, there is an extended discussion of different practices, with no explanation how any of this is related to the law of nations.[150]

Overall, then, these few examples fail to clarify issues raised by the definition of the law of nations and provide no indication whether or not Grotius envisaged the world in terms of an international society. At this stage the search for more substance behind his evocative language remains unsuccessful.

[147] Ibid., pp. 343–61, 391–408, 805–20.
[148] Ibid., pp. 450–61.
[149] Ibid., p. 226.
[150] Ibid., pp. 267–94.

Good Faith

Continuing the search, one meets with the principle of good faith. In the context of human society, Grotius clearly sees it as a bond. But with respect to the relations between states and 'the supreme rulers of men', he makes no such claim. He discusses the principle in relation to allies and enemies, he asserts its importance – good faith must not be violated – and he mentions breaches of good faith;[151] but he seems reluctant to expose his reasons for insisting that good faith should be observed.[152] There is the idea that good faith imposes 'a restriction for warfare'; and the conclusion to *De Jure Belli ac Pacis* admonishes rulers to keep good faith 'more earnestly than others' because 'they violate it with greater impunity'. For the sake of their conscience, they should 'cherish good faith', and in the interest of their reputation as it supports 'the authority of the royal power'.[153] It is a virtue of the individual, but is it conducive to society among states and rulers? Grotius does not present it as such.

Religion

Searching for further possible links between states and rulers, one encounters the idea of religion. Within the state, Grotius plays down its importance as a unifying force: here 'the laws and the easy execution of the laws' take the place of religion. At the level of human society, however, where the laws are few and their enforcement is difficult, religion – which in the form of piety is of universal extent – is of great consequence: 'If piety is removed ... with it go good faith and the friendly association of mankind, and the one most excellent virtue, justice'.[154]

When Grotius places religion in the context of states and rulers, he becomes more specific: he is concerned with the Christian religion which must be defended; but it is difficult to see what follows for the relations among states and rulers, in general.

151 See, for example, Grotius, *De Jure Praedae*, vol. 1, pp. 194–202, 330–31; and Grotius, *De Jure Belli ac Pacis*, vol. 2, pp. 20, 814–20.

152 See, for example, Grotius, *De Jure Praedae*, vol. 1, pp. 117, 302; and Grotius, *De Jure Belli ac Pacis*, vol. 2, pp. 792, 798–99. As Fikentscher puts it in his study of an early Grotius work, '*Fides* is described and demanded, but it is not philosophically substantiated'. W. Fikentscher, 'De Fide et Perfidia – Der Treuegedanke in den "Staatsparallelen" des Hugo Grotius aus heutiger Sicht' [On Honesty and Perfidy – The Idea of Truthfulness in Hugo Grotius's "State Parallels" Viewed from the Present], *Sitzungsberichte der Bayerischen Akademie der Wissenschaften*, vol. 1, 1979, p. 51.

153 Grotius, *De Jure Belli ac Pacis*, vol. 2, pp. 860–61.

154 Ibid., pp. 509 (quoting Cicero), 510.

To demonstrate this briefly: according to *De Jure Praedae*, Christian states may justly conclude alliances and treaties with non-Christians against Christians. Such alliances may be 'encouraged to persist', and even be 'expanded'. In *De Jure Belli ac Pacis* they are presented as being permissible, but caution is advised – 'the power of the heathen' may greatly increase by such alliances. Christian 'peoples and kings' are encouraged to form an alliance 'while an impious enemy is raging in arms', for in this way they will be able to serve Christ with the power that is theirs.[155]

In *True Religion*, Grotius exhorts his countrymen to take the Christian religion to non-Christian countries, to

> Pagans, such as live in China, Arabia, and Guinea; ... Mahumetans, as those under the dominion of the Turks, the Persian, and Moores of Barbarie; or ... the Jewes themselves, at this day the professed enemies of Christianity.[156]

His reason is that the Christian religion 'excells' all others. The religious differences within Christianity are discounted. Does not disagreement happen in 'all kinde of Arts and Sciences'? Is not this variety 'contained within certain bounds'?[157]

Thus the effects of religion are variable. Christianity is sometimes a bond between Christian states and rulers, but not always; it sometimes makes for a division between Christian and non-Christian states, again not always. When it comes to the laws of war, discussed in a later section, the same harsh law applies equally to both, Christian and non-Christian alike.

Civilization

While searching for further possible links, one notes the idea that there are 'civilized nations', 'nations more advanced in civilization', 'more civilized peoples', 'nations of the better sort' as against 'uncivilized peoples'.[158] Grotius normally identifies the former only indirectly as European, only

[155] Grotius, *De Jure Praedae*, vol. 1, pp. 283, 315–17, 345–48; Grotius, *De Jure Belli ac Pacis*, vol. 2, pp. 397–403.

[156] Grotius, *True Religion*, pp. 4–5. Wolf credits Grotius with 'tolerance *vis-à-vis* all religions and forms of worship', but he does this without revealing the evidence on which he bases his view. See E. Wolf, *Grosse Rechtsdenker der deutschen Geistesgeschichte* [Great Legal Thinkers in German Intellectual History] (Tuebingen: Mohr (Paul Siebeck), 1963), p. 260.

[157] Grotius, *True Religion*, pp. 128, 131. This may be contrasted with his comments in the 'Prolegomena' to *De Jure Belli ac Pacis* deploring the lack of restraint in war 'throughout the Christian world'. Grotius, *De Jure Belli ac Pacis*, vol. 2, p. 20.

[158] See, for example, Grotius, *De Jure Belli ac Pacis*, vol. 2, pp. 42–43, 208, 266, 507, 624, 652, 657, 738.

once establishing a direct link between 'civilized' and 'European': 'But this also [to poison weapons or water] is contrary to the law of nations, not indeed of all nations, but of European nations, and of such others as attain to the higher standard of Europe.'[159] Grotius does not dwell on this idea; he mentions it only in passing.

With this, the search for ingredients to put substance into the idea of international society may be concluded. Its findings: there is the idea of a plurality of independent states and rulers; and also of their formal equality. The law of nations is poorly developed as a link between states and rulers, and the principle of good faith, as also the ideas of religion and civilization, do little to strengthen that link. Does a clearer picture emerge when we turn to more concrete aspects of international society?

Commerce

Grotius's ideas on commerce are adapted to the occasion on which he pronounces them. Within the framework of *De Jure Praedae*, two lines of argument are developed.

Free Commerce between Private Individuals in the Interest of Human Society

In the first place, under the heading 'Wherein It Is Shown that even if the War Were a Private War, It Would Be Just ...', Grotius invites the reader to assume that the United East India Company is a group of private individuals who represent no particular state and whose war against the Portuguese and Spaniards in the East Indies is a private war fought in defence of the freedom of commerce.[160]

To engage freely in commerce, Grotius argues, is a right conferred by the law of nature on all human beings, and no one is entitled to deprive anybody of this right. 'Freedom of trade ... springs from the primary law of nations, which has a natural and permanent cause, so that it cannot be abrogated.'[161] God distributed the goods of the earth unevenly and endowed different people with different skills because He wanted 'human friendship' to be 'fostered by mutual needs and resources'. Hence, 'anyone who abolishes this system of exchange, abolishes also the ... fellowship in which humanity is united'.[162]

[159] Ibid., p. 653.
[160] Grotius, *De Jure Praedae*, vol. 1, Ch. XII, pp. 216–82.
[161] Ibid., p. 257.
[162] Ibid., p. 218.

Given this, the individuals in question would be entitled to trade with the East Indians even if the Portuguese were 'the owners' of those regions. But – and Grotius borrows from Vitoria and other Spanish thinkers – the Portuguese 'lack possession' because those regions have their own rulers, and they lack all 'title to possession' because theirs is not the right of discovery nor the right of war, nor do they derive the right to take possession from the papal donation.[163] Equally, the Portuguese have no exclusive possession of the sea nor of the right of navigation. '[N]ature ... commands ... that the sea shall be held in common.'[164] And the pope cannot donate what is the property of no one in particular. Nor does prescription or custom apply, for, besides being 'rooted in civil law', it also can have no force when opposed to the law of nature.[165]

Thus, the Portuguese have no exclusive possession of the right to engage in commerce with the East Indians, and equity demands that the profits from commerce be not reaped by anyone alone, but be to the advantage of all.

> [T]he ... practice [of monopoly] ... is regarded as gravely pernicious when carried on within a single state ... [S]hould [it] be tolerated within that great community made up of the human race, thus enabling the Iberian nations to establish a monopoly over the whole earth?[166]

This, then, is Grotius's case for free commerce between private individuals in the interest of human society.

Free Commerce in the Interest of the State

Second, however, commerce is not really a private activity. As Grotius points out in the beginning of *De Jure Praedae*, and again in its concluding chapter, there is a close link between commerce and the well-being of the state. '[W]ho is so ignorant of the affairs of the Dutch', he asks, as not to know that 'the sole source of support, renown, and protection for those affairs lies in navigation and trade?' In particular, the commerce with Asia is the main, if not the whole, source of 'the wealth of our state'.[167]

[163] Ibid., pp. 220–26.

[164] Ibid., p. 232. De Pauw mentions that the principle of the freedom of the seas was already proclaimed by Pope Alexander III in 1169. See de Pauw, *Grotius and the Law of the Sea*, p. 8. Part of de Pauw's treatise (pp. 46–76) is reproduced in L. E van Holk and C. G. Roelofsen (eds), *Grotius Reader: A Reader for Students of International and Legal History* (The Hague: T. M. C. Asser Instituut, 1983), pp. 145–75.

[165] Grotius, *De Jure Praedae*, vol. 1, pp. 244–55.

[166] Ibid., p. 261.

[167] Ibid., pp. 1, 338–66.

More generally, 'in all lands the management of shipping falls within the sphere of supreme governmental power', so that anybody who returns with supplies from abroad is considered as having been away 'practically on state business'. When the Dutch rulers founded the United East India Company, nobody doubted that with it, 'the surest possible foundations of public prosperity had been laid'.[168] Look at the Spaniards and Portugese, he invites the reader: from what poverty to what wealth have they risen!

As a matter of fact, the war which the Dutch fight in the East Indies is not a private war, but a public war. Grotius presents a number of reasons why, in this war, Holland and its allies have justice on their side. One such reason is the interference by the Portuguese and Spaniards with the principle of free commerce, and it figures, not as a direct, but as an indirect cause. The Dutch do not fight the Portuguese and Spaniards because they obstruct commerce; they fight because such obstruction constitutes an injury to 'the welfare of the state' and the state has the right to defend itself against such injury.[169]

Grotius's second argument for free commerce does not refer to human society nor does it imply the existence of international society. It centres on the state, and a particular state at that, Holland.

Within *Mare Liberum*, another line of argument is developed.

Free Commerce between States in the Interest of Human Society

Grotius's next statement on commerce appears anonymously in 1609. Addressed to the rulers and free peoples of Christendom, it requests their opinion on a case which it wishes to draw to their attention. As Grotius puts it, to the 'double tribunal' of 'conscience' and 'public opinion' we submit a new case.

The case concerns 'practically the entire expanse of the high seas, the right of navigation, the freedom of trade', and involves the Dutch on the one side and the Spaniards and Portuguese on the other. Grotius argues it along the same lines as his first case in *De Jure Praedae* but, by giving it a different wrapping, he makes it appear different, and hence it can be interpreted differently.

The old title 'Wherein It Is Shown that even if the War Were a Private War, It Would Be Just …' has been removed and, in its place, a new title has been put: *Mare Liberum*.

[168] Ibid., pp. 340–41.
[169] Ibid., pp. 283–317.

The original proposition that the Dutch fighting in the East Indies be considered private individuals representing no particular country has disappeared, and Grotius now introduces the Dutch as 'the subjects of the United Netherlands'.[170] Only one law now applies, and Grotius presents it in the following way:

> The law by which our case must be decided is ... the same among all nations ... it is innate in every individual ... [I]t is a law derived from nature, the common mother of us all.[171]

The case may be seen as the case of the United Provinces whose right of commerce – a right conferred by the law of nature – is interfered with by the Spaniards and Portuguese who, on their side, are unable to claim any right in support of their action.[172] And the Dutch 'are to maintain at all hazards that freedom which is [theirs] by nature', even if it means continuing the war. They are enjoined to 'fight boldly, not only for your own liberty, but for that of the human race'.[173] The obstruction of commerce appears as a direct cause of a public war.

In *Mare Liberum*, then, Grotius may be seen as arguing for free commerce between states, but he still cannot be seen as arguing for international society. His reference, in the last quotation above and on other occasions, is to human society. It is human society rather than international society which suffers as a result of the violation of the principle of free commerce. Dutch interests and the interests of human society are in harmony.

'The Colonial Conferences between England and the Netherlands in 1613 and 1615' submits yet another line of argument.

Monopolized Commerce in the Interest of the State

In 1613 Grotius 'by order from the States of Holland' heads a delegation of three commissioners of the United East India Company to London, and he is again the spokesman for his country's interests when, two years later, an English delegation comes to The Hague.[174] The main item on

170 Grotius, *Mare Liberum*, pp. 3–7.

171 Ibid., p. 5. This does not mean that the terms primary law of nations and secondary or volitional law of nations do not occasionally appear in the text. See, for example, pp. 23, 53, 55, 57, 63.

172 Ibid., pp. 11–71.

173 Ibid., pp. 72, 73. This passage, as also the opening chapter, suggests that *Mare Liberum* was meant to lend support to the policies of the Stadhouder, Prince Maurits, rather than to those pursued by Oldenbarneveldt. If this were the case, it might help to explain why it was published anonymously in 1609.

174 Clark and van Eysinga, 'The Colonial Conferences', vol. 15, p. 85. Both editors emphasize that Grotius was the spokesman on the Dutch side at both conferences. See vol. 15, pp. 1, 13–14, 26, 85; vol. 17, pp. 19–20, 100.

the agenda is the commerce with the East Indies: The English demand 'free Trade into the East Indies and every part thereof', to which they are entitled 'as well by the Law of the Nations, as by the admittance of the Kings and Princes there';[175] the Dutch find reasons why this should be denied to them.

The argument presented by Grotius centres on the following three points. First, there is the question of law. The 'laws of nature and nations' are limited and defined by the laws and institutions of peoples. For example, there is no realm where it is lawful 'for every man to buy every commodity of every person, in every place, and at all times'. The rulers and peoples of the East Indies have chosen to agree to sell their spices to the Dutch alone, and nothing accords more with the laws of nature and nations than that these agreements be kept.[176]

The Dutch do not generally deny that the English, in accordance with the law of nations, are entitled to trade with the East Indies, but they maintain that the English have no right to buy that which is contracted by its owners to someone else: '[O]ur defence is based on the rule of the same law which says that agreements must be kept'.[177]

Above all, the Dutch insist on the very just cause of these contracts, which is the continuous defence on their part of those with whom they have entered the contracts, the rulers and peoples of the East Indies, against the Spaniards and Portuguese. Who wants to deny that it is a man's right to contract his products, present and future, in order to save his life?

Second, there is the question of equity. The commerce with the East Indies, Grotius argues, is impossible unless those regions are defended against the Spaniards and Portuguese. This defence has been and continues to be undertaken by the Dutch at great cost. But the English want to partake in the profits derived from that commerce without partaking in the expenses necessary to arrive at these profits. This is not equitable.[178]

And third, there is the question of common utility. The cost of the war has eaten into Dutch profits. If the Dutch have to share the profits with the English, but may not share the expenses, it will not be possible for the Dutch to continue paying for the war. But without it, neither the Dutch nor the English can have any hope of retaining the trade, for the Spaniards and Portuguese would take over.

175 Clark and van Eysinga, 'The Colonial Conferences', vol. 15, p. 118.
176 Ibid., pp. 101, 118–19.
177 Ibid., p. 188.
178 Ibid., pp. 181–82; see also pp. 192–93.

> [I]f free trade is granted to everybody, the French, the English, ourselves, and whoever else might be interested, where would you find ... the order and money necessary to push back the force of Spain.[179]

As the English observe, the Hollanders do not 'declare themselves in the behalf of free Trade, and to all nations, with as much liberty and freedom as [in] *mare liberum*'.[180]

The argument of 1613–15 does not depict commerce as a link between states or as a link between individuals. The idea of international society is absent, and so is the idea of human society. The case it makes is for the monopolization of commerce by one state – the state on whose behalf the argument is put forward.

Towards the end of the (inconclusive) negotiations of 1613–15, only the question of common utility is retained. Given that the concern is with working out what is to be done rather than what is just and right, the Dutch suggest, the English should look at the problem in such a way as might result in a satisfactory solution, in which case the question of law could, by mutual consent, be dropped without having been decided.[181]

De Jure Belli ac Pacis

Notwithstanding its importance as a cause of war in this period, Grotius limits his discussion to a few paragraphs in the course of the chapter, 'Of Things Which Belong to Men in Common'. He outlines the essentials of the case for free commerce in the interest of human society, but a few pages later claims that 'it is not at variance with the law of nature' for a people 'to make an agreement with another people to sell to it alone products of a certain kind, which do not grow elsewhere' provided that 'the people which buys is prepared to sell to others at a fair price'.[182] He also mentions commerce in the context of the classification of treaties, but does not engage in further argument.

Grotius's main statements on commerce are those of an advocate for the United East India Company for the Dutch government. It is not surprising that there are inconsistencies between pleas made in different contexts. In *De Jure Belli ac Pacis* he makes no attempt to resolve these, but plays down the issue of commerce. Some of his arguments are supportive of human society, but there is no indication of support for international society – or indeed of such a concept.

179 Ibid., pp. 193–94; see also pp. 182–83.
180 Ibid., p. 120.
181 Ibid., pp. 212–14.
182 Grotius, *De Jure Belli ac Pacis*, vol. 2, pp. 199–200, 205.

Diplomacy

Grotius's definition of ambassador identifies diplomacy as a link between rulers. Ambassadors, he writes, 'are those representatives whom rulers with sovereign powers send to one another'. That this extends also to states or peoples is clear from the context.[183] But the context is no more informative about the nature of this link between states and rulers than the definition.

In fact, Grotius says little about diplomacy. Apart from a few remarks which he includes in *De Jure Praedae*,[184] his ideas on the subject are contained in one short chapter in *De Jure Belli ac Pacis*, entitled: 'On the Right of Legation'.[185] In the first place, Grotius maintains that the law relating to embassies belongs to the law of nations: '[T]his law does not certainly arise from definite reasons, as the law of nature does, but takes its form according to the will of nations'.[186] That is, the law relating to embassies is positive law.

Second, two rights derive from this law: the right to be admitted; and the right to be free from violence.

On the first point, Grotius has little to say about the reasons why it was 'the will of nations' to establish the institution, diplomacy. It is 'useful' because:

> [N]ot only do very many matters come up in war which cannot be handled except through ambassadors, but also peace itself is hardly to be made by any other means.[187]

In a later chapter he mentions 'a conference' as 'a method' of preventing a dispute from developing into a war.[188] In his other works, too, diplomacy is placed in the context of conflict and war rather than peace. In *De Jure Praedae*, for example, the purpose of the embassies sent by the East Indian states and rulers to The Hague is identified as seeking 'a general combination of forces' to attack the Portuguese; and the negotiations of 1613–15 aim not so much at resolving a commercial conflict as at winning the English over for an offensive alliance against the Portuguese.[189]

183 Ibid., pp. 439–40.
184 See, for example, Grotius, *De Jure Praedae*, vol. 1, pp. 26, 96, 201–02, 291–92, 334.
185 Grotius, *De Jure Belli ac Pacis*, vol. 2, pp. 438–49.
186 Ibid., p. 442.
187 Ibid., p. 446.
188 Ibid., pp. 560–61.
189 Grotius, *De Jure Praedae*, vol. 1, p. 346; Clark and van Eysinga, 'The Colonial Conferences', vol. 15, p. 148.

This rather limited conception of the purposes of diplomacy may be contrasted with Gentili's view that it is not a product of volitional law but arose from necessity, and is grounded in the law of nature: '[S]ince it was inevitable that obligations and negotiations should arise between organisations having such reciprocity of rights as exists between nations, commonwealth and kings',[190] it was necessary for them to appoint representatives to conduct negotiations.

Turning to the law relating to embassies, this does not, as Grotius sees it, command the admission of ambassadors, but 'it does forbid the rejection of ambassadors without cause'.[191] He mentions three causes which justify the refusal to receive an ambassador:

- the one who dispatches the ambassador may be 'an enemy in arms' or 'planning war';
- the ambassador may have an objectionable belief system, such as being 'an atheist'; or he may be unacceptable for reasons of 'personal hatred'; and
- the embassy or mission may be suspected of 'stirring up the people'; its rank may not be 'proper'; it may arrive at an 'inopportune time'; or it may be permanent.

Grotius formulates the last point in the following way:

> But permanent legations, such as are now customary, can be rejected with the best of right; for ancient custom, to which they were unknown, teaches how unnecessary they are.[192]

These three causes and the way he illustrates them make it clear that he favours a right of admission which can be easily inactivated.

The right of the ambassador to be free from violence, Grotius points out, has been and continues to be subject to different interpretations. Livy, the Roman historian, for example, was of the opinion that ambassadors should be safe even if 'they commit hostile acts', whereas Sallust, also a historian, held that 'equity and justice' permit the punishment of ambassadors who are found to have committed a wrong.[193] He goes on to record other divergent opinions. Nonetheless, Grotius's own view is not slow to crystallize: '[I]t is contrary to the law of nations

[190] A. Gentili, *De Legationibus Tres*, vol. 2, transl. G. J. Laing, intro. E. Nys, *The Classics of International Law* (New York: Oxford University Press, 1924, reprinted New York and London: Oceana Publications and Wildy & Sons, 1964), pp. 51–52.

[191] Ibid., p. 440.

[192] Ibid., p. 441.

[193] Ibid., p. 442.

that ambassadors should be brought to trial'. The reasons which he gives are:

- there is nothing 'great' or 'outstanding' about a law which protects ambassadors 'only from unjust violence';
- any advantage which may be derived from punishment is outweighed by the disadvantage of jeopardizing the security of ambassadors. Punishment can be exacted by the one who sends the ambassador or, if he is unwilling, by means of a war; and
- if ambassadors are required to explain their behaviour to any person other than the one who sends them, their safety rests on an 'extremely precarious footing'.

Grotius offers his 'unqualified conclusion' when he says:

> [T]he rule has been accepted by the nations that the common custom, which makes a person who lives in foreign territory subject to that country, admits of an exception in the case of ambassadors. Ambassadors as if by a kind of fiction are considered to represent those who sent them ... [B]y a similar fiction, ambassadors [are] held to be outside of the limits of the country to which they [are] accredited.[194]

Hence a wrong committed by an ambassador should either be overlooked, or the ambassador should be ordered to leave. If the wrong is 'particularly atrocious', the ambassador should be sent back with the demand that he be punished or surrendered. He admits two exceptions only. '[D]ire necessity' such as 'guarding against serious hurt, especially to the state', permits the detention and questioning of an ambassador; and 'natural defence' allows the killing of an ambassador if he attempts to use armed force. For the rest, an ambassador, once admitted, is 'under the protection of the law of nations even among public enemies'. Grotius declares this law, which extends full security to ambassadors, to be binding on the state or ruler who admits the ambassador, but exempts from it any state or ruler through the territory of whom the ambassador passes without a safe conduct.[195]

When Grotius identifies the law relating to embassies as belonging to the law of nations, this must mean that it expresses the agreement of states, supported by the views of wise authorities. But when he discusses the inviolability of the ambassador, it appears that there exists no such agreement, but only the differing opinions of the wise men down the ages, and the precedents are conflicting. Thus Grotius's 'unqualified conclusion' and the points supporting it cannot be taken as a statement

[194] Ibid., p. 442–43.
[195] Ibid., p. 443–46.

of what the law is, but only his opinion of what it should be. The juridical basis which he claims for it is uncertain indeed. Again, Grotius's tortuous discussion may be contrasted with Gentili's wholehearted endorsement of the principle.

Grotius depicts diplomacy as a link which operates between mainly suspicious or hostile states and rulers. Its juridical basis is uncertain, and it is easy for states and rulers to interfere with it. As in the case of commerce, there is no conception of diplomacy as an institution of international society.

The Question of War

When Grotius defines war, he includes private as well as public war. Thus, in *De Jure Praedae* he writes: 'Armed execution against an armed adversary is designated by the term war', and in *De Jure Belli ac Pacis* he puts it this way: '[W]ar is the condition of those contending by force'.[196] In *De Jure Belli ac Pacis* he offers a justification for his definition:

> And usage does not reject this broader meaning of the word. If, to be sure, the term war is at times limited to public war, that implies no objection to our view, since it is perfectly certain that the name of a genus is often applied in a particular way to a species especially a species that is more prominent.[197]

For Grotius the question of war is: Can any war be just? His reply: Some wars are just.[198] To the question what wars are just he offers an answer which, after careful scrutinizing of his writings, may be read to mean that he has room for four kinds of just war.[199]

Just Private War

First, there is the just private war in *De Jure Praedae*.[200] Like his predecessors, he makes Aristotle's idea of the four causes its constituent

[196] Grotius, *De Jure Praedae*, vol. 1, p. 30; Grotius, *De Jure Belli ac Pacis*, vol. 2, p. 33; see also p. 832. Haggenmacher compares and contrasts the two definitions and concludes that the change from the first to the second definition, 'as radical as it appears at first sight, is only superficially radical; fundamentally it hardly modifies Grotius's views'. See Haggenmacher, *Grotius et la Doctrine de la Guerre Juste*, pp. 457–62.

[197] Grotius, *De Jure Belli ac Pacis*, vol. 2, p. 34.

[198] Grotius, *De Jure Praedae*, vol. 1, pp. 31, 42; Grotius, *De Jure Belli ac Pacis*, vol. 2, pp. 20, 34, 51–90.

[199] For an interpretation which discerns three 'images of war' in Grotius, see M. Donelan, 'Grotius and the Image of War', *Millennium: Journal of International Studies*, vol. 12, no. 3, 1983.

[200] The ingredients of this idea are also present in *De Jure Belli ac Pacis*, although less well developed, but Grotius does not integrate them nor does he provide a means by which to do so.

principle: for a private war to be just, its four causes – the efficient cause, the material cause, the formal cause and the final cause – need to be just.[201]

Regarding the efficient cause, 'any person whatsoever' may justly resort to war. An individual may wage it on his own behalf or on behalf of 'allies', and these may be relatives, neighbours, fellow citizens or simply fellow human beings. An individual may be helped by allies (voluntary agents) and by those who are under that individual's authority (subjects), children, slaves, servants and so on.[202]

In relation to voluntary agents, Grotius admits four kinds of material cause as just: self-defence; the defence of one's property; exacting payment of that which is one's due; and the inflicting of punishment – these are just because they correspond to rights conferred by the law of nature.[203] In relation to subjects or instruments, there is only one just material cause of war: the order of the one in authority. It is just, provided 'the reason of the subjects is not opposed thereto after weighing the probabilities'.[204]

The question of whether a just material cause can exist on both sides is answered by Grotius in two ways. As far as voluntary agents are concerned, his answer is 'no': '[T]here can be no war that is just for both parties'. Regarding subjects, his answer is 'yes': '[T]here is nothing to preclude the possibility of a war that is just on both sides'.[205]

The just formal cause of war consists of 'just form in undertaking war' and 'just form in waging war'. The former condition is met 'when judicial means for the attainment of our rights are defective'.[206] Just form in waging war is observed when 'the requisite of moderation' – a requirement of natural law – is fulfilled. For voluntary agents, this means that they must remain within the limits of the right for which they wage war; for subjects or instruments, it means that they must remain within the limits of orders given by their superior(s).[207]

201 Grotius, *De Jure Praedae*, vol. 1, p. 59; although Grotius also says that '[a] war is said to be just if it consists in the execution of a right' (p. 30). Aristotle's idea of the four causes does not reappear explicitly in *De Jure Belli ac Pacis*.

202 Grotius, *De Jure Praedae*, vol. 1, pp. 61–62; see Grotius, *De Jure Belli ac Pacis*, vol. 2, pp. 164–65.

203 Grotius, *De Jure Praedae*, vol. 1, pp. 67–68, 70; see Grotius, *De Jure Belli ac Pacis*, vol. 2, pp. 171–72. Grotius uses the word 'right' [*jus*] here, even though two of the precepts to which he refers the reader – Laws I and II – are formulated in terms of what is permissible.

204 Grotius, *De Jure Praedae*, vol. 1, p. 80; Grotius, *De Jure Belli ac Pacis*, vol. 2, pp. 587–95.

205 Grotius, *De Jure Praedae*, vol. 1, pp. 76–77, 83.

206 Ibid., pp. 87–88, 135–37; Grotius, *De Jure Belli ac Pacis*, vol. 2, p. 92.

207 Grotius, *De Jure Praedae*, vol. 1, pp. 104, 108, 118. Grotius's chapters on moderation in war in Book Three of *De Jure Belli ac Pacis*, vol. 2, pp. 716–82, refer only to public war.

Regarding the purpose or final cause of war, Grotius is brief: voluntary agents wage war in order to attain their right(s); and subjects wage it 'in order to render obedience to a superior'.[208]

The just private war as presented by Grotius in *De Jure Praedae* is in agreement with human society because it attempts to secure the justice which is embodied in its law – the law of nature.

Just Public War

De Jure Praedae contains a second kind of just war – the just public war. Its constituent principle is the same as for the just private war: a public war, in order to be just, must derive 'entirely from just causes'.[209]

As Grotius portrays it, the just public war has the same material and final cause – at the more general and less concrete level – as the just private war; the former differs from the latter merely with respect to its efficient and formal cause.[210]

The just efficient cause is the state or ruler – 'the supreme magistrate'. Also admitted is 'the magistrate next in rank', for the supreme magistrate may be 'absent or negligent'. The ally in a just public war is another state or magistrate. The one who is 'bound by the laws of [the] state' – the citizen – is the subject or instrument.[211]

When discussing the just formal cause, Grotius counsels against rushing into war, 'a matter not so much of right as of discretion',[212] and treats arbitration as honourable but purely voluntary: '[N]o-one is compelled to entrust his rights to this or that person'.[213]

Just form in undertaking a public war consists in its conformity with the law of nations. States and rulers, Grotius argues, have agreed that the injured state should offer the transgressing state the opportunity to present its case and, if the latter fails to discharge its 'judicial duty', pass judgement itself; and it should issue the declaration of war.[214] Neither of these procedures is required when things do not permit of a delay, for example, when an unjust war has been commenced against the state.

[208] Grotius, *De Jure Praedae*, vol. 1, pp. 66, 113, 118, 126–29, 277, 295.

[209] Grotius, *De Jure Praedae*, vol. 1, p. 59; although Grotius, referring to Bartolus, also says that a public war is just 'when waged between two free states' (p. 63).

[210] Ibid., pp. 68, 125–29. At the less abstract level, as Chs. XII and XIII demonstrate, the material causes of a private war differ from those of a public war (see pp. 216–317).

[211] Ibid., pp. 62–65.

[212] Ibid., p. 69. The better translation would seem to be 'a matter not so much of *law* as of discretion'. See Grotius, *De Jure Praedae*, vol. 2, p. 30.

[213] Grotius, *De Jure Praedae*, vol. 1, p. 98.

[214] Ibid., pp. 28–29, 98–103. Grotius uses the terminology of jurists of Antiquity – *clarigatio* and *rerum repetitio*. As the translator explains, *clarigatio* is 'a demand for redress

Just form in waging a public war, on the other hand, is related to the law of nature and, with one exception, is the same as for private war, that is, 'the requisite of moderation' must be observed. For example, while it is lawful to attack enemy subjects who resist, subjects who do not – women, children, farmers, prisoners and so on – should be spared; or, while it is lawful to despoil all enemy subjects, nothing should be taken which is in excess of what is due; and faith should be kept with the enemy.[215]

The exception is introduced in connection with the question of war being just for subjects on both sides. Grotius posits the existence of a rule that 'by the law of nations', subjects on both sides in war rightfully acquire spoils. To which, in a later chapter, he adds the further rule that 'whatever is acquired through the citizens by the command and in the interests of the state is acquired for the state'.[216]

This tends to undermine his case for the just public war, and this for two reasons. First, it undermines the just material cause as an essential ingredient of the just public war, because spoils are rightfully acquired, seemingly without limit, by both the state which lacks a just material cause as much as by the state which wages war for a just cause. Second, it goes against 'the requisite of moderation' as embodied in the just formal cause.

Grotius's case in *De Jure Praedae* for the just public war is not fully supportive of human society. And it does not suggest the existence of international society, for there is no indication that this is the war which states and rulers have agreed to regard as just.

Formal War

De Jure Belli ac Pacis presents the reader with what Grotius variously calls the 'complete war', the 'formal public war', the 'just or formal war' or simply the 'formal war'. It is just because it accords with the law of nations, and this is because it meets two requirements: first, it is waged by the state or ruler on each side; and, second, it is publicly declared.[217]

A just material cause is not a requisite of Grotius's third kind of just war: '[T]o harm an enemy ... is permissible ... for either side indiscriminately'.

and a declaration of war if redress [is] not received within thirty-three days', and *rerum repetitio* means 'reclamation of goods or rights' (p. 98).

215 Ibid., pp. 104, 108–18.

216 Ibid., pp. 124, 144. For the whole argument, see pp. 142–56.

217 See, for example, Grotius, *De Jure Belli ac Pacis*, vol. 2, pp. 57, 97, 630, 633. The corresponding Latin terms are: *bellum plenum, bellum publicum solenne, bellum justum sive solenne, bellum solenne*. Grotius, *Hugonis Grotii De Jure Belli et Pacis*, vol. 1, pp. 39, 104; vol. 3, p. 53.

Moreover, 'in a public[218] war ... anyone at all becomes owner, without limit or restriction, of what he has taken from the enemy'.[219] Nor does the final cause of war come into the discussion. The important point is that a war waged by sovereigns on both sides, and publicly declared, has particular legal effects, and is in this sense just. In Grotius's language,

> If we interpret the word just in relation to certain legal effects, in this sense surely it may be admitted that a war may be just from the point of view of either side.[220]

The formal war is 'extremely frequent',[221] and Grotius devotes six chapters to an exposition of its effects.[222] They distinguish themselves by their severity. To give a few examples:

- the right of killing, which is a right of war, 'extends not only to those who actually bear arms, or are subjects ... but ... to all persons who are in the enemy's territory'. Foreigners who have failed to depart are regarded as enemies. Subjects may be killed in 'any place whatsoever'. Children and women may be killed, also prisoners, suppliants or hostages;[223]
- whole cities may be destroyed; walls may be levelled to the ground; and fields devastated. Sacred things are not exempt from destruction;
- the property of the enemy may be acquired 'without limit or restriction';[224]
- not only do prisoners become slaves, but '[t]here is no suffering which may not be inflicted with impunity upon such slaves'.[225]

Grotius mentions only a few exceptions to his dictum that according to the 'law of nations ... anything is permissible as against an enemy'. For example, it is not permissible to kill the enemy by poison, to poison weapons or water, to use assassins or to rape women. And there is the

[218] The Latin word is *solenne*, which should be translated as 'formal'. Grotius, *Hugonis Grotii De Jure Belli et Pacis*, vol. 3, p. 108.

[219] Grotius, *De Jure Belli ac Pacis*, vol. 2, p. 664; see also pp. 565, 630, 643–44.

[220] Ibid., p. 566; see also pp. 435–36, 630, 639, 641.

[221] Ibid., p. 799.

[222] Ibid., chs. 4–9, pp. 641–715. According to Haggenmacher, fourteen chapters of Book Three, chs. 3 – are concerned with the effects of the formal war. (Ch. 3 is strictly speaking not about the effects of the formal public war but about its prerequisites.) Haggenmacher, *Grotius et la Doctrine de la Guerre Juste*, p. 571. Yet the Latin text makes it clear that only chs. 3–9 relate to the formally just public war (*bellum solenne jure gentium* or *bellum jure gentium*), and that chs. 10–16 relate to the materially just/unjust war (*bellum justum/injustum*). See, for example, Grotius, *Hugonis Grotii De Jure Belli et Pacis*, vol. 3, pp. 53, 70, 97, 105, 148, 165; 188, 196, 248, 254, 269, 281.

[223] Grotius, *De Jure Belli ac Pacis*, vol. 2, pp. 646–51.

[224] Ibid., pp. 658–62, 664.

[225] Ibid., p. 691.

rule that faith must be kept with the enemy, for otherwise there would be 'no limit nor termination' to such wars.[226]

Such effects 'met with the approval of nations':

To undertake to decide regarding the justice of a war between two peoples had been dangerous for other peoples, who were on this account involved in a foreign war ... Furthermore, even in a lawful war,[227] from external indications it can hardly be adequately known what is the just limit of self-defence, of recovering what is one's own, or of inflicting punishments; in consequence it has seemed altogether preferable to leave decisions in regard to such matters to the scruples of the belligerents.[228]

It is evident that Grotius's states and rulers do not see themselves as forming a society: the idea of 'a greater whole' is not a part of 'the scruples of the belligerents'. As Grotius does not fail to point out, they have regard only for what is advantageous for themselves.[229] The formal war is an expression of a plurality of states and rulers, negating both international society and human society.

Materially or Morally Just Public War

De Jure Belli ac Pacis also contains the idea of what may be called the materially or morally just public war. Grotius refers to it sometimes as the 'just war' or the 'less formal war', at other times simply as 'public war'.[230] Its efficient cause is generally the state or ruler, but it need not be, and likewise, the enemy. There may be a public declaration of war, but there need not be.[231]

Its claim to justice derives from the nature of its material cause. This needs to be just or, as he also formulates it: '[I]f the cause of a war should be unjust, even if the war should have been undertaken in a lawful[232] way, all acts which arise therefrom are unjust'. They are unjust, not in terms

226 Ibid., pp. 651–57, 792, 798–99.

227 The Latin term is *bellum justum*, which should be translated as 'just war'. Grotius, *Hugonis Grotii De Jure Belli et Pacis*, vol. 3, p. 75.

228 Grotius, *De Jure Belli ac Pacis*, vol. 2, p. 644.

229 Ibid., pp. 651, 654.

230 See, for example, ibid., pp. 57, 97, 164. The corresponding Latin terms are: *bellum justum, bellum minus solenne, bellum publicum*. Grotius, *Hugonis Grotii De Jure Belli et Pacis*, vol. 1, pp. 39, 104, 198. That Grotius distinguishes between two kinds of just war in *De Jure Belli ac Pacis* is obvious not only from what he says (for example, vol. 2, pp. 57, 97, 639, 664 and 689), but also from his presentation of the formal cause of war in Book Three.

231 Grotius, *De Jure Belli ac Pacis*, vol. 2, p. 164; see also pp. 97–101.

232 The Latin word is again *solenne*, best translated as 'formal'. Grotius, *Hugonis Grotii De Jure Belli et Pacis*, vol. 3, p. 192.

of natural law nor the law of nations, but from the point of view of 'moral injustice'.[233]

In opposition to the just or justifiable cause, he places the unjust cause, which he also identifies as 'persuasive' 'nominal' or 'real cause'.[234] This language suggests, and Grotius leaves it as a suggestion, that the material cause of war, which is just, is the apparent and not the real cause.

The unjust or real cause of war receives only a few pages' coverage. Its main instances are: '[t]he fear of something uncertain'; 'advantage apart from necessity'; 'the refusal of marriage'; 'the desire for richer land'; 'the discovery' of what is held by another; 'the desire to rule others against their will on the pretext that it is for their good'; the claim to universal empire by emperor or pope; 'the desire to fulfil prophecies, without the command of God'; and the desire to force the Christian religion on those who are unwilling to accept it.[235]

The just or justifiable cause of war, on the other hand, occupies most of Book Two of *De Jure Belli ac Pacis* – or this, at least, is what the opening paragraph of its first chapter suggests: 'Let us proceed to the causes of war – I mean the justifiable causes.'[236] Yet much of what Grotius covers in Book Two is not about just causes of war but about rights and, occasionally, about an obligation – a fact communicated by the opening words of many a chapter.[237]

It is, of course, possible to see each of these chapters as containing the unwritten invitation to identify the violation of a right discussed, or the neglect of an obligation mentioned, as a just cause of war, but to do so would mean to say something which – a very few exceptions apart – Grotius himself chooses not to say.[238] And frequently, as in the discussion of rights within the family or the varied rules of succession, it is difficult to discern how a violation would provide a justification of war.

The rights presented in book 2 are mainly rights 'for which we are endebted to the law of nature'. As such they do not belong to those things which this law enjoins or forbids, but relate to that which it permits[239] – and this, as we found earlier, is accompanied by uncertainty.

233 Grotius, *De Jure Belli ac Pacis*, vol. 2, pp. 718–19; see also p. 170.
234 Ibid., pp. 546–47; see also p. 169.
235 Ibid., pp. 516–17, 549–56.
236 Ibid., p. 169.
237 See chs. 1–21 of book 2, in Grotius, *De Jure Belli ac Pacis*, vol. 2, pp. 169–545, of which Chs. 10 and 17, pp. 320–27 and 430–37, are about obligations.
238 See, for example, Grotius, *De Jure Belli ac Pacis*, vol. 2, the ill-treatment of ambassadors (p. 449); the denial of burial (p. 460); and cruelty to Christians (p. 518).
239 Grotius, *De Jure Belli ac Pacis*, vol. 2, p. 438. Regarding Grotius's identification of these 'natural' rights with that which is permissible according to the law of nature see, for example, pp. 54, 172, 179, 184, 201, 207. For a more general discussion of Grotius's

Thus, much of what book 2 is concerned with may be seen as being about causes of war, rather than just causes, and this is what Grotius himself indicates in the 'Prolegomena': 'The second book', he writes, 'having for its object to set forth all the causes from which war can arise'.[240]

The generous-looking coverage of the just or justifiable causes of war does not, then, provide much information on the main ingredient of Grotius's morally just public war – the just material cause. So, what is the little that it does provide?

At the general and abstract level Grotius identifies four just causes: '[D]efence, the obtaining of that which belongs to us or is our due, and ... punishment'.[241] At the less general and more concrete level he distinguishes between what may be referred to as 'just causes concerning self' and 'just causes concerning another'. These have a familiar ring.

Concerning self, it is just for states and rulers to resort to war in order:

- to defend themselves against a 'threatened' injury: 'it is permissible [for public powers] to forestall an act of violence which is not immediate, but which is seen to be threatening from a distance', but not to 'weaken a growing power which, if it become too great, may be a source of danger';[242]
- to seek reparation for an injury received; and
- to inflict punishment for an injury received.[243]

Concerning another, it is just for states and rulers to resort to war in order:

- to assist their subjects;
- to help allies or friends;
- to help 'any persons whatsoever', for 'liberty to serve the interests of human society through punishments ... is in the hands of the highest authorities';[244] and

'theory of natural rights', see R. Tuck, *Natural Rights Theories: Their Origin and Development* (Cambridge: Cambridge University Press, 1979), pp. 58–81.

240 Grotius, *De Jure Belli ac Pacis*, vol. 2, p. 21. For a different reading of Grotius's materially just cause of war, see Haggenmacher, 'Grotius and Gentili', pp. 163–67.

241 Grotius, *De Jure Belli ac Pacis*, vol. 2, p. 171. More general and abstract than this is the statement in the 'Prolegomena': 'War ought not to be undertaken except for the enforcement of rights' (p. 18).

242 Grotius, *De Jure Belli ac Pacis*, vol. 2, p. 184; see also pp. 503–04, and his argument in *De Jure Praedae*, vol. 1, pp. 329–30.

243 Grotius, *De Jure Belli ac Pacis*, vol. 2, pp. 449, 460–61, 601–03, 624.

244 Ibid., pp. 504–05, 578, 581, 582.

- to defend God. In Grotius's words, 'those who … abolish [religion] may be restrained in the name of human society'.[245]

The right to assist another, it is worth noting, is accompanied by qualifications.[246]

To turn to the just formal cause of war, according to Grotius, just form in waging the materially or morally just public war consists in observing moderation – a theme to which he devotes seven chapters.[247] He introduces the discussion by remarking that he must now retrace his steps and 'deprive those who wage war of nearly all the privileges which I seemed to grant, yet did not grant to them'.[248] However, this is misleading: he has granted no privileges, but has set out the accepted law of war, as he sees it, and this remains in the text, alongside the precepts which he now advocates – the much admired *temperamenta*. It is not clear which is the more authoritative.

Among the more important are:

- innocent persons such as women, children, and old men should not be killed; religious men or men of letters, farmers or merchants should not be injured; prisoners of war or hostages should not be deprived of life;
- devastation of that which belongs to the enemy should be refrained from, and sacred and consecrated things should be preserved;
- the enemy's property should not be retained beyond the amount of his debt; and
- sovereignty over the vanquished should not be acquired.[249]

These precepts resemble those presented in *De Jure Praedae*, but, in contrast with the earlier work,[250] he does not portray them as being imposed by the law of nature 'properly so-called', but ascribes them to moral justice, goodness, highmindedness, what is right from the point of view of religion and morals, a sense of shame, mercy, clemency, humaneness, rules of love, fairness, kindness, prudence and generosity[251] – which reason declares to be honourable and praiseworthy, but not obligatory.[252]

[245] Ibid., p. 514; see also pp. 508–10.
[246] Ibid., pp. 578–80; 581; 582–83; 507–08; 514–17, 518–21.
[247] Ibid., chs. 10–16, pp. 716–82. To be quite correct, two of the seven chapters, 10 and 16, are concerned with the materially or morally unjust war.
[248] Ibid., p. 716.
[249] Ibid., pp. 733–43, 746–54, 757.
[250] Grotius, *De Jure Praedae*, vol. 1, pp. 103–04, 108–19, especially p. 110.
[251] Grotius, *De Jure Belli ac Pacis*, vol. 2, pp. 716–82.
[252] Ibid., pp. 38, 39.

It is not clear why Grotius abandoned the imperatives of natural law for moral exhortations, appealing in themselves but lacking philosophical foundation, creating a stark dichotomy between what is lawful and 'the rule of right'.[253] This juxtaposition of opposites has troubled many commentators. G. I. Draper, delivering one of the harsher judgements, goes so far as to maintain that 'the exposition of the laws of war … is vitiated by the abandonment of the main purpose with which the author set out, namely, the humanization of the law of war'. He finds no satisfactory explanation why Grotius 'conceded that the Law of Nations permitted many atrocities, and seemed to relegate the *temperamenta* to hortatory status'.[254]

The end and aim of war, its final cause, is scarcely mentioned in *De Jure Belli ac Pacis* until, as an afterthought in the final chapter, Grotius invokes Augustine's dictum: 'Peace is not sought that war may be followed, but war is waged that peace may be secured.'[255] The closest he comes to a definition is that: 'Peace … is an act of the state on behalf of the whole body or on behalf of its parts.'[256] The chapter 'On the Good Faith of States by Which War Is Ended' discusses a variety of legal questions concerning the making of peace and the provisions of peace treaties, but does not present peace as the final goal of war nor discuss the general principles of the just peace.[257]

The materially or morally just public war in *De Jure Belli ac Pacis* neither strengthens the idea of human society nor points to the existence of international society, mainly because its essential ingredient – the just material cause – is poorly developed and there are no binding rules for the just conduct of war.

Indeed, none of Grotius's four kinds of just war suggests that there is an international society with which it must not come into conflict if it wants to retain the quality of being just. The just wars in *De Jure Praedae* are concerned with human society but there is no hint of an idea of international society. The formal war in *De Jure Belli ac Pacis* reflects the idea of a plurality but not a society of states, and the materially or morally just public war not only fails as an argument, but its moral appeals are to the ruler's sense of virtue, not to a sense of a greater whole. The search for Grotius's conception of international society remains fruitless.

[253] Ibid., p. 716.
[254] G. I. A. D. Draper, 'Grotius' Place in the Development of Legal Ideas about War', in Bull, Kingsbury and Roberts (eds), *Hugo Grotius and International Relations*, pp. 197, 198.
[255] Grotius, *De Jure Belli ac Pacis*, vol. 2, p. 861.
[256] Ibid., p. 816.
[257] Ibid., pp. 805–31.

Moderation

Moderation is a prominent theme in Grotius's writings; it is less noticed that immoderation is also present, and not only in the chapters on the formal war. Various instances of both have appeared in the course of this chapter, and it remains to bring them together and evaluate them.

The idea of moderation occurs in four variants. First, it presents itself as the idea of the 'middle ground'. Grotius identifies as the *medium* or *modus* or *mediocritas* 'that which lies between extremes' and, on numerous occasions, expresses himself in favour of it. For example, he 'most commends' the government of the Hollanders because it is 'placed between the Regall Authority, and the Authority of the Common People', and hence 'avoideth the evils of both of them, and draweth unto it selfe from them all which is good after it'.[258] Or, in *De Jure Praedae*, he declares: 'Justice consists in taking a middle course. It is wrong to inflict injury, but it is also wrong to endure injury.'[259] Or, in *De Jure Belli ac Pacis*, there is the well-known comment on war, cited earlier: 'For both extremes ... a remedy must be found.'

The idea of using words rather than force is a second form of moderation present in his writings. He mentions numerous thinkers of Antiquity, such as Herodotus, Euripides, Thucydides, Terence, Livy and Tacitus, as having expressed themselves in favour of settling disputes by 'discussion' rather than 'violence', and, in *De Jure Belli ac Pacis*, he adds instances of arbitration.[260] Yet he does not portray himself as an advocate of the use of words in place of the use of force. In *De Jure Praedae* he identifies it as an 'honourable' but not a 'necessary measure'; and in *De Jure Belli ac Pacis*, he sees arbitration as a possible method, in case of doubt, of avoiding war, even declaring that '[e]specially ... Christian kings and states are bound to pursue this method'. However, he undermines it when finding that, in such matters, states and rulers prefer not 'to have recourse to the judgements of others'.[261]

Third, moderate is that which accords with the law of nature. Grotius makes this point 'forcefully' in *De Jure Praedae* when discussing just form in waging war, private and public, identifying any act which is committed in excess of that which the law of nature prescribes as transgressing the 'requisite of moderation'. Does not 'that most sacred of natural precepts'

[258] Grotius, *A Treatise on the Antiquity*, pp. 6–7, see also p. 27.
[259] Grotius, *De Jure Praedae*, vol. 1, p. 3, see also pp. 2, 69.
[260] Ibid., pp. 97–98; Grotius, *De Jure Belli ac Pacis*, vol. 2, pp. 560–63.
[261] Grotius, *De Jure Praedae*, vol. 1, p. 98; Grotius, *De Jure Belli ac Pacis*, vol. 2, pp. 563, 644.

decree that 'man must not be prodigally misused by his fellow man'?[262] In *De Jure Belli ac Pacis*, however, he does not reaffirm this link.[263]

And fourth, when, in *De Jure Belli ac Pacis*, Grotius links the idea of moderation to just form in waging the morally just public war, he invokes 'higher grounds', reasons less 'forceful' than law – moral justice, high-mindedness, a sense of shame, mercy, goodness, kindness, and so on. Moderation also has 'its advantages', he points out, and should be 'valued' on that account: it takes away from the enemy 'a great weapon, despair'; it gives the impression of 'great assurance of victory'; it is likely to win the minds of men, and not only the enemy; and it identifies him who wages war as a Christian.[264]

Grotius's four variants of the idea of moderation suggest that his commitment to this idea, while genuine, is qualified – an impression which is reinforced by the existence in his writings of the idea of immoderation.

The idea of immoderation occurs mainly in connection with volitional law – law within the state and law between states. Grotius admits the idea of immoderation into the state when he discusses 'a human law ... approved by God': the law of non-resistance. A ruler may resort to injustice, arbitrariness, violence, oppression and the subject has no right to resist.[265] Immoderation goes with impunity because,

> [B]eyond doubt the most important element in public affairs is the constituted order of bearing rule and rendering obedience ... This truly cannot coexist with individual licence to offer resistance.[266]

As discussed above, Grotius finds a place for the idea of immoderation between states and rulers in that part of the law of nations which concerns itself with what is permitted in the formal war.

Moderation and immoderation exist side by side in Grotius's writings, and there is no attempt on his part to reconcile the one with the other except to declare the former to be 'right' and the latter to be 'permissible'.[267] He sometimes links the idea of moderation to the law of nature but attaches it to different 'phases', which may be interpreted to mean that he does not regard it as an essential ingredient of the idea of human society. He never establishes a link between moderation and the law of nations. It may be seen as benefitting states and rulers in their

262 Grotius, *De Jure Praedae*, vol. 1, p. 110.
263 In ch. 1 of book 3, Grotius discusses that which is permissible in war according to the law of nature, presenting the principle of proportionality not as moderate but as just. Grotius, *De Jure Belli ac Pacis*, vol. 2, pp. 599–605.
264 Grotius, *De Jure Belli ac Pacis*, vol. 2, pp. 754–56; see also p. 20.
265 Ibid., pp. 138–56.
266 Ibid., p. 143.
267 Ibid., p. 643.

relations with one another, but he rarely portrays it that way. On the other hand, he does not hesitate to associate the law of nations with the idea of immoderation, negating the idea of international society.

Conclusion

Under the heading 'Ambiguity and Complexity', Wight comments: 'Grotius can be posthumously all things to all men; he is interpretable in various ways. Lauterpacht draws him in the image of Lauterpacht.'[268] And, one is tempted to add, Wight draws him in the image of Wight. But, as we have seen, Gierke, Wight and Bull concur in placing him in the same tradition: the *via media*, whose leitmotiv is the idea of international society. And it is true that some of Grotius's observations appear to give expression to this idea, sometimes in memorable language.

However, it is the surprising thesis of this chapter that the promise held out by these expressions remains unfulfilled. The feature which stands out in the picture that has been taking shape is the absence, in a world of independent states, of any notion of their forming an international society. The initial discussion of this issue, in the context of the law of nations, left open the question whether in its application to specific topics, that law might provide indications of norms in international society. The findings were disappointing. Grotius's brief discussion of diplomacy falls well short of this; the most prominent strand in his discussion of commerce is the right of the state to control commerce in the national interest; and with respect to war, the law of nations permits an array of extreme practices that exclude any notion of international society. The moral principles which Grotius advances in the concluding chapters of *De Jure Belli ac Pacis*, the *temperamenta*, are expressed in vague, general terms, in particular in terms of personal morality – appeals to the ruler's conscience or sense of honour – and, with one solitary exception, make no reference to the wider association of states.[269]

This suggests the question of whether, if Grotius cannot be placed within the *via media* tradition, he may more plausibly be located in one of the other designated traditions. This could only be the realist: notwithstanding his rejection of realism in general terms in the person of Carneades, his chosen spokesman for this approach, there are many indications that in practice Grotius holds views usually associated with

[268] Wight, *Four Seminal Thinkers in International Theory*, p. 32.

[269] 'For not only is every state sustained by good faith, as Cicero says, but also that greater society of states' – one of those elusive phrases which is not taken up in the course of the relevant discussion. See Grotius, *De Jure Belli ac Pacis*, vol. 2, p. 860.

realism. His views on commerce and the law of nations concerning war point in this direction, and more generally he depicts states as self-regarding, and justifiably so: the preservation of self and the necessities for life take precedence over obligations to others. In this context, Richard Tuck's thesis of Grotius's surprising closeness to Hobbes lends philosophical support to the practical examples of Grotius's realist inclinations, further exemplified in the staunch Dutch nationalism expressed in his legal advocacy and his historical writings.[270]

However, Grotius cannot simply assigned to the realist tradition. His starting point is natural law, not reason of state; his central questions concern the moral and legal justification of war. Concepts such as human society are not part of the realist worldview. Indeed, this concept evokes universalism, but it remains in the background, posing no threat to the world of sovereign states. Indeed in some sense his general outlook may be closer to the *via media* than to realism, bearing in mind the importance he accords to moderation as well as more generally to morality and law. He combines realist and *via media* themes, but not as an intellectual synthesis: rather, differing theses jar uneasily against one another. This is true, especially, of his *magnum opus*, the source of most of the problems identified in this chapter. *De Jure Praedae*, on the other hand, offers a tightly structured natural law – based argument. Indeed, Grotius appears more comfortable in the role of advocate, marshalling his arguments for a pre-assigned conclusion, than in the much more ambitious role he aspires to in *De Juri Belli ac Pacis*: '[T]o contribute somewhat to the philosophy of law ... the noblest part of jurisprudence'.[271] Like a mathematician, he will reason abstractly, excluding 'every particular fact'. Sadly, the arguments thus constructed do not come together. Could it be that, notwithstanding his immense erudition, this is where his lack of thorough grounding in one of the major disciplines – philosophy, law or theology – made itself felt?

Or it may be that the explanation of the weaknesses of the work is to be found in Roelofsen's hypothesis that Grotius was, first and foremost, a politician.[272] His family tradition valued humanist learning but the supreme aspiration was to hold high public office. Grotius rose swiftly to political prominence, and during the early years of exile in Paris he watched eagerly for any opportunity to return to Dutch public life. In his later years an honoured university position would surely have been open to him, but he opted for the Swedish diplomatic service. The intellectual

[270] Tuck, *The Rights of War and Peace*, pp. 78–108.
[271] Grotius, *De Jure Belli ac Pacis*, vol. 2, p. 21.
[272] Roelofsen, 'Grotius and the International Politics of the Seventeenth Century'.

skills and propensities appropriate to such a career would not make for rigorous philosophical reasoning.

Doubtless Grotius's work will continue to be open to differing interpretations, partly because readers will come to it with different interests and questions, but also for the broader reasons that Wight alludes to. The overall coherence and significance of his writings is likely to remain subject to contention. But this does not preclude well-grounded conclusions on specific issues: not every interpretation can stand. It has been contended here that the assigning of Grotius to the tradition that bears his name cannot withstand a thorough reading of the texts – always assuming that more is required than taking note of scattered expressions that evoke an image of international society. If it means an outlook on international relations shaped by a certain 'vision' – a perpetual struggle for mastery, or a rudimentary society or community of independent sovereigns, or perhaps an unacceptable international anarchy requiring the creation of a universal political authority – it is evident that Grotius's thought is informed by no such coherent vision.

Conclusion

The conclusion is presented in three sections:

1. The pattern of ideas sums up the findings, abstracting from the details in the individual chapters.
2. The question of a tradition discusses whether and in what sense the term 'tradition' is appropriate in this context.
3. Implications and questions look more broadly at implications for the history of international thought and questions that arise concerning the contemporary discipline.

The Pattern of Ideas

The essential elements of the concept of international society are the political entities – the independent or sovereign states – and the links between them, positive and normative. The primary concern of all four thinkers is normative: the principles that the prince should follow, the rights and obligations of states and rulers, the just reasons for waging war and the just conduct of war. Only Erasmus, with his comments on the effects of the new learning, offers more than commonplace observations on the empirical character of the links between states.

States and Rulers

All four authors have the idea of a plurality of political entities, and notwithstanding their differing terminology – Christian princes, perfect communities, free princes and free peoples, states and rulers – these are independent, essentially sovereign, states although only Gentili and Grotius use the term 'sovereignty'. The states have the essential feature of external sovereignty: the right to make their own laws, and to wage war and make peace, free from any external authority. There may be a nominal superior, for example, the Holy Roman Emperor over some of the German and Italian rulers, but if this does not restrict their de facto power to legislate or to go to war, they are treated as sovereign. The three jurists are prepared to follow contemporary practice rather than outdated formalities. But when it concerns the spiritual power of the pope, Vitoria takes the traditional view, maintaining that the pope has the authority, *in extremis*, to require Christian rulers to go to war in defence of the Christian faith: a serious restriction on sovereignty in principle, however anachronistic in practice.

They show little interest in forms of government, and thus the question of who exercises sovereignty is not a major concern for them, and it may be answered differently from community to community. What matters – at least to Erasmus, Vitoria and Gentili – is that sovereignty, irrespective of who exercises it, is exercised justly: power is not for the purposes of tyranny, but for purposes of administration. This idea recurs like a refrain from Erasmus to Vitoria, and from Vitoria to Gentili. The wise and good prince, Erasmus holds, respects the laws, and the laws embody 'the fundamental principles of equity and honesty'. The ruler who is entrusted with the administration of the perfect community, Vitoria sets forth, considers what is lawful and what creates and conserves felicity. However 'absolute' power may be, Gentili submits, 'nothing unseemly is admitted'. Grotius, while agreeing that it is unjust to show disrespect for the laws, condones it in the one who exercises the sovereign power that he rightfully possesses: more important than justice is the 'constituted order'. Thus Grotius rejects any right of resistance against an oppressive ruler, unless the ruler himself violates the constituted order.

But perhaps here Grotius is making explicit what the others leave unstated. Neither Vitoria nor Gentili allows a right of resistance except, in Gentili's case, for those holding high public office. Erasmus does not go into the issue. For the three jurists, the victims of tyranny can look only to the uncertain prospect of intervention from outside – uncertain, because although this is a just cause of war, rulers have no obligation to intervene.

That Which Links and Circumscribes

All four thinkers devote far more attention to the links between political communities, in particular their mutual rights and obligations. Erasmus stands apart from the other three, not in his conclusions but in the way he reaches them. He is *sui generis*: he does not employ either of the conceptual languages that Edward Keene identifies in this period: reason of state or natural law.[1] He is no theorist, but offers a wealth of observations which in the end come together as a coherent image.

[1] E. Keene, *International Political Thought: A Historical Introduction* (Cambridge: Polity Press, 2005), pp. 99–100.

He presents three sets of ideas. His international society being limited to Christendom, the first and most important is 'the philosophy of Christ', the source of the norms that should govern the society. This makes for 'a firm and holy bond' between Christian princes. Supplementing the Christian religion are all those ideas which lie embedded in 'the noble old systems of thought' of Antiquity, perhaps also inspired by Christ. Sharing these ideas means to be linked by 'learning'. He places less emphasis on a third set of ideas, those which are contained in a just positive law of nations – that is, a law which Christian princes impose upon themselves.

Religion, learning and law provide Christian princes with a code of conduct which tells them, on the one hand, to respect one another's separateness and sovereignty. The temporal Christian prince, as Erasmus puts it, should not inflict harm on another prince; he should not attack him, he should not take his riches, he should not subject him to his rule or religion and he should not break a promise made to him. The temporal Christian prince is entitled to go to war, but only if it is unavoidable and a question of defending his country or religion. On the other hand, the Christian princes's code of conduct prescribes cooperation. The temporal Christian prince should act in common with other Christian princes in achieving peace when war has broken out; in strengthening and beautifying their respective realms; and in helping a Christian people in distress. The spiritual Christian prince is subject to the same two kinds of precept. On the one hand, he should not become involved in 'worldly things' but should uphold the rule of Christ; on the other hand, he should be prepared to use the authority of his office to arbitrate and mediate in conflicts among temporal Christian princes. Erasmus's way of seeing that which links, although formulated in terms of obligations rather than rights, supports both the idea of separateness and sovereignty and that of society.

The other three thinkers fall within the broad category of natural law theorising. Notwithstanding their different intellectual origins – Thomist, Bartholist/humanist and eclectic humanist – the similarities among them are more striking than the differences, with the important exception of the crucial points on which Grotius diverges from the other two. It is therefore convenient to consider them together.

For all three, the Christian religion is no longer the primary bond among states; rather, it is law, natural law and the law of nations. These are universal, and thus for those who envisage an international society, it is worldwide. The primary bond is more abstract than Erasmus's philosophy of Christ. Religion plays a lesser role, varying from thinker to thinker, and human society figures quite prominently, although its precise role is not easy to determine.

They have a common understanding of natural law as deriving from God, in the sense that God created humans with the capacity to reason, through which they can ascertain right and wrong, and thus the basic rules that should govern human and social life. In principle these are known with certainty, but they acknowledge that in practice there are differences over complex moral issues and it may be difficult to discern what the natural law requires. The others appear implicitly to follow Vitoria's distinction between very basic laws known with certainty and generally accepted, along with direct inferences from them, and inferences through a longer chain of reasoning, where different opinions arise.

On the other hand, they differ on the status of the law of nations – the law governing relations between states but often, confusingly, referred to as the law common to all states. For Gentili it is part of natural law, for Grotius it is positive, or volitional, law. Vitoria is inconsistent, but his main concern is that it should be as binding, as authoritative, as natural law.

They agree, nonetheless, that it promotes cooperation and openness to outsiders, thus rights to travel and sojourn in other lands, and to engage in commerce which, they hold, promotes not only material well-being, through goods not available in one's own country, but also makes for friendship amongst peoples. Diplomatic relations are important for resolving the problems that arise between sovereigns who acknowledge no superior authority, and diplomacy needs to be regulated by laws, the most significant of which is the principle of diplomatic inviolability.

It is with respect to the practical application of the law of nations in areas such as these that Grotius stands apart from the other two. He supports the right to engage in commerce only in certain contexts, in others arguing for the right of one state to monopolize commerce of a particular kind or with a particular partner. Similarly, the rights he accords to diplomats are more qualified than for Gentili, and their legal basis less secure. For Gentili they are grounded in natural law, for Grotius in volitional law, thus dependent on the continuing agreement of rulers.

The same pattern is evident with respect to the law of war: a large measure of agreement, but divergence at a crucial point. All three stand in the long tradition of classical and medieval thought on the just war. They treat self-defence, the right to repel attack, as self-evident, but only Gentili extends this to include pre-emptive or preventive war: Grotius rejects this and Vitoria's text is open to different interpretations. Beyond this, they hold that the maintenance of order and justice in the world legitimizes offensive war – to punish wrong-doing – injuries inflicted on oneself or others, for example, to restore property wrongfully seized, to assist allies or others unjustly attacked, to protect subjects whose lives are endangered by tyrannical rule, and the like. Just wars must satisfy strict criteria, not only for the grounds for waging war but also for the manner of conducting it, and justice must be observed in the subsequent peace-making. Vitoria and Gentili spell out these ideas, the latter more elaborately, their reasoning grounded in a natural law.

In his youthful work, *De Jure Praedae*, Grotius made this traditional line of argument, but in *De Jure Belli ac Pacis*, he insists on a strict distinction between natural and positive law, the law of nations as volitional law coming under the latter category. Thus depending on what states have agreed to, it imposes only very limited restrictions: legal requirements for the declaration of war but virtually no constraints on its conduct. Thus his category 'formal war' circumvents his laborious account of the just causes of war and he legitimizes the lack of restraint of which he complains eloquently in the 'Prologomena' and which he seeks to mitigate in the chapters on moderation. The contradiction between legality and morality is exposed starkly but remains unresolved. Whereas the traditional just war can, in an appropriate context, be interpreted as an aspect of the idea of international society, Grotius's account of the law of war is incompatible with it. And more generally, while the thought of the other two can readily be interpreted in terms of an underlying concept of international society, Grotius shows himself at various points in the discussion to be unaware of any such concept.

In the case of these three thinkers, other potential bonds between states which might be significant for international society prove to be more limited. The Christian religion, for Erasmus the primary bond, complicates Vitoria's account but is not a major factor for the other two. For Vitoria it forms the basis of a second community, that of all Christians, a spiritual community where the head of the Church is superior to the temporal rulers, but their temporal power is respected unless the survival of the Church is at stake, and the rules of the Christian community do not override the general rules of the community of all states.

For the Protestant Gentili, religion is a matter between man and God, not between man and man, and should have no place in political life. Thus it is not part of his lofty structure. He allows that it does have some political effects: a common religion is an especially strong bond among states. But it is only one of several reasons making for alliances. For Grotius, despite his intense interest in theology, religion has an even slighter role in international relations. A common religion may, but need not, make for amity or alliance. Religious differences may, but need not, make for enmity. He does not, like Gentili, rule out alliances between Christian and non-Christian states but, like the others, is concerned over the danger of an excessively powerful Ottoman empire. But all four thinkers are opposed to making religion a ground for war; nothing of the crusading spirit remains.

The idea of human society, the essential unity of mankind, is more prominent in Gentili and Grotius; in Vitoria it travels under another name: the world as a whole. The creation of states has not entirely superseded the unity of the human race and the natural law which governed human relationships from the outset. It is in the name of human society that rulers may intervene to protect innocent victims of tyranny. Like human rights in the present era, human society presents an intellectual problem for the concept of the sovereign state. It authorizes action to safeguard rights proclaimed by natural law, thus limits the scope of sovereignty; the sovereign is not subject to an external political power but is bound by universal rules, derived from God, to which all rational beings must assent. But since rulers are not obliged to intervene in such cases, the practical significance of human society remains unclear; all that is clear is that it can be invoked as a legitimizing symbol rather like the international community at the present time. Where other norms of international society are present, as in Vitoria and Gentili, the idea of human society may be seen as complementing them. But when, as in Grotius, such norms cannot be identified and there is no implicit concept of international society, it becomes a substitute for that concept.

That Which Is Desirable: Values

The final question that was raised at the outset was whether, in addition to the points abstracted from Martin Wight and Hedley Bull, the four authors suggested any further ideas relevant to international society. It became evident that moderation was such an idea – initially as a way of bringing practice more into accord with the normative ideals being advocated, but also as a political value in itself. And this leads naturally to the question: what other values do they share?

They support many values, varying from author to author, but a valid abstract of what they have in common may be obtained by focusing on five ideas: independence, cooperation, justice, peace and finally moderation. Again, Grotius stands somewhat apart from the other three.

Independence All four thinkers find it good that princes, communities, peoples, states and rulers are free to make decisions and act accordingly. 'The King cannot be compelled or passed over by any one' (Erasmus). Vitoria's perfect community, with its own laws, meets with God's approval. Gentili is satisfied that the law of nations accords final control over their own affairs to his free princes and free peoples. And Grotius celebrates the independent spirit of his fellow Hollanders.

Their opposition to political universalism confirms their attachment to independence. It also points to some other values which they see as being supported by independence. Erasmus links it to security and prosperity, Vitoria and Gentili to justice, and Grotius to usefulness. Independence, they agree, is worth preserving, and they all make its defence against unjust attack a just cause of war. Only if such a war risks destroying community, people, or state, must it not be fought. Survival is more important than independence.[2]

Co-operation Cooperation is dear to three of the four thinkers, although it does not have exactly the same meaning for them. Erasmus sees it as collaboration or acting in common. For Vitoria and Gentili, it sometimes has the same meaning; at other times, the one depicts it as openness or non-exclusion, and the other as participation or sharing. Wise and good Christian princes, Erasmus submits, cooperate in maintaining peace and work together to strengthen and beautify their respective countries. Perfect temporal communities, Vitoria argues, are not closed to one another, but receive one another's traders and travellers, and those who wish to sojourn; they defend not only friends and allies, but anybody who 'suffers unjustly'; and Christian perfect temporal communities, in addition, help Christian spiritual power 'to preserve and protect itself'. Free princes and free peoples, Gentili insists, do not exclude themselves from commerce and diplomacy, nor do they exclude others. They are prepared to defend another prince or people against unjust attack. Cooperation is not only satisfying in itself, it also promotes other values. Erasmus connects it with peace, prosperity, justice and independence, Vitoria with justice, happiness, peace, independence and security, and Gentili sees it as contributing to material equality, friendship, justice, peace and independence.

Clearly, cooperation is worth preserving. Yet, the refusal to co-operate is not normally a just cause of war. When cooperation means acting in common, none of the three thinkers makes non-cooperation punishable in war. Erasmus perceives it as a lack of wisdom and goodness, and prescribes greater learning as a means to counteract it. Vitoria permits

[2] Erasmus, Vitoria and Grotius make this point explicitly. In the case of Gentili, it may be inferred from his general position that 'the principle on which states are governed is to avoid suffering harm'. See Gentili, *De Jure Belli Libri Tres*, vol. 2, transl. J. C. Rolfe, intro. C. Phillipson, *The Classics of International Law*, Oxford and London: Clarendon Press and Humphrey Milford, 1933, reprinted New York and London: Oceana Publications and Wildy & Sons, 1964), pp. 44, 82, 87, 102.

various forms of punishment short of war, but places these in the context of Christian temporal power refusing to co-operate with Christian spiritual power. Gentili does not suggest any countermeasures. When co-operation means openness and participation, both Vitoria and Gentili identify non-cooperation as a just cause of war, but neither of them regard war as the only possible answer. If cooperation means 'suffering harm', and Erasmus, Vitoria and Gentili are at one again, it may be refused without inviting any remedial action.

Grotius does not reveal a concern for cooperation, but only mentions, as a matter of right, that states and rulers may defend subjects, allies, friends and 'any person whatsoever' against wrongful treatment.

Justice Erasmus, Vitoria and Gentili present justice as equity, fairness, reasonableness or appropriateness. Justice, they are agreed, is imperative in the rule over political communities and in the relations between them. For Erasmus it is, along with cooperation, a guiding principle for the Christian prince's conduct of affairs. Laws must be equitable, and the administration of justice is one of the prince's highest duties. For Vitoria, the original formation of political communities was necessary not only for security but also for the realization of positive values, among them the achievement of justice. He includes the just execution of power among the prince's obligations in working for the temporal good of the community. Gentili has less to say in this context, but justice is included in his definition of the legitimate exercise of power and in his concept of administration as the task of the king, distinguishing him from the tyrant. Grotius has even less to say: it may be implied that the king has an obligation to rule justly, but this is never spelled out. What is emphasized is the need to maintain the constituted order.

On the just war, as we have seen, there are wide divergences. As regards the making of peace, both Vitoria and Gentili place special emphasis on justice, even while allowing that there may be cases where only a harsh peace can achieve security. From this and similar examples it can be seen that although none of the thinkers emphasizes the tension between justice and order which was a central concern for Bull, they were aware of it, and more generally were aware of potential conflicts among the values they supported so vigorously, as will be noted further below.

Peace For Erasmus, Vitoria and Gentili, peace is among the highest goods; Grotius again stands apart from the other three. Erasmus equates it with concord, harmony and tranquillity, and Vitoria expresses similar sentiments. And Gentili is not against citing St. Augustine: 'Peace', he says, 'is ordered harmony', adding that 'order is the proper distribution of things, which … is the nature of justice'.

Peace, as they perceive it, is order joined by justice. For Erasmus, it opens the way to the prosperity and well-being of Christendom, Vitoria sees it as a precondition for 'natural felicity', and Gentili takes it as an indication that things are as they should be according to nature.

Peace, the three agree, is such a good that it must not be abandoned lightly. Erasmus never tires of portraying the physical and moral devastations that result from war. Vitoria and Gentili do not use the same method of dissuasion, but they join Erasmus in requiring princes, communities and peoples to go to war only if all attempts at peaceful settlement have failed. And Erasmus and Vitoria make it clear that, at times, peace without justice may be preferable to the 'justest' of wars. Such is the case, they hold, when the choice is not between justice and injustice, but between more and less injustice.

Despite these areas of agreement, there is a striking contrast in tone between Erasmus at one extreme and Gentili at the other, with Vitoria in between. Whereas Erasmus vehemently condemns the wars of his time, conceding reluctantly that war can sometimes be a necessity, Gentili expresses no strong emotion, but maintains that both sides are frequently justified in going to war. Vitoria, denying this and more sensitive to the costs of war, offers practical advice to the ruler quite close to that of Erasmus. The concept of international society, then, can accommodate a wide range of attitudes to war – a proposition that invites more discussion than can be undertaken in the present context.

Grotius says relatively little about peace, and for the most part concerns himself with the 'when' and the 'how' of peacemaking, not with general principles. He saves his brief general reflections until the final pages of *De Jure Belli ac Pacis*, where he agrees with Augustine that 'war is waged that peace may be secured',[3] and also with the view that it may be preferable to accept an unjust peace if it becomes too costly to continue the struggle.

Moderation Erasmus never defines moderation, but his attachment to it is such that it has been called a passion. Vitoria presents it as 'temperance' or that which 'has regard for proportion'. Grotius is especially attracted by the middle ground. Gentili undertakes a more thorough conceptual analysis. While placing a high value on moderation, he

[3] H. Grotius, *De Jure Belli ac Pacis Libri Tres* [Three Books On the Law of War and Peace], vol. 2, transl. Latin edition of 1646 by F. W. Kelsey, with the collaboration of others, *The Classics of International Law* (Oxford: Clarendon Press, 1913–27, reprinted New York and London: Oceana Publications and Wildy & Sons, 1964), p. 861.

maintains that it can become excessive – for example, against a ruthless or uncompromising enemy. It must be exercised with discretion. Restraint, or for that matter the middle ground, are not always appropriate. He prefers the idea of observing the proper limit. The moderate ruler will not go to extremes but may resort to severe measures if restraint is not effective. This clarification is important because moderation is, in a sense, a controlling value which limits the range of application of the others. Carried to an extreme, any of the others can become dangerous.

Moderation tempers independence. Princes, communities and peoples, while free to make decisions and act accordingly, are not free to make any decisions whatsoever. They must not violate that which links. It imposes limits on co-operation. Prince cooperates with prince, community with community, and people with people, but not at the cost of 'suffering harm'. Moderation inheres in their idea of justice, and it is there to modify conduct which, while just, may, in particular circumstances, not be 'wise' or 'advisable' or 'proper'. And the peace which they endorse is not peace at any price, but peace based on justice; and if justice is violated, peace may be abandoned. War itself, as they agree, is not beyond the reach of moderation: its conduct must accord with it.

Grotius's frequent support for moderation seems to place him alongside the other three until his account of the law of war introduces a discordant note. Although he dissociates himself from this, his category 'formal war' stands as a statement of what is legally permitted, and is in this sense just. His overall discussion of moderation remains self-contradictory. He diverges from the others, to a greater or lesser extent, on all the values except independence, thus confirming by another route the conclusion reached earlier.

Beyond the Via Media

The term *via media* was chosen provisionally at the outset to designate the tradition of thought under investigation, not because it seemed optimal but because the terms that had been applied – rationalist, Grotian, internationalist – each presented difficulties. The disadvantage of *via media* is that it suggests a lack of its own distinctive ideas. It seems to imply a watered-down version of the ideas of the other two traditions – each having, as it were, a higher profile.

The pattern of values presented above suggests otherwise: a set of positive values which, taken together, serve to identify a body of ideas with its own distinctive character, not depending at all on the ideas held by other schools of thought. And they give greater substance to the basic elements of international society, also identified at the outset: political plurality, major linkages among the units, and rules accepted as binding. This does not, of course, resolve the question of nomenclature or even suggest any particular option, but perhaps leaves one with the question: why not simply refer to an international society tradition?

The Question of a Tradition

As noted earlier, there has recently been extensive discussion of problems inherent in the concept of tradition, both in general and specifically in international relations. The issues here go beyond criticisms of Wight's three traditions. They raise the question of the appropriateness of the concept of tradition itself, as employed by Wight and Bull. It has become a commonplace that many traditions are 'invented', i.e. claims that certain practices or ideas date back to a distant past, which cannot withstand historical scrutiny. Overlapping with this is the concept of an analytical tradition, where a contemporary scholar, not the persons referred to, specifies certain ideas as constituting a tradition. Here it tends to be implied that the claimed tradition distorts or falsifies the actual record. This is typically contrasted with the self-constituted tradition, which is defined by its participants. This latter appears more authentic, and is closer to the original usage of the term as a set of practices or ideas 'handed down' from one generation to the next.[4]

But this way of presenting the concepts overlooks the main reason for postulating an analytical tradition. While it may, like the invented tradition, be claiming a false pedigree for a contemporary construct, it typically has a different purpose. Wight, and others like him, employ the term 'tradition' as a way of bringing intellectual order into what may appear a hopelessly complex and confusing array of opinions about international relations. They postulate that these may be grouped in a few basic categories, within which the various opinions can be ordered. Thus George Kennan and Hans Morgenthau imposed a certain framework for a more systematic discussion of foreign policy in the United States in the early Cold War years by postulating a dichotomy, realism versus idealism/utopianism. Wight countered that this distorted the history of international thought, which was better depicted in terms of three broad clusters of ideas: his three traditions. There is no suggestion that all thinkers and disputants saw themselves in these terms, but rather that their underlying

[4] B. Schmidt, *The Political Discourse of Anarchy: A Disciplinary History of International Relations* (New York: State University of New York Press, 1998), pp. 25–26. For a survey of the controversy on the concept of tradition, see R. Jeffery, *Hugo Grotius in International Thought* (New York: Palgrave Macmillan, 2006), pp. 17–25.

assumptions fall within one or other of the patterns. Nor is this comparable to contriving a groundless historical foundation to bolster a controversial contemporary political claim. Indeed, Wight's stance may be contrasted with that of Kennan and Morgenthau: the latter were postulating a general framework in order to support a particular set of views on current foreign policy; Wight sought to correct this framework because it presented a radically incomplete view of international thought.[5]

The term 'analytical tradition' was not available to Wight and Bull, but it seems clear that Wight was well aware of using 'tradition' in this sense. He refers to a recurring pattern of ideas, and does not claim that the thinkers he names in relation to each tradition saw themselves in this light. It is of interest, nonetheless, whether the four thinkers examined here had any sense of sharing a common view of international relations. This is not explicit in their writings, and indeed it may appear unlikely. There was as yet no concept of international relations: the relations between states, or between their rulers, was not a subject for systematic study. Moreover, Erasmus's intellectual framework was so different from that of the other three that they refer to him very little, and then superficially. Both Gentili and Grotius, in his earlier works, refer favourably to Vitoria, but only as one of many sources. Gentili's colleague, Jean Hotman, provides an apt comment on the scholarly practice of the time:

> From century to century, from hand to hand, we learn from each other. Few writers have done otherwise, especially in serious discussion and matters of importance. Such a work without aid and counsel would be both too defective and too sterile ... [T]hey all borrow from each other, although each one of them has labored independently.[6]

Grotius may well have understated his borrowing from Gentili, but this would have been on specific points, not the overall framework – the 'lofty structure'. There is no hint in Grotius of such an image of the international system. There could be a tacit awareness on the part of the three jurists of participating in a tradition of thought on the just war, but this

[5] Wight saw the dichotomy as 'the reflection of a diseased situation' in the 1930s and 1940s. His 'conscious aim' was to show that the two-schools analysis was inadequate. If there is an unstated political motive, it is to broaden the scope of the foreign policy debate, not to support a particular view. See M. Wight, *International Theory: The Three Traditions*, ed. G. Wight and B. Porter (Leicester: Leicester University Press for the Royal Institute of International Affairs, London, 1991), p. 267.

[6] E. Nys, 'Introduction', in A. Gentili, *De Legationibus Libri Tres*, vol. 2, transl. G. J. Laing, *The Classics of International Law* (New York: Oxford University Press, 1924, reprinted New York and London: Oceana Publications and Wildy & Sons, 1964), vol. 2, pp. 22a–23a. Hotman describes this process of borrowing in response to the accusation of plagiarism.

was a literature with a specific focus, which does not bring in the wider international context.[7]

Likewise, although all four authors reject realism and universalism, there is no indication that they see these as longstanding or rival ways of thinking about international relations. They do not seek to engage with the arguments of the other viewpoints; rather, they present them as stereotypes, often dismissively. Erasmus's satire on Pope Julius II stands alone; i.e. there is no context; his critical comments on universalist imperial claims have varied, but quite specific contexts. Vitoria's rejection of realism remains implicit; his argument against imperial or papal claims to universal rule is made in terms of the present, not longstanding debates. Gentili takes up a position but does not pursue either issue. Grotius deals briefly with universalism but takes up the issue of realism at the outset of *De Jure Belli ac Pacis*, treating Carneades as his chosen representative of the many who deny that law or morality have any place in relations between states. He recognizes a long-standing debate in political thought, but as a dichotomy. Thus in none of the thinkers is there a sense of three rival ways of thinking, let alone three potential traditions, with regard to international relations. There is, then, no self-constituted tradition in the early modern period, and in all probability in later periods, given the diversity of those named in Wight's and Bull's accounts.

This naturally raises the question whether the term 'tradition' is appropriate: may it not create confusion? And indeed Brian Schmidt claims that, especially in International Relations, there is a tendency to view an analytical tradition as an actual historical one.[8] However, as we have seen, Wight does not do this and nor, I shall argue, does Bull. When a term is so widely used and familiar, not only in this instance but in many others, it would seem impractical to seek to change it; rather, like many other terms in the study of politics, 'tradition' is used in more than one sense. Students of politics are quite familiar with this situation, and aware of the need to be clear in which sense a given term is being used.

Bull's question is not whether Wight's traditions are analytical or 'historical', in the sense of self-constituted, but whether they are historical in the sense of offering a valid interpretation of the thought of earlier periods, not simply an imaginary philosophical conversation, in the manner

[7] Grotius's comments in the 'Prolegomena' would imply that there was no such tradition: he refers disparagingly to Vitoria and others as having 'said next to nothing' on the subject. But perhaps, it was suggested earlier, this is not to be taken seriously. See Grotius, *De Jure Belli ac Pacis*, vol. 2, p. 22.

[8] 'Historical' is used here in the sense 'self-constituted'. Schmidt, *The Political Discourse of Anarchy*, pp. 24–32. Many of his examples depict realism as the primary or classical tradition.

of Plato's dialogues. This question is often not raised in discussions of analytical traditions, which tend to take the form of exposing their historical errors.

Renee Jeffery's account of the vicissitudes of the Grotian tradition concludes with an extensive discussion of differences between Wight and Bull, which raises important questions concerning Bull's approach, both his concept of tradition and his interpretation of Grotius's thought.[9] It is true that Bull presents a more hard-edged version of the traditions than Wight, insisting on conceptual precision where Wight tends to circle around an issue, offering varying formulations, leaving a certain impression of vagueness. And Bull's initial account of the traditions in *The Anarchical Society* is disconcertingly categorical, seemingly an unproblematic historical 'given' – although this becomes much more nuanced when he comes to discuss different periods.[10] But Jeffery does not adequately substantiate her contention that Bull 'viewed Wight's analytical traditions as actual historical ones ... with discernible patterns of transmission',[11] using 'historical' in the sense of 'self-constituted'. All of Bull's references, no less than Wight's, are to the pattern of ideas, not to the presence of a self-conscious tradition and its mode of transmission. While there is no awareness of the relevant tradition on the part of the four thinkers, the pattern of ideas postulated by Wight and Bull is already clearly present in the pre-Grotian period, and in this sense the Grotian tradition (under whatever name) predates Grotius himself.

Implications and Questions

The wider conclusions that may be drawn from the study are divided into three sections: the history of international thought, the English School and the discipline.

History of International Thought

Although the period has attracted a great deal of attention among political theorists, this has not extended to international thought except for selected themes. There is no narrative of the thought on international relations, as distinct from the history, or prehistory, of international law. Keene provides the best short overview, based on the distinction between two conceptual 'languages': the political, reason of state and the legal,

[9] Jeffery, *Hugo Grotius in International Thought*, pp. 124–35.

[10] H. Bull, *The Anarchical Society: A Study of Order in World Politics* (London: Macmillan, 1977), pp. 24–27.

[11] Jeffery, *Hugo Grotius in International Thought*, p. 126.

natural law approaches.[12] The second was not narrowly legal: as we have seen, there is a wider political context in the thought of the three jurists examined here. Hartmut Behr's broad-brush universalist interpretation of the period is, at least for this reader, less convincing.[13]

The present study can make only a partial contribution to an overall narrative of the period. It deals with only one strand, albeit an important one. It does not include the reason of state thinkers or the defenders of universal empire, and at least one natural law theorist, Suárez, is missing, for reasons explained earlier. Nonetheless, it is possible to comment on the period as a whole and on the place of the four thinkers, and to suggest some questions for further inquiry. And the study has discovered one thinker, Erasmus, who stands outside both of Keene's categories, although his substantive views are close to those of the natural law school.

The view of the period that emerges in this study differs significantly from Bull's interpretation in *The Anarchical Society*. Bull emphasizes the extent to which the thinkers could not shake off earlier, essentially medieval, assumptions, and how far they were from a well-developed theory of the modern states system.[14] Their international society was based on Christian values, there was 'no fundamental constitutive principle or criterion of membership' of international society; surviving universalist assumptions and confusion over the *ius gentium* impeded the development of international law and a clear concept of the sovereign state; and they had not yet developed an account of the institutions of international society.

The present interpretation places the emphasis quite differently: on the extent to which the thinkers had cast off medieval universalist assumptions and habits of mind, thus on their view of the international system as one of independent, de facto sovereign states. On this reading, the thinkers were essentially pragmatic, guided by the new political realities, disregarding the legal superstructure of the Holy Roman Empire and proceeding on the assumption that the 'subordinate' princes were the real rulers, and thus entitled to the appropriate rights and obligations. It is true that the abstract concept of the state remained undeveloped, hence the varying terminology, but the idea of sovereignty itself was clear in Gentili and Grotius. It is of course true that the idea of the institutions of international society was not yet present, even in Gentili; this is further discussed in the next section. Most of Bull's other comments follow from the time lag between recognizing new political situations which render

12 Keene, *International Political Thought*, pp. 98–133.

13 H. Behr, *A History of International Political Theory: Ontologies of the International* (Houndsmills: Palgrave Macmillan, 2010), pp. 75–129.

14 Bull, *The Anarchical Society*, pp. 27–33.

old concepts obsolete, characterizing them in practical political terms, and the full codification of the new situation in legal terms. The interpretations are not necessarily at odds, but are written from different perspectives. The present one has sought to recreate the intellectual world of the four thinkers; Bull is viewing it in the light of later developments in legal thought.

The four thinkers have been examined with a particular question in mind. More generally, how might they find their place in a general history of international thought in that period? As regards Erasmus, it has long been recognized that he offers valuable insights into the history of his times, but his views on international relations more generally remain unexplored. It is clear that he merits a place in the history. In this study he stands alone, but it would be of interest to establish whether there is a context of humanist thinking to which he could be related – for example, whether his conception of a society of Christian princes is foreshadowed in other humanist writings. As we have seen, the quality of his political thought has been a topic of controversy, but the view taken here is that he was a shrewd observer, not only of abuses of power but also, for example, of the weaknesses of hereditary monarchy as a system of rule and also that, in the light of the literary conventions of the day, some of his seemingly naïve expressions can be seen to be well calculated. His denunciations of war were widely known, but it is unlikely that his view of international society attracted attention, given the dispersed nature of the sources.

Vitoria is the first of the thinkers named by Wight and Bull. It would be of interest to establish whether his image of international society is foreshadowed by any earlier scholastic thinkers, and to take up the question of the originality of his political thought, for example, how far his political assumptions differed from those of Aquinas. He is a major figure, the initiator of a new intellectual tendency, the Salamanca School or 'new scholasticism' and a leading contributor to the debates on the American Indians. His influence is not surprising: his brief writings reveal the philosopher's capacity to discern the central issues, and the reader becomes aware of his judicious judgements. His work offers a concise statement of the core issues of the just war tradition and, however one interprets his position on the American Indians, it well captures the dilemmas of the attempts to justify Spanish imperialism. His refusal to publish his works remains unexplained – this could well have been dangerous, but he refers only to his reluctance to engage in public controversy;[15] and in any case

[15] Vitoria, letter to Miguel de Arcos, 8 November 1534, in A. Pagden and J. Lawrance (eds), *Francisco de Vitoria: Political Writings* (Cambridge: Cambridge University Press, 1991), pp. 331–32.

he could be confident that they would be read by colleagues and that his views would become known in the highest circles.

Gentili emerges as the central figure in the narrative. Whereas Erasmus's account of international society had to be pieced together and Vitoria limits himself to a powerful sketch, Gentili's lofty structure is an explicit image of the international system – a society of a unique kind. For the first time some of its institutions begin to come into focus, although this concept never becomes explicit. He lacks Vitoria's philosophical depth but he has the jurist's concern for systematic exposition and for practical detail. The discussion of particular points sometimes becomes rambling, but overall he follows a clear line of argument, albeit sometimes gliding over difficulties and complications, of which Grotius was more aware but was often unable to resolve. Bull credits Gentili with being 'far-sighted' – for anticipating some of the developments which transformed the ancient law of nations into the modern international law.[16]

Why, then, given its merits and the lack of comparable works, was Gentili's contribution so long neglected and is only now beginning to receive sustained scholarly attention? It is unfortunate that there is no modern biography that might provide more adequate information on the context in which he worked, which might well throw light on this question. But it is evident that he did not enjoy the exceptional standing of the other three. Erasmus attained a unique standing as a European man of letters; Vitoria initiated a new direction in scholastic theology, a new 'School', and it is clear that he enjoyed an exceptional personal authority; Grotius, a celebrated child prodigy, reached a high political office and, in a society which valued humanist learning, had the rare distinction of the scholar-statesman, his works highly esteemed. Although Gentili, an Italian exile in England, had a successful career, he could point to no such exceptional accomplishments. A respected scholar and professional jurist – his appointment to the Spanish embassy attests to his reputation for professional integrity – he had relatively limited political connections, and this was his highest position in public life. Thus Gentili's works, it would appear, suffered the usual fate of academic publications: to be eclipsed by later publications, perhaps in this case helped along by Grotius's ungenerous comments. It is clear that he merits a more permanent place in the historical record.

Grotius's role in the history of international thought, on the other hand, is greatly diminished. He is no longer the first major exponent of international society; indeed, he fails to develop a clear idea of it. The various expressions seeming to suggest it prove to lack substance. He

16 Bull, *The Anarchical Society*, p. 31.

would still have a place in a broader history of international thought, but for different reasons, even though the study has exposed further serious limitations in his *magnum opus*: inconsistencies and above all the failure of his overall argument to come together.

One aspect which has not been emphasized is his sense of the complexity of moral and political issues – much admired by Wight – such that he identifies complications and problems which Gentili, as just noted, had passed over. The ambitious scope of the work and his eclectic approach mean, as Wight also points out, that readers can follow up particular themes without concern for the whole. Thus political theorists can focus on his concept of natural law but need not concern themselves with how adequately he applies it in practice, or others can take up his ideas on moral restraint in war, disregarding their weak philosophical grounding or the problem of reconciling them with other parts of his text. His '"Prolegomena" is a skilful introduction and his first Book holds the promise of a systematic exposition which the later Books fail to fulfil'.[17] Such factors, along with his general reputation, may help to explain the continuing prominence of his work.

The English School

The most significant conclusion is not the deposing of Grotius, but the finding that the other three thinkers fall squarely within one of the three traditions, their thinking guided by an underlying concept of international society. While it must be acknowledged that no general conclusion can be drawn from such a small number of cases, it is noteworthy that in the first phase of the modern states system, presumably furthest removed from the contemporary intellectual world, their basic ideas can be interpreted in terms of Wight's framework.

Since the publication of *The Anarchical Society*, there has been a tendency to conceptualize international society in terms of its institutions; but, as we have seen, only Gentili begins to hint at this possibility. But prior to the institutions is the outlook to which they give expression, and it is in terms of differing basic outlooks or ways of viewing international relations that Wight and Bull define the three traditions. And it is at this level that Wight explored the many facets of the traditions in his lectures.

[17] Cf O'Connell's assessment: 'Like other infant prodigies, however, his knowledge was disorganized ... his enormous reputation was due to intense industry which enabled him to reinforce his writings with a crushing weight of academic authority and precedent; and it was this reputation which gave him his pre-eminent place in the science of international law,' and he goes on to refer to his eclecticism and philosophical confusion. D. P. O'Connell, *Richelieu* (London: Weidenfeld & Nicolson, 1968), pp. 303–04.

Such outlooks, sometimes referred to as worldviews or perhaps paradigms, are in a sense prior to theories.[18] Over time, a variety of theories developed within each outlook, in accordance with changes in philosophy and other relevant disciplines.

The finding that the three fall so clearly within one of the traditions is notable also in view of Wight's comment – responding to the criticism that classification can become stultifying – that such a system is most valuable at the point when it breaks down, and that the major political theorists seldom remained within the parameters of a single tradition.[19] Wight, as we saw, proposed subdividing the traditions to reflect this overlap, and Barry Buzan, in his proposed revision of English School theory, puts forward a much more elaborate breakdown to account for the development of many more theoretical variants in the contemporary period.[20]

However, there is a certain logic to seeing the three traditions as exclusive categories: three fundamentally different normative reactions to a world of sovereign states. First, on the realist view, sovereignty is absolute: there can be no restriction on the sovereign's freedom of choice, hence no binding moral or legal norms, but only rules to which he has agreed and may rescind. On the second, *via media* view, sovereignty is not absolute: it means no more than the absence of any political or legal superior, but sovereigns are subject to binding norms. A variety of theories have been put forward to justify this standpoint. The third option is to reject the pluralist world as unacceptable, morally and on practical grounds, as incapable of maintaining the order necessary for a tolerable existence; thus there is the advocacy of some form of universal political authority which can adequately represent the underlying unity of mankind.

But Wight and Bull did not pursue this line of argument. Wight's lectures acquaint the student with the views on major themes in international relations that have been advanced by thinkers in all three traditions. An understanding of international relations, it is implied, is achieved through dialogue among the three. This is close to the view that it is the hallmark of the English School to offer a synthesis of different perspectives on the subject. Bull was more concerned to develop his own theoretical position, but he did this in part through a critical examination of

18 The term 'paradigm' is not used here because there is no established usage in the social sciences, and it tends to create confusion. For a discussion of worldviews, paradigms and theories, see M. Griffiths, 'Worldviews and IR Theory: Conquest or Coexistence?' in M. Griffiths (ed.), *International Relations Theory for the Twenty-First Century: An Introduction* (London: Routledge, 2007).

19 Wight, *International Theory*, pp. 259–60.

20 B. Buzan, *From International to World Society? English School Theory and the Social Structure of Globalisation* (Cambridge: Cambridge University Press, 2004), pp. 90–160.

views from one or other rival tradition. More recently, Buzan has sought to bring world society more strongly into focus in English School theorizing, and Tim Dunne has argued that theories of international society should include its relationship to the international system and to world society.[21] Thus they would take account of those material considerations bearing on the distribution of power, including levels of technology, and the constraints that they impose – i.e. basic premises of realist theory. Bringing in world society would seek to identify shared values and interests worldwide – a universalist perspective – but Dunne allows that there may be clashing universalisms, Western and anti-Western: world society is not harmonious.

Thus the idea of the three traditions as exclusive categories has been discarded, and for good reason. It identifies basic normative choices, but theory is also empirical, and here it lacks plausibility. At times the world appears to be much as the realists depict it: deeply conflict-ridden, the powers struggling for dominance yet all fearing for their security; in such periods there is an absence of trust, and norms of international society are disregarded. At other times conditions favour, or at least permit, the development of an ordered system. Theories seeking to account for all this cannot be squeezed into a single category.

Yet the four thinkers studied here – Grotius now included – do not appear to take cognizance of the rival traditions. They deal summarily or even dismissively with some of their claims; there is nothing of Wight's dialogue or Bull's engaging seriously with their arguments. But on closer examination they do take account of considerations essentially drawn from the other traditions, albeit unobtrusively. For example, in urging that rulers take account not only of what is justifiable but also of what is prudent or advisable, and that they consider the costs of a just war, they are bringing in characteristic realist concerns for the consequences of actions or the chances of success, and making assumptions about a fundamental realist premise, the distribution of power. If realist borrowings remain implicit, their universalist elements – in particular the concept of human society or its equivalent – are quite prominent in the thinking of the jurists, leading Gierke and others to see them as universalists. Its place in their overall thinking remains rather hazy. It is the realm of human relations where the state is absent or failing to perform its essential role, where the law of nations cannot be invoked, thus is subject only to natural law. Thus if a ruler takes or threatens the lives of innocent

[21] Ibid., pp. 27–89; T. Dunne, 'The English School', in C. Reus-Smit and D. Snidal (eds), *The Oxford Handbook of International Relations* (Oxford: Oxford University Press, 2008), pp. 270–79.

subjects, outsiders may intervene to protect them, under natural law, in the name of human society. No universal political authority is implied. Its place in their thinking may be likened to that of world society in Bull's conceptual schema: of fundamental moral significance but mainly remaining in the background.[22]

The present study has included one additional element which was not part of the original framework derived from Wight and Bull: the discussion of the values endorsed by the four thinkers. These go beyond Bull's dichotomy, order and justice. The latter is included, but the other four values could not be subsumed under 'order', but are more specific. 'Order' may be implicit, but only in a very general sense: it is a more abstract concept than most of theirs, and more readily spelled out in the context of the institutions of international society, which only one of the four, Gentili, was beginning to glimpse.

It is unlikely that precisely the same pattern of values would be reproduced down the ages, but it would be of interest to pursue this issue in relation to later exponents of the idea of international society. Of greater interest than the specific set of values would be the general pattern of values, partly supporting one another but also, it must be assumed, partly at odds, and in particular the presence of a regulative principle such as moderation in the sense of observing the proper limit. This is of course not a precise controlling principle, but conveys a certain disposition and intent. Moreover, this approach to values may be contrasted with the idea of a hierarchy or strict ordering of priority among values, to be found in economics and in some liberal political theorists. It would be of interest to establish whether the sense of value differences being ultimately irreconcilable and capable of resolution only through some form of compromise – *modus vivendi*, moderation, acceptance of limits – is characteristic of the English School.[23]

The early modern thinkers, then, may be related in various ways to current theorizing. Do they have anything to offer to those more concerned with practice, i.e. the issues of contemporary foreign policy? This could only be at the level of basic assumptions or approach. Here, it may be suggested, a perusal of the old works might be surprisingly fruitful. Two examples must suffice.

[22] Bull, *The Anarchical Society*, pp. 20–22. Bull concludes his complex argument thus: 'World order, finally, is morally prior to international order … if any value attaches to order in world politics, it is order among all mankind which we must treat as being of primary value, not order within the society of states.' But he does not develop this line of reasoning.

[23] For a discussion of value pluralism and the principle of the *modus vivendi*, see J. Gray, *Two Faces of Liberalism* (Cambridge: Polity Press, 2000).

First, at present, deliberation about war or intervention tends to be in very specific terms, such as comparisons with recent experience. Questions of justification tend to be taken for granted. But it would be more appropriate that they be brought in explicitly, and here the thinkers in the just war tradition could provide a useful starting point, since they offer a systematic discussion of fundamentals, free from the many contemporary references which tend to complicate more recent discussions.

A second example may be drawn from the contrast between widely shared assumptions in that period and the present. It was noted that each of the authors left political communities free to determine their own form of government, and they did not see this as at all controversial. The present climate of thinking in the West, still the most influential if no longer dominant grouping in world politics, is strikingly different. It is taken for granted that democracy is the best form of government and the general policy of democracy promotion is seldom questioned; the only restriction which, since the Iraq War, is normally acknowledged is that this should not be through war. There is no awareness of how unusual this is, historically, nor of the extent to which it could promote international disorder – the perception of authoritarian governments. The issue surfaced briefly in the wake of the Arab Spring, with some American commentators prepared to argue in favour of promoting disorder in this particular instance. But in general it is assumed that the West is the essential and primary sponsor of international order, and the active promotion of democracy raises no concerns.

This is not the place to engage in a discussion of the complex issues involved. The point here is that the comparison of past and present brings out a little noted aspect of the present which could well be more significant than it might initially appear. It is evident that the international order from the sixteenth to the nineteenth centuries would have been quite different if the European governments had been under steady pressure from an external power to adopt a form of government which would have entailed radical differences in their societies, to which their rulers were opposed.

The Discipline

Can a study relating to the prehistory of the study of international relations have anything further of a general kind to offer to the present discipline? In all probability, not directly – but perhaps it can raise significant questions. Wight was concerned to escape from the *Zeitgeist*, but here it may be a matter of becoming more aware of it: more aware, that is to say, of the particular character of the discipline in this particular phase of its history and thus, again taking a cue from Wight, questioning whether all the developments over recent decades amount to scholarly progress.

Discussions of the discipline tend to focus on theory – including metatheory and methodology – and on content – the 'old' and the 'new' agendas. Here the sixteenth century can have little to say – although it may be noted that Erasmus has recently figured prominently in a proposal to develop the idea of a satiric vision of politics and international relations alongside the more familiar 'tragic vision'.[24]

One may suspect that Erasmus, were he to contemplate the present state of scholarship, might be tempted to see a return of scholasticism: highly sophisticated abstract arguments, absorbing to the initiated but incomprehensible to the ordinary reader. This would be unfair, as indeed he was unfair to many scholastic thinkers, and he could not maintain that the issues now being debated were trivial. But perhaps he might have a point, or even more than one. Is the complex terminology – the 'jargon' – really necessary, or is it more a barrier to protect a mode of theorizing against rival approaches? Could not greater effort be devoted to expressing theory in ways more readily understood by those of other theoretical persuasions, students and other readers? This may indeed be taking place, but there is still some way to go.

Erasmus might also be perplexed over some other features of the current discipline. Why, he might wonder, is there so uniform a format in the journals? The articles all of a similar length and heavily footnoted, normally addressing a theoretical question or at least placing emphasis on the theory being employed to address the problem, leaving many of its aspects unexplored. Can all the questions short of those requiring book-length treatments really be adequately discussed in an article of a standard length? And is there no place for lively interventions not requiring such scholarly overkill? He had always allowed the nature of the problem to determine the length of his writings, and would find such a system stifling. He would not readily understand the career incentives and institutional rigidities supporting such practices, but would question whether they could foster genuine originality of thought.

He would need some time to accustom himself to the idea of international relations as an academic discipline, but then he would light on John Ruggie's question: 'What makes the world hang together?' – only to be disappointed, because he could find no answer.[25] With a certain effort he would come to see the need for specialization to advance this new

[24] I. Hall, 'The Satiric Vision of Politics: Ethics, Interests and Disorders', *European Journal of International Relations*, vol. 20, no. 1, 2014, pp. 217–36.

[25] J. G. Ruggie, 'What Makes the World Hang Together? Neo-Utilitarianism and the Social Constructivist Challenge', *International Organization*, vol. 52, no. 4, 1998, p. 855.

kind of knowledge that had brought about unbelievable material progress, but was this so effective in the human sciences? Much more was known on specific topics, but was there greater understanding of human and social well-being, was there moral progress?

The Erasmian perspective raises many issues, three of which will be taken up here. (1) Has specialization gone too far? Has the discipline lost sight of Ruggie's question? Is there a need for more syntheses, more studies that integrate the fragments? (2) Is research too theory-driven, insufficiently shaped by the problems that we choose or that thrust themselves before us? (3) Whom do we write for? In particular, why is there so little communication with the public, and should this be rectified?

Whole and Part The sense of specialization taking over is especially pronounced in the journals, but perhaps one should rather look to books for broader overviews or attempts at synthesis. But here, too, such studies are remarkably infrequent. Works such as Buzan's redefining and broadening the scope of English School theorizing, or Andrew Hurrell's comprehensive theoretical and institutional study of the present 'global order', remain exceedingly rare.[26] And journals could indeed respond to the need for a stronger focus on the whole, for example through review articles (why have these gone out of fashion?) or through special issues, often very rewarding but more likely to be devoted to a new issue seeking a place on the agenda.

The editors of *The Oxford Handbook of International Relations* have taken several steps toward a more integrated presentation of the discipline. They preface their broad selection of theoretical approaches with two introductory chapters: their own, which locates the various theories within a common framework, and a chapter calling for eclectic theorizing, by which the authors mean recognizing the strengths of different theoretical perspectives and how they may be fruitfully combined in studying concrete problems.[27] The *Oxford Handbook* also offers a sustained attempt to bring together the empirical and the normative, each theoretical approach being examined in terms of both dimensions. A section of the *Oxford Handbook* is devoted to bridging the boundaries between subfields, and a few eminent scholars are invited to share their

[26] A. Hurrell, *On Global Order: Power, Values and the Constitution of International Society* (Oxford: Oxford University Press, 2007).

[27] See C. Reus-Smit and D. Snidal, 'Between Utopia and Reality: The Practical Discourses of International Relations', in Reus-Smit and Snidal (eds), *The Oxford Handbook of International Relations*; P. Katzenstein and R. Sil, 'Eclectic Theorizing in the Study and Practice of International Relations', in Reus-Smit and Snidal (eds), *The Oxford Handbook of International Relations*.

thinking on the 'big questions', or on the direction in which the discipline should be moving.

However, the *Oxford Handbook* could also be seen as showing how far we remain from an answer to Ruggie's question. An overview of the theoretical landscape is a promising start, but provides no more than the overall framework: a set of theoretical languages, images of the international system and some notions of how the players interact. But who the key actors are and how outcomes are determined remain hazy. It is not so much that the issues are contested, but rather that they are not clearly defined. It has been said of the branch of international relations which addresses this range of issues – foreign policy analysis – that 'the subject matter is excruciatingly resistant to systematic analysis'.[28] There are many excellent studies on aspects of foreign policy decision-making – for example, the role of internal politics, of bureaucratic structures and traditions, of rational choice and impediments to it, perception and misperception, personality types – but the whole field is somehow less than the sum of its parts.[29]

But perhaps this is less dismaying than it might appear. Consider the case of economics, long established as an academic discipline, where the theories and the issues are much more sharply focused. Its practitioners can be taken by surprise by a major event such as the global financial crisis, no less than were International Relations scholars by the end of the Cold War. For a brief moment there appeared to be an unfamiliar climate of soul-searching in that discipline, but before long most economists seem to have found an explanation for the shortcomings which left their theories intact. Yet serious differences over policy remain, and there is much that the discipline cannot explain, let alone predict. Perhaps the situations of the two disciplines are more similar than economists would like to think, but in the one case the shortcomings are obvious to all, and in the other they are mostly well concealed and little acknowledged. The challenge to International Relations remains: to provide a more reliable map of the terrain and thus a better guide to action – but the same is true of all the social sciences.

A Question of Priorities One may accept the editors of the *Oxford Handbook's* contention that 'theoretical assumptions (and debates surrounding them) determine the contours of the field and inform even the most empirical research',[30] and yet suspect that there is an over-emphasis on theoretical publications, especially in the journals. It is not that the

[28] D. T. Stuart, 'Foreign-Policy Decision-Making', in Reus-Smit and Snidal (eds), *The Oxford Handbook of International Relations*, p. 590.
[29] For the diversity of approaches and findings, see the journal *Foreign Policy Analysis*.
[30] Reus-Smit and Snidal, 'Between Utopia and Reality', p. 5.

topics are inconsequential, but that other, highly significant issues are under-researched, while theoretical issues of lesser order are elaborately examined.

The most prominent issue area that comes to mind is the environmental, and above all the issue of climate change, which arguably has taken the place of nuclear weapons as the main threat to civilization in the present era. But while the issues raised by the former were for long a central concern of the discipline, the latter remains at the periphery. This is inherently an interdisciplinary area and one which presents obstacles to theorizing analogous to those of foreign policy analysis. Yet international relations theories could offer orientations to its study, and the international political dimension is understood only rather superficially in the public discourse. The economic issues have been far more clearly defined and brought into the policy debate. The most obvious finding from international relations may well be the difficulty of reaching international agreement, and the reasons for this, but there must surely be scope for more imaginative research into how these might be overcome. The potential for transnational coalitions might be one such topic. Is it that career incentives militate against time spent in mastering the essentials of other, unfamiliar disciplines, and against arduous empirical research, perhaps with little prospect of theoretical innovation?

Another example is the discipline's failure to anticipate the end of the Cold War. Arguably this was not an outcome that should, or could, have been predicted, but it should not have come as a shock; it should have been envisaged as a possibility. After the event there was a vigorous debate between advocates of explanations in terms of material causes versus ideational causes of the Soviet collapse – structures versus ideas. But there was little reflection on the reasons for the discipline's being taken by surprise. A certain kind of historical knowledge might have provided more adequate preparation; that is to say, knowledge of the reasons making for the erosion of support for political regimes and for their final collapse, including the danger that attempts at reform may prove fatal. But international history is something of a poor relation in both disciplines, history and international relations. Perhaps historical sociology could best promote the kind of broad historical awareness that would reduce the likelihood of future shocks.

The Public Profile A third issue for the discipline is raised more indirectly by the study: whom do we write for? Is there an important relationship, or audience, beyond the discipline itself and its students? The *Oxford Handbook* devotes two chapters to one such readership, the policy community. And this indeed has been a long-standing preoccupation. But a wider public readership remains unmentioned.

The four subjects of this study wrote with differing readerships in mind. Erasmus wrote for the reading public of his day, and corresponded with monarchs and their advisers. Vitoria's manuscripts would be read by colleagues and perhaps more widely in the Dominican order, but his views might be made known in the highest political circles. Gentili, it would seem, wrote for professionals and students; his political connections were more modest. Grotius alone held high political appointments, and it seems that he had such readers in mind, as well as professionals, but also a wider readership, in writing *De Jure Belli ac Pacis*. Thus all four had policymakers in mind, and two were accustomed to writing for a wider public.

To return to the contemporary discipline: the issue of communicating with the policy community has been extensively canvassed elsewhere and will not be further discussed, but the question of writing for a broader public readership warrants further attention. There is a high level of public interest in certain international issues and a more diffuse interest in works that offer a perspective on the overall international scene, a sense of orientation in the confusing impressions constantly transmitted through the media. Perhaps the most effective communicators in the discipline are area specialists. Their expertise is immediately relevant and sought after; and it is possible to maintain high scholarly standards while writing for a wide readership.

At a more general level, neighbouring disciplines are more effective in producing works which are widely read and at the same time have something significant to say to the profession. These are never numerous, but it can be expected that a few historians will be offering a perspective on major issues or themes which rightly attract attention. At the time of writing, the First World War is such a theme, no longer a living memory but close enough that a skilful synthesis which brings out ways in which those events shaped the present can appeal to many interests while making a significant contribution to scholarship. It is difficult to think of parallels in the international relations discipline.

Economists in the public domain tend to be engaged in policy debates, mostly ephemeral, but occasionally, like Paul Krugman, persisting in developing a particular line of argument, or exceptionally, like Milton Friedman, presenting a new doctrine in a way that is accessible to the general reader. Among policy-oriented international relations theorists, only Hans Morgenthau has had such a strong public presence. Closely related to the policy debates is the capacity to define a central issue in a situation where there is a pervasive lack of clarity. Well-known examples would be the theses advanced by Francis Fukuyama and Samuel Huntington on the nature of the international milieu after the end of the Cold War. Such theses seldom prove longlasting, but they contribute to clarifying perceptions, prompt debate and may open up fruitful lines of further inquiry. But both these theorists were at the periphery of international relations, based essentially in a neighbour discipline.

The lack of a stronger public profile may be regrettable, but does it matter? There are numerous contributions to the policy debate; the lack of 'big names' should not be a major concern. More significant is the absence of the broad perspective, the kind of major work which places the passing events in an illuminating context, which automatically attracts attention, in the discipline as in the public domain. Is there any way in which such projects might be promoted?

No compelling answer suggests itself, beyond the thought that this would require a change in the discipline's ethos. Erasmus might have an answer, but his practical sense would warn him that it would fall on stony ground. What this generation needs, he might muse, is a strong infusion of humanist culture – but could that be more than a tantalizing dream?

Bibliography

PRIMARY SOURCES

Desiderius Erasmus of Rotterdam

Allen, P. S. (ed.), *Opus Epistolarum Des. Erasmi Roterodami*, vol. 2, *1514–1517*, Oxford: Clarendon Press, 1910.

Allen, P. S. and Allen, H. M. (eds), *Opus Epistolarum Des. Erasmi Roterodami*, vol. 3, *1517–1519*, Oxford: Clarendon Press, 1913.

(eds), *Opus Epistolarum Des. Erasmi Roterodami*, vol. 6, *1525–1527*, Oxford: Clarendon Press, 1926.

(eds), *Opus Epistolarum Des. Erasmi Roterodami*, vol. 7, *1527–1528*, Oxford: Clarendon Press, 1928.

Allen, P. S., Allen, H. M. and Garrod, H. W. (eds), *Opus Epistolarum Des. Erasmi Roterodami*, vol. 11, *1534–1536*, Oxford: Clarendon Press, 1947.

Collected Works of Erasmus, vol. 1, *The Correspondence of Erasmus: Letters 1 to 141, 1484 to 1500*, transl. R. A. B. Mynors and D. F. S. Thomson, annotated W. K. Ferguson, Toronto: University of Toronto Press, 1974.

Collected Works of Erasmus, vol. 2, *The Correspondence of Erasmus: Letters 142 to 297, 1501 to 1514*, transl. R. A. B. Mynors and D. F. S. Thomson, annotated W. K. Ferguson, Toronto: University of Toronto Press, 1975.

Collected Works of Erasmus, vol. 3, *The Correspondence of Erasmus: Letters 298 to 445, 1514 to 1516*, transl. R. A. B. Mynors and D. F. S. Thomson, annotated J. K. McConica, Toronto: University of Toronto Press, 1976.

Collected Works of Erasmus, vol. 4, *The Correspondence of Erasmus: Letters 446 to 593, 1516 to 1517*, transl. R. A. B. Mynors and D. F. S. Thomson, annotated J. K. McConica, Toronto: University of Toronto Press, 1977.

DeMolen, R. L. (ed.), *Erasmus*, London: Edward Arnold, 1973.

Dolan, J. P., *The Essential Erasmus: Selected and Translated with Introduction and Commentary*, New York and Scarborough, Ontario: Meridian/The New American Library, 1964.

Erasmus, D., *Enchiridion: Handbuechlein eines christlichen Streiters*, transl. and ed. W. Welzig, Graz and Koeln: Hermann Boehlaus Nachf., 1961.

Papst Julius vor der Himmelstür: Julius exclusus e coelis. Lateinisch-deutsch, transl. and annotated W. von Koppelfels, Mainz: Dieterich'sche Verlagsbuchhandlung, 2011.

'The Antibarbarians', transl. and annotated M. M. Phillips, in *Collected Works of Erasmus*, vol. 23, *Literary and Educational Writings 1*, ed. C. R. Thompson, Toronto: University of Toronto Press, 1978, pp. 1–122.

The Education of a Christian Prince, transl. and intro. L. K. Born, New York: Columbia University Press, 1936.

The Julius Exclusus of Erasmus, transl. P. Pascal, intro. and critical notes J. K. Sowards, Bloomington, IN: Indiana University Press, 1968.

'Vtilissima Consvltatio de Bello Tvrcis Inferendo, et Obiter Enarratvs Psalmvs XXVIII', ed. A. G. Weiler, in *Opera Omnia Desiderii Erasmi Roterodami*, V–III, vol. 15, Amsterdam: North Holland Publishing Co., 1986, pp. 31–82.

Flower, B. and Rosenbaum, E. (compil.), *Opus Epistolarum Des. Erasmi Roterodami*, vol. 12, *Indices*, Oxford: Oxford University Press, 1958.

Froude, J. A., *Life and Letters of Erasmus: Lectures Delivered at Oxford 1893–1894*, New York: Charles Scribner's Sons, 1927.

Gerlo, A. (ed.), *La Correspondance d'Érasme*, vols 5, 6 and 8, Brussels: University Press, 1976–1979.

Hillerbrand, J. (ed.), *Erasmus and His Age: Selected Letters of Desiderius Erasmus*, New York: Harper & Row, 1970.

Margolin, J. C., *Guerre et Paix dans la Pensée d'Érasme*, Paris: Aubier Montaigne, 1973.

Nichols, F. M., *The Epistles of Erasmus From His Earliest Letters to His Fifty-First Year Arranged in Order of Time: English Translations from the Early Correspondence with a Commentary Confirming the Chronological Arrangement and Supplying Further Biographical Matter*, vols 2 and 3, London: Longmans/Green & Co., 1904–1918. Vol. 3 extends to 'His Fifty-Third Year'.

Olin, J. C. (ed.), *Christian Humanism and the Reformation: Selected Writings of Erasmus, with the Life of Erasmus by Beatus Rhenanus*, New York: Fordham University Press, 1980.

Phillips, M. M., *The Adages of Erasmus: A Study with Translations*, Cambridge: Cambridge University Press, 1964.

Thompson, C. R. (transl.), *The Colloquies of Erasmus*, Chicago and London: University of Chicago Press, 1965.

Francisco de Vitoria

Barbier, M., 'Introduction', in M. Barbier (ed.), *Francisco de Vitoria: Leçons sur les Indiens et sur le Droit de Guerre* [Francisco de Vitoria: Lectures on the Indians and on the Law of War], Geneva: Droz, 1966, pp. vii–lxxxii.

Getino, L. (transl.), *Francisco de Vitoria: Derecho Natural y de Gentes*, intro. E. de Hinojosa, Buenos Aires: Ernecé Editores, 1946.

Nys, E. (ed.), *Francisci de Victoria De Indis et De Iure Belli Relectiones, The Classics of International Law*, Washington, DC: Carnegie Institution, 1917, reprinted New York: Oceana Publications, 1964.

Pagden, A., and Lawrance, J. (eds), *Francisco de Vitoria: Political Writings*, Cambridge: Cambridge University Press, 1991.

Pereña, L. (ed.), *Francisco de Vitoria: Escritos Políticos*, Buenos Aires: Ediciones Depalma, 1967.

Pereña, L. and Pérez Prendes, J. M. (eds), *Francisco de Vitoria: Relectio de Indis o Libertad de los Indios*, Madrid: Consejo Superior de Investigaciones Científicas, 1967.

Scott, J. B., *The Spanish Origin of International Law: Francisco de Vitoria and His Law of Nations*, Oxford and London: Clarendon Press and Humphrey Milford, 1934.

Urdánoz, T., 'Introducción Biográfica', in T. Urdánoz (ed.), *Obras de Francisco de Vitoria: Relecciones Teológicas*, Madrid: Autores Cristianos, 1960, pp. 1–107.

(ed.), *Obras de Francisco de Vitoria: Relecciones Teológicas*, Madrid: Autores Cristianos, 1960.

Wright, H. F., 'Prefatory Remarks Concerning the Text', in E. Nys (ed.), *Francisci de Victoria De Indis et De Iure Belli Relectiones*, *The Classics of International Law*, Washington, DC: Carnegie Institution, 1917, reprinted by Oceana Publications, New York, 1964, pp. 191–207.

Alberico Gentili

Comines, P. de, *Memoirs*, transl. and annotated Mr. Uvedale, 2nd edn, vol. 1, London: Bettesworth & Pemberton, 1723.

Gentili, A., *De Jure Belli Libri Tres*, vol. 1, A Photographic Reproduction of the Edition of 1612, *The Classics of International Law*, Oxford and London: Clarendon Press and Humphrey Milford, 1933.

De Jure Belli Libri Tres, vol. 2, transl. J. C. Rolfe, intro. C. Phillipson, *The Classics of International Law*, Oxford and London: Clarendon Press and Humphrey Milford, 1933, reprinted New York and London: Oceana Publications and Wildy & Sons, 1964.

De Legationibus Libri Tres, vol. 1, A Photographic Reproduction of the Edition of 1594, intro. E. Nys, *The Classics of International Law*, New York: Oxford University Press, 1924.

De Legationibus Libri Tres, vol. 2, transl. G. J. Laing, intro. E. Nys, *The Classics of International Law*, New York: Oxford University Press, 1924, reprinted New York and London: Oceana Publications and Wildy & Sons, 1964.

Hispanicae Advocationis Libri Duo, vol. 1, A Photographic Reproduction of the Edition of 1661, intro. F. F. Abbott, *The Classics of International Law*, New York: Oxford University Press, 1921, reprinted New York and London: Oceana Publications and Wildy & Sons, 1964.

Hispanicae Advocationis Libri Duo, vol. 2, transl. F. F. Abbott, *The Classics of International Law*, New York: Oxford University Press, 1921.

Markowicz, L. (transl. with intro.), 'Latin Correspondence by Alberico Gentili and John Rainolds on Academic Drama', in J. Hogg (ed.), *Elizabethan and Renaissance Studies*, no. 68, Salzburg: Institut fuer Englische Sprache und Literatur, 1977, pp. 1–141.

Nys, E., 'Introductio', in A. Gentili, *De Legationibus Libri Tres*, vol. 2, transl. G. J. Laing, *The Classics of International Law*, New York: Oxford University Press, 1924, reprinted New York and London: Oceana Publications and Wildy & Sons, 1964, pp. 11a–37a.

'Introduction', in E. Nys (ed.), *Francisci de Victoria De Indis et De Iure Belli Relectiones*, transl. J. Pawley Bate, *The Classics of International Law*, Washington, DC: Carnegie Institution, 1917, reprinted New York: Oceana Publications, 1964, pp. 55–100.

Rainolds, J., *The Overthrow of Stage-Plays by the Way of Controversy between D. Gager and D. Rainolds*, 1599, New York and London: Johnson Reprint, 1972.

Hugo Grotius

Briefwisseling van Hugo Grotius, vol. 3, eds P. C. Molhuysen and B. L. Meulenbroek, 'S-Gravenhage: Martinus Nijhoff, 1961.

Briefwisseling van Hugo Grotius, vol. 4, ed. B. L. Meulenbroek, 'S-Gravenhage: Martinus Nijhoff, 1964.

Briefwisseling van Hugo Grotius, vol. 5, ed. B. L. Meulenbroek, 'S-Gravenhage: Martinus Nijhoff, 1966.

Briefwisseling van Hugo Grotius, vol. 7, ed. B. L. Meulenbroek, 'S-Gravenhage: Martinus Nijhoff, 1969.

Briefwisseling van Hugo Grotius, vol. 11, eds B. L. Meulenbroek and P. P. Witkam, 'S-Gravenhage: Martinus Nijhoff, 1981.

Clark, G. N., and Eysinga, W. J. M. van, 'The Colonial Conferences between England and the Netherlands in 1613 and 1615', Part I, *Bibliotheca Visseriana*, vol. 15 (Lugdunum Batavorum: E. J. Brill, 1940), pp. 1–270.

'The Colonial Conferences between England and the Netherlands in 1613 and 1615', Part II, *Bibliotheca Visseriana*, vol. 17 (Lugdunum Batavorum: E. J. Brill, 1951), pp. 1–155.

Filmer, Sir R., 'Observations Upon H. Grotius De Jure Belli ac Pacis', in J. P. Sommerville (ed.), *Sir Robert Filmer: Patriarcha and Other Writings*, Cambridge: Cambridge University Press, 1991, pp. 208–34.

Grotius, H., *A Treatise on the Antiquity of the Commonwealth of the Battavers, Which Is Now the Hollanders*, transl. T. Woods, London: John Walker, 1649.

Annales et Histoires des Troubles du Pays-Bas, Amsterdam: Iean Blaev, 1662.

De Jure Belli ac Pacis Libri Tres, vol. 2, transl. Latin edition of 1646 by F. W. Kelsey, with the collaboration of others, *The Classics of International Law*, Oxford: Clarendon Press, 1913–1927, reprinted New York and London: Oceana Publications and Wildy & Sons, 1964.

De Jure Praedae Commentarius, vol. 1, transl. Original Manuscript of 1604 by G. L. Williams, collab. W. H. Zeydel, *The Classics of International Law*, Oxford and London: Clarendon Press and Geoffrey Cumberlege, 1950, reprinted New York and London: Oceana Publications and Wildy & Sons, 1964.

De Jure Praedae Commentarius, vol. 2, *The Collotype Reproduction of the Original Manuscript of 1604, The Classics of International Law*, Oxford and London: Clarendon Press and Geoffrey Cumberlege, 1950.

'De Republica Emendanda: A Juvenile Tract by Hugo Grotius on the Emendation of the Dutch Polity', eds A. Eyffinger, P. A. H. de Boer, J. T. de Smidt and L. E. van Holk, *Grotiana*, New Series, vol. 5, 1984, pp. 3–135.

'Defensio', in H. F. Wright, 'Some Less Known Works of Hugo Grotius', *Bibliotheca Visseriana*, vol. 7, Lugdunum Batavorum: E. J. Brill, 1928, pp. 154–205.

Hugonis Grotii De Jure Belli et Pacis Libri Tres, ed. W. Whewell, 3 vols, Cambridge: Cambridge University Press, 1853.

Mare Liberum, Sive De Iure Quod Batavis Competit Ad Indicana Commercia Dissertatio, transl. with a revision of the Latin text of 1633 R. van Deman Magoffin, ed. with an intro. note J. B. Scott, *The Classics of International Law*, New York and London: Oxford University Press and Humphrey Milford, 1916.

The Jurisprudence of Holland, transl. with brief notes and a commentary R. W. Lee, vol. 1, Oxford: Clarendon Press, 1926.

True Religion, Amsterdam: Theatrum Orbis Terrarum, 1971.

Holk, L. E. van and Roelofsen, C. G. (eds), *Grotius Reader: A Reader for Students of International and Legal History*, The Hague: T. M. C. Asser Instituut, 1983.

Wright, H. F., 'Some Less Known Works of Hugo Grotius', *Bibliotheca Visseriana*, vol. 7, Lugdunum Batavorum: E. J. Brill, 1928, pp. 133–238.

SECONDARY SOURCES

Abbott, F. F., 'Introduction', in A. Gentili, *Hispanicae Advocationis Libri Duo*, vol. 1, *A Photographic Reproduction of the Edition of 1661, The Classics of International Law*, New York: Oxford University Press, 1921, pp. 11a–44a.

Anghie, A., *Imperialism, Sovereignty and the Making of International Law*, Cambridge: Cambridge University Press, 2004.

Aston, T. (ed.), *Crisis in Europe: 1560–1660: Essays from Past and Present*, London: Routledge & Kegan Paul, 1965.

Augustijn, C., *Erasmus: His Life, Works and Influence*, Toronto: University of Toronto Press, 1991.

Bainton, R. H., *Erasmus of Christendom*, Glasgow: Fontana/Collins, 1977, first published 1969.

Barker, E., 'Introduction', in O. von Gierke, *Natural Law and the Theory of Society 1500–1800*, vol. 1, Cambridge: Cambridge University Press, 1934, pp. ix–xci.

Bataillon, M., *Érasme et l'Espagne*, vol. I, nouvelle edn, Paris: Droz, 1991, first published 1937.

Behr, H., *A History of International Political Theory: Ontologies of the International*. Houndsmills: Palgrave Macmillan, 2010.

Beumer, J., *Erasmus der Europaeer: Die Beziehungen des Rotterdamers zu den Humanisten seiner Zeit unter den verschiedenen Nationen Europas*, Werl, Westfalia: Dietrich Coelde, 1969.

Biermann, B. M., 'Bartolomé de Las Casas and Verapaz', in J. Friede and B. Keen (eds), *Bartolomé de Las Casas in History: Toward an Understanding of the Man and His Work*, DeKalb, IL: Northern Illinois University Press, 1971, pp. 443–84.

Binns, J. W., 'Alberico Gentili in Defense of Poetry and Acting', *Studies in the Renaissance*, vol. 19, 1972, pp. 224–72.

Borschberg, P., *Hugo Grotius 'Commentarius in Theses XI'*, Berne: Peter Lang, 1994.

Boucher, D., *Political Theories of International Relations: From Thucydides to the Present*, Oxford: Oxford University Press, 1998.

Brett, A., 'Francisco de Vitoria (1483–1546) and Francisco Suárez (1548–1617)', in B. Fassbender and A. Peters (eds), *The Oxford Handbook of the History of International Law*, Oxford: Oxford University Press, 2013, pp. 1086–91.

Brett, A. S., *Changes of State: Nature and the Limits of the City in Early Modern Natural Law*, Princeton, NJ: Princeton University Press, 2011.

Bull, H., 'Martin Wight and the Theory of International Relations', in M. Wight, *International Theory: The Three Traditions*, ed. G. Wight and B. Porter, Leicester: Leicester University Press for the Royal Institute of International Affairs, London, 1991, pp. ix–xxiii.

'Society and Anarchy in International Relations', in H. Butterfield and M. Wight (eds), *Diplomatic Investigations: Essays in the Theory of International Politics*, London: George Allen & Unwin, 1969, pp. 35–50.

The Anarchical Society: A Study of Order in World Politics, London: Macmillan, 1977.

'The Grotian Conception of International Society', in H. Butterfield and M. Wight (eds), *Diplomatic Investigations: Essays in the Theory of International Politics*, London: George Allen & Unwin, 1969, pp. 51–73.

'The Importance of Grotius in the Study of International Relations', in H. Bull, B. Kingsbury and A. Roberts (eds), *Hugo Grotius and International Relations*, Oxford: Clarendon Press, 1990, pp. 65–93.

Butterfield, H. and Wight, M. (eds), *Diplomatic Investigations: Essays in the Theory of International Politics*, London: George Allen & Unwin, 1969.

Buzan, B., *From International to World Society? English School Theory and the Social Structure of Globalisation*, Cambridge: Cambridge University Press, 2004.

Campagna, N., *Francisco de Vitoria: Leben und Werk*, Zurich and Munster: LIT Verlag, 2010.

Choue, Y. S. (ed.), *World Encyclopedia of Peace*, 2nd edn, vol. IV, New York: Oceana Publications, 1999.

Comas, J., 'Historical Reality and the Detractors of Father Las Casas', in J. Friede and B. Keen (eds), *Bartolomé de Las Casas in History: Toward an Understanding of the Man and His Work*, DeKalb, IL: Northern Illinois University Press, 1971, pp. 487–537.

Davies, R. T., *The Golden Century of Spain: 1501–1621*, London: Macmillan, 1961.

Dickens, A. G. and Jones, W. R. D., *Erasmus the Reformer*, London: Methuen, 1994.

Donelan, M., 'Grotius and the Image of War', *Millennium: Journal of International Studies*, vol. 12, no. 3, 1983, pp. 233–43.

Doyle, M. W., *Ways of War and Peace: Realism, Liberalism, Socialism*, New York: Norton, 1997.

Draper, G. I. A. D., 'Grotius' Place in the Development of Legal Ideas about War', in H. Bull, B. Kingsbury and A. Roberts (eds), *Hugo Grotius and International Relations*, Oxford: Clarendon Press, 1990, pp. 177–207.

Dresden, S., 'Présence d'Érasme', in Académie Royale Néerlandaise des Sciences et des Sciences Humaines, *Actes du Congrès Érasme, Rotterdam, 27–29 Octobre*

1969, Amsterdam and London: North Holland Publishing Company, 1971, pp. 1–13.

Dumbauld, E., *The Life and Legal Writings of Hugo Grotius*, Norman, OK: University of Oklahoma Press, 1969.

Dunne, T., 'The English School', in C. Reus-Smit and D. Snidal (eds), *The Oxford Handbook of International Relations*, Oxford: Oxford University Press, 2008, pp. 267–85.

Dunning, W. A., *A History of Political Theories: From Luther to Montesquieu*, New York and London: Macmillan, 1949.

Edwards, C. S., *Hugo Grotius: The Miracle of Holland: A Study in Political and Legal Thought*, intro. R. A. Falk, Chicago: Nelson-Hall, 1981.

Ehrlich, L., 'L'Interprétation des Traités', *Recueil des Cours*, vol. 24, IV, 1928, pp. 5–145.

Elliott, J. H., *Europe Divided: 1559–1598*, Glasgow: Fontana/Collins, 1977.

Imperial Spain: 1469–1716, London: Edward Arnold, 1963.

Elton, G. R., *England under the Tudors*, London: Methuen, 1956.

Reformation Europe: 1517–1559, Glasgow: Fontana/Collins, 1977.

Eyffinger, A., 'In Quest of Synthesis: An Attempted Synopsis of Grotius' Works According to their Genesis and Objective', *Grotiana*, New Series, vol. 4, 1983, pp. 76–88.

Fabisch, P., *Julius Exclusus e Coelis: Motive und Tendenzen gallikanischer und bibelhumanistischer Papstkritik im Umfeld des Erasmus*, Münster: Aschendorhh Verlag, 2008.

Fernández, J. A., 'Erasmus on the Just War', *Journal of the History of Ideas*, vol. 34, no. 2, 1973, pp. 209–26.

Fikentscher, W., 'De Fide et Perfidia – Der Treuegedanke in den "Staatsparallelen" des Hugo Grotius aus heutiger Sicht', *Sitzungsberichte der Bayerischen Akademie der Wissenschaften*, vol. 1, 1979, pp. 7–160.

Friedrich, C. J., 'Gierke, Otto von', in E. R. A. Seligman (ed.-in-chief), *The Encyclopaedia of the Social Sciences*, vol. 6, New York: Macmillan, 1931, pp. 655–66.

Fruin, R., 'An Unpublished Work of Hugo Grotius', transl. from an Essay in Dutch (1868), *Bibliotheca Visseriana*, vol. 5, Lugdunum Batavorum: E. J. Brill, 1925, pp. 3–74.

Geldner, F., *Die Staatsauffassung und Fuerstenlehre des Erasmus von Rotterdam*, Berlin: Emil Ebering, 1930.

Geyl, P., *The Netherlands in the Seventeenth Century: I. 1609–1648*, London: Ernest Benn, 1961.

The Revolt of the Netherlands: 1555–1609, 2nd edn, London and New York: Ernest Benn and Barnes & Noble, 1980).

Gierke, O. von, *Das Deutsche Genossenschaftsrecht*, 4 vols, Graz: Akademische Druck und Verlagsanstalt, 1954.

Johannes Althusius und die Entwicklung der naturrechtlichen Staatstheorien, 5th edn, Aalen: Scientia, 1958.

Natural Law and the Theory of Society 1500–1800, transl. with intro. E. Barker, 2 vols, Cambridge: Cambridge University Press, 1934.

Giménez Fernández, M., 'Fray Bartolomé de Las Casas: A Biographical Sketch', in J. Friede and B. Keen (eds), *Bartolomé de Las Casas in History: Toward an Understanding of the Man and His Work*, DeKalb, IL: Northern Illinois University Press, 1971, pp. 67–125.

Griffiths, M., 'Worldviews and IR Theory: Conquest or Coexistence?' in M. Griffiths (ed.), *International Relations Theory for the Twenty-First Century: An Introduction*, London: Routledge, 2007, pp. 1–10.

Gray, J., *Two Faces of Liberalism*, Cambridge: Polity Press, 2000.

Guggenheim, P., 'Contribution à l'Histoire des Sources du Droit des Gens', *Recueil des Cours*, vol. 94, II, 1958, pp. 1–84.

Haggenmacher, P., 'Grotius and Gentili: A Reassessment of Thomas E. Holland's Inaugural Lecture', in H. Bull, B. Kingsbury and A. Roberts (eds), *Hugo Grotius and International Relations*, Oxford: Clarendon Press, 1990, pp. 133–76.

Grotius et la Doctrine de la Guerre Juste, Paris: Presses Universitaires de France, 1983.

'On Assessing the Grotian Heritage', in T. M. C. Asser Instituut (ed.), *International Law and the Grotian Heritage: A Commemorative Colloquium Held at The Hague on 8 April 1983 on the Occasion of the Fourth Centenary of the Birth of Hugo Grotius*, The Hague: T. M. C. Asser Instituut, 1985, pp. 150–60.

Hale, J. R., *Renaissance Europe: 1480–1520*, London: Fontana/Collins, 1979.

Halkin, L., *Erasmus: A Critical Biography*, Oxford: Oxford University Press, 1993.

Hall, I. 'The Satiric Vision of Politics: Ethics, Interests and Disorders', *European Journal of International Relations*, vol. 20, no. 1, 2014, pp. 217–36.

Hamilton, B., *Political Thought in Sixteenth-Century Spain: A Study of the Political Ideas of Vitoria, De Soto, Suárez and Molina*, Oxford: Clarendon Press, 1963.

Hanke, L., *Bartolomé de Las Casas: An Interpretation of His Life and Writings*, The Hague: Martinus Nijhoff, 1951.

The Spanish Struggle for Justice in the Conquest of America, Boston, MA: Little Brown & Co., 1965.

Hart, A. C. 't, 'Hugo de Groot and Giambattista Vico', *Netherlands International Law Review*, vol. 30, no. 1, 1983, pp. 5–41.

Headley, J. M., 'Gattinara, Erasmus and the Imperial Configurations of Humanism', *Archiv fuer Reformationsgeschichte*, vol. 71, 1980, pp. 64–98.

Heath, M. J., 'Introductory Note' to 'Julius Excluded from Heaven: A Dialogue', in *Collected Works of Erasmus*, vol. 27, *Literary and Educational Writings 5*, ed. A. H. T. Levi, Toronto: University of Toronto Press, 1986, pp. 155–67.

Herz, J. H., *Political Realism and Political Idealism: A Study in Theories and Realities*, Chicago: University of Chicago Press, 1951.

Vom Ueberleben: Wie ein Weltbild entstand, Duesseldorf: Droste, 1984.

Hinsley, F. H., *Power and the Pursuit of Peace: Theory and Practice in the History of Relations between States*, Cambridge: Cambridge University Press, 1963.

Holland, T. E., 'Gentili, Alberico (1552–1608)', in L. Stephen and S. Lee (eds), *The Dictionary of National Biography*, vol. 7, London: Oxford University Press/Humphrey Milford, 1937–1938, pp. 1003–06.

Studies in International Law. Oxford: Clarendon Press, 1898.

Howard, M., *War and the Liberal Conscience*, London: Temple Smith, 1978.

Huizinga, J., *Dutch Civilization in the Seventeenth Century and Other Essays*, sel. P. Geyl and F. W. N. Hugenholtz, transl. A. J. Pomerans, London: Collins, 1968.

Hume, D., 'Of the Balance of Power', in P. Seabury (ed.), *Balance of Power*, San Francisco, CA: Chandler, 1965, pp. 32–36.

Hurrell, A., *On Global Order: Power, Values and the Constitution of International Society*, Oxford: Oxford University Press, 2007.

Jeffery, R., *Hugo Grotius in International Thought*, New York: Palgrave Macmillan, 2006.

Kalkhoff, P., 'Die Vermittlungspolitik des Erasmus und sein Anteil an den Flugschriften der ersten Reformationszeit', *Archiv fuer Reformationsgeschichte*, vols 1–2, 1903–1905, pp. 1–83.

Kaltenborn, C. von, *Die Vorlaeufer des Hugo Grotius auf dem Gebiete des Jus naturae et gentium sowie der Politik im Reformationszeitalter*, Leipzig: Gustav Mayer, 1848, reprinted Frankfurt am Main: Sauer & Anvermann, 1965.

Katzenstein, P. and Sil, R., 'Eclectic Theorizing in the Study and Practice of International Relations', in C. Reus-Smit and D. Snidal (eds), *The Oxford Handbook of International Relations*, Oxford: Oxford University Press, 2008, pp. 109–30.

Keene, E., *Beyond the Anarchical Society: Grotius, Colonialism and Order in World Politics*, Cambridge: Cambridge University Press, 2002.

International Political Thought: A Historical Introduction, Cambridge: Polity Press, 2005.

Kingsbury, B. and Straumann, B. (eds), *The Roman Foundations of the Law of Nations: Alberico Gentili and the Justice of Empire*, Oxford: Oxford University Press, 2010.

(eds), D. Lupher (transl.), *The Wars of the Romans: A Critical Edition and Translation of* De Armis Romanis, Oxford: Oxford University Press, 2011.

Kisch, G., *Erasmus und die Jurisprudenz seiner Zeit*, Basel: Helbing & Lichtenhahn, 1960.

Knight, W. S. M., *The Life and Works of Hugo Grotius*, The Grotius Society Publications No. 4, London: Sweet and Maxwell, 1925.

Knowles, D., *The Evolution of Medieval Political Thought*, London: Longmans, 1962.

Koenigsberger, H. G., *The Habsburgs and Europe: 1516–1660*, Ithaca and London: Cornell University Press, 1971.

Koerber, E. von, *Die Staatstheorie des Erasmus von Rotterdam*, Berlin: Duncker & Humblot, 1967.

Lange, C. L., 'Histoire de la Doctrine Pacifique et de son Influence sur le Développement du Droit International', *Recueil des Cours*, vol. 13, III, 1926, pp. 175–426.

Lauterpacht, H., 'The Grotian Tradition in International Law', in E. Lauterpacht (ed.), *International Law: Being the Collected Papers of Hersch Lauterpacht*, vol. 2, Part I, Cambridge: Cambridge University Press, 1975, pp. 307–65.

Lesaffer, R., 'Alberico Gentili's *ius post bellum* and Early Modern Peace Treaties', in B. Kingsbury and B. Straumann (eds), *The Roman Foundations of the Law of Nations: Alberico Gentili and the Justice of Empire* (Oxford: Oxford University Press, 2010), pp. 210–40.

Malcolm, N., 'Alberico Gentili and the Ottomans', in B. Kingsbury and B. Straumann (eds), *The Roman Foundations of the Law of Nations: Alberico Gentili and the Justice of Empire*, Oxford: Oxford University Press, 2010, pp. 127–45.

Mansfield, B., *Erasmus in the Twentieth Century: Interpretations c1920–2000*, Toronto: University of Toronto Press, 2003.

Martínez, M. M., 'Las Casas on the Conquest of America', in J. Friede and B. Keen (eds), *Bartolomé de Las Casas in History: Toward an Understanding of the Man and His Work*, DeKalb, IL: Northern Illinois University Press, 1971, pp. 309–49.

Mattingly, G., *Renaissance Diplomacy*, Harmondsworth: Penguin, 1965.

Meinecke, F., *Machiavellism: The Doctrine of Raison d'État and Its Place in Modern History*, transl. from German D. Scott, intro. W. Stark, New York and Washington, DC: Praeger, 1965.

Menéndez Pidal, R., 'Formación del Fundamental Pensamiento Político de Carlos V', in P. Rassow and F. Schalk (eds), *Karl V: Der Kaiser und seine Zeit*, Koeln and Graz: Boehlau Verlag, 1960, pp. 144–66.

Mesnard, P., *L'Essor de la Philosophie Politique au XVIe Siècle*, Paris: J. Vrin, 1951.

Meulen, J. Ter, and Diermanse, P. J. J., *Der Gedanke der Internationalen Organisation: 1300–1800*, The Hague: Martinus Nijhoff, 1968.

Molen, G. H. J. van der, *Alberico Gentili and the Development of International Law: His Life, Work and Times*, 2nd rev. edn, Leyden: A. W. Sijthoff, 1968.

Muenkler, H., *Im Namen des Staates: Die Begruendung der Staatsraison in der Fruehen Neuzeit*, Frankfurt am Main: Fischer Verlag, 1987.

Nicolson, H., *Diplomacy*, 3rd edn, London and New York: Oxford University Press, 1965.

Norena, C., *Studies in Spanish Renaissance Thought*, The Hague: Nijhoff, 1975.

Nussbaum, A., *A Concise History of the Law of Nations*, rev. edn, New York: Macmillan, 1954.

O'Connell, D. P., 'Rationalism and Voluntarism in the Fathers of International Law', *Indian Year Book of International Affairs*, vol. 13, Part II, 1964, pp. 3–32.

Richelieu, London: Weidenfeld & Nicolson, 1968.

Onions, C. T. (ed.), *The Shorter Oxford English Dictionary on Historical Principles*, 3rd edn, 2 vols, Oxford: Clarendon Press, 1967.

Pagden, A., 'Dispossessing the Barbarian: The Language of Spanish Thomism and the Debate over the Property Rights of the American Indians', in A. Pagden (ed.), *The Languages of Political Theory in Early Modern Europe*, Cambridge: Cambridge University Press, 1987, pp. 79–98.

Panizza, D., *Alberico Gentili, giurista ideologo nell'Inghilterra elisabettiana*, Padua: La Garangola, 1981.

Parker, G., *Europe in Crisis: 1598–1648*, Glasgow: Fontana, 1979.

Parkinson, F., *The Philosophy of International Relations: A Study in the History of Thought*, London: Sage, 1977.

Pauw, F. de, *Grotius and the Law of the Sea*, transl. P. J. Arthern, Editions de l'Institut de Sociologie, Brussels: Université de Bruxelles, 1965.

Phillips, M. M., *Erasmus and the Northern Renaissance*, New York: Collier Books, 1965.

Phillipson, C., 'Albericus Gentilis', in Sir J. Macdonell and E. Manson (eds), *Great Jurists of the World*, London: John Murray, 1913, pp. 109–43.
'Franciscus a Victoria (1480–1546): International Law and War', *Journal of the Society of Comparative Legislation*, New Series, vol. 15, 1915, pp. 175–97.
'Introduction', in A. Gentili, *De Jure Belli Libri Tres*, vol. 2, transl. J. C. Rolfe, The Classics of International Law, Oxford and London: Clarendon Press and Humphrey Milford, 1933, reprinted New York and London: Oceana Publications and Wildy & Sons, 1964, pp. 9a–51a.
'Preface', *Netherlands International Law Review*, vol. 30, no. 1, 1983, p. 3.
Price, J. L., *Culture and Society in the Dutch Republic During the Seventeenth Century*, New York: Charles Scribner's Sons, 1974.
Pürimäe, P., 'Alberico Gentili's Doctrine of Defensive War and Its Impact on Seventeenth Century Normative Views', in B. Kingsbury and B. Straumann (eds), *The Roman Foundations of the Law of Nations: Alberico Gentili and the Justice of Empire*, Oxford: Oxford University Press, 2010, pp. 187–209.
Ranke, L. von, 'The Great Powers', in G. G. Iggers and K. von Moltke (eds), *The Theory and Practice of History by Leopold von Ranke*, Indianapolis and New York: Bobbs-Merrill, 1973, pp. 65–101.
Renoudet, A., *Études Érasmiennes: 1521–1529*, Paris: E. Droz, 1939.
Reus-Smit, C. and Snidal, D., 'Between Utopia and Reality: The Practical Discourses of International Relations', in C. Reus-Smit and D. Snidal (eds), *The Oxford Handbook of International Relations*, Oxford: Oxford University Press, 2008, pp. 3–37.
Roberts, M. (ed.), *Sweden's Age of Greatness: 1632–1718*, London: Macmillan, 1973.
Roelofsen, C. G., 'Grotius and the International Politics of the Seventeenth Century', in H. Bull, B. Kingsbury and A. Roberts (eds), *Hugo Grotius and International Relations*, Oxford: Clarendon Press, 1990, pp. 95–131.
'Some Remarks on the "Sources" of the Grotian System of International Law', *Netherlands International Law Review*, vol. 30, no. 1, 1983, pp. 73–79.
Ruggie, J. G., 'What Makes the World Hang Together? Neo-Utilitarianism and the Social Constructivist Challenge', *International Organization*, vol. 52, no. 4, 1998, pp. 855–85.
Scheltens, D. F., 'Grotius' Doctrine of the Social Contract', *Netherlands International Law Review*, vol. 30, no. 1, 1983, pp. 43–60.
Schmidt, B., *The Political Discourse of Anarchy: A Disciplinary History of International Relations*. New York: State University of New York Press, 1998.
Schoeck, R. J., *Erasmus of Europe*, vol. I, *The Making of a Humanist, 1467–1500*, Edinburgh: Edinburgh University Press, 1990.
Erasmus of Europe, vol. II, *The Prince of Humanists, 1501–1536*, Edinburgh: Edinburgh University Press, 1993.
Schwarzenberger, G., 'The Grotius Factor in International Law and Relations: A Functional Approach', in H. Bull, B. Kingsbury and A. Roberts (eds), *Hugo Grotius and International Relations*, Oxford: Clarendon Press, 1990, pp. 301–12.

Simmonds, K. R., 'Alberico Gentili at the Admiralty Bar, 1605–1608', *Archiv des Voelkerrechts*, vol. 7, 1958–1959, pp. 3–23.

'Gentili on the Qualities of the Ideal Ambassador', *Indian Year Book of International Affairs*, vol. 13, II, 1964, pp. 47–58.

Skinner, Q., *The Foundations of Modern Political Thought*, vol. 1, *The Renaissance*, Cambridge: Cambridge University Press, 1978.

The Foundations of Modern Political Thought, vol. 2, *The Age of Reformation*, Cambridge: Cambridge University Press, 1978.

Soder, J., *Die Idee der Voelkergemeinschaft: Francisco de Vitoria und die Philosophischen Grundlagen des Voelkerrechts*, Frankfurt am Main/Berlin: Alfred Metzner, 1955.

Stuart, D. T., 'Foreign-Policy Decision-Making', in C. Reus-Smit and D. Snidal (eds), *The Oxford Handbook of International Relations*, Oxford: Oxford University Press, 2008, pp. 576–93.

Tex, J. den, *Oldenbarneveldt*, 2 vols, transl. from Dutch R. B. Powell, Cambridge: Cambridge University Press, 1973.

Thomas, J. A. C., *The Institutes of Justinian: Text, Translation and Commentary*, Amsterdam: North-Holland, 1975.

Thompson, C. R., 'Erasmus as Internationalist and Cosmopolitan', *Archiv fuer Reformationsgeschichte*, vol. 46, 1955, pp. 167–95.

Thomson, J. A. K., 'Desiderius Erasmus', in F. J. C. Hearnshaw (ed.), *The Social and Political Ideas of Some Great Thinkers of the Renaissance and the Reformation*, New York: Barnes & Noble, 1949, pp. 149–70.

Tracy, J. D., *Erasmus of the Low Countries*, Berkeley, CA: University of California Press, 1996.

The Politics of Erasmus: A Pacifist Intellectual and His Political Milieu, Toronto: University of Toronto Press, 1978.

Tuck, R., *Natural Rights Theories: Their Origin and Development*, Cambridge: Cambridge University Press, 1979.

'Peter Haggenmacher, Grotius et la Doctrine de la Guerre Juste', *Grotiana*, New Series, vol. 7, 1986, pp. 87–92.

The Rights of War and Peace: Political Thought and the International Order from Grotius to Kant, Oxford: Oxford University Press, 1999.

Vermeulen, B.P., 'Grotius and Geneva', *Bibliotheca Visseriana*, vol. 6, Lugdunum Batavorum: E. J. Brill, 1926, pp. 5–81.

'Grotius' Methodology and System of International Law', *Netherlands International Law Review*, vol. 30, no. 1, 1983, pp. 374–82.

Vollenhoven, C. van, 'On the Genesis of *De Jure Belli ac Pacis* (Grotius, 1625)', *Verspreide Geschriften*, vol. 1, Haarlem and 'S-Gravenhage: Tjeenk Willink & Zoon and Martinus Nijhoff, 1934, pp. 352–68.

The Framework of Grotius' Book De Jure Belli ac Pacis (1625), Amsterdam: Noord-Hollandsche Uitgeversmaatschappij, 1931.

'The Growth of Grotius' *De Iure Belli ac Pacis* as It Appears from Contemporary Correspondence', *Bibliotheca Visseriana*, vol. 8 (Lugdunum Batavorum: E. J. Brill, 1929), pp. 105–70.

Vreeland, Jr., H., *Hugo Grotius the Father of the Modern Science of International Law*, New York: Oxford University Press, 1917.

Waldron, J., '*Ius Gentium*: A Defence of Gentili's Equation of the Law of Nations and the Law of Nature', in B. Kingsbury and B. Straumann (eds), *The Roman Foundations of the Law of Nations: Alberico Gentili and the Justice of Empire*, Oxford: Oxford University Press, 2010, pp. 283–96.

Weiler, A. G., 'Einleitung' to 'Vtilissima Consvltatio de Bello Tvrcis Inferendo, et Obiter Enarratvs Psalmvs XXVIII', in *Opera Omnia Desiderii Erasmi Roterodami*, V–III, vol. 15, Amsterdam: North Holland Publishing Co., 1986, pp. 3–28.

Wight, M., 'An Anatomy of International Thought', *Review of International Studies*, vol. 13, no. 3, 1987, pp. 221–27.

Four Seminal Thinkers in International Theory: Machiavelli, Grotius, Kant, and Mazzini, ed. G.Wight and B. Porter, Oxford: Oxford University Press, 2005.

International Theory: The Three Traditions, ed. G. Wight and B. Porter, Leicester: Leicester University Press for the Royal Institute of International Affairs, London, 1991.

Power Politics, ed. and intro. H. Bull and C. Holbraad, Harmondsworth: Pelican, 1979.

Systems of States, ed. and intro. H. Bull, Leicester: Leicester University Press for the London School of Economics and Political Science, 1977.

'Western Values in International Relations', in H. Butterfield and M. Wight (eds), *Diplomatic Investigations: Essays in the Theory of International Politics*, London: George Allen & Unwin, 1969, pp. 89–131.

'Why Is There No International Theory?', in H. Butterfield and M. Wight (eds), *Diplomatic Investigations: Essays in the Theory of International Politics*, London: George Allen & Unwin, 1969, pp. 17–34.

Williams, R., *Politics and Letters: Interviews with New Left Review*, London: N. L. B., 1979.

Williams, Jr, R. A., *The American Indian in Western Legal Thought*, New York: Oxford University Press, 1990.

Wilson, C., *The Transformation of Europe: 1558–1648*, London: Weidenfeld & Nicolson, 1976.

Wolf, E., *Grosse Rechtsdenker der deutschen Geistesgeschichte*, Tuebingen: Mohr (Paul Siebeck), 1963.

Zweig, S., *Triumph und Tragik des Erasmus von Rotterdam*, Wien: Herbert Reichner, 1935.

Index